NASCAR'S BEST

WILLIAM BURT

MOTORBOOKS
INTERNATIONAL

First published in 2004 by Motorbooks International, an imprint of MBI
Publishing Company, Galtier Plaza, Suite 200, 380 Jackson Street, St. Paul, MN
55101-3885 USA

Motorbooks International titles are also available at discounts in bulk quantity
for industrial or sales-promotional use. For details write to Special Sales
Manager at Motorbooks International Wholesalers & Distributors, Galtier Plaza,
Suite 200, 380 Jackson Street, St. Paul, MN 55101-3885 USA.

ISBN 0-7603-1797-6

Edited by Heather Oakley and Peter Bodensteiner
Designed by Kari Johnston

On the cover: Tony Stewart, Bobby Allison, Dale Earnhardt Jr., Junior Johnson,
Richard Petty.

On the frontispiece: Benny Parsons, Darrell Waltrip, Cale Yarborough, Dale
Earnhardt, Jimmie Johnson.

On the back cover, top: Dale Earnhardt
Bottom: Cale Yarborough

Printed in the United States

CONTENTS

The Grand National Days 268

Current
Nextel

JOHN ANDRETTI
JOHNNY BENSON
GREG BIFFLE
JEFF BURTON
WARD BURTON
KURT BUSCH
DERRIKE COPE
RICKY CRAVEN
DALE EARNHARDT JR.
BILL ELLIOTT
JEFF GORDON
ROBBY GORDON
JEFF GREEN
KEVIN HARVICK
DALE JARRETT
JIMMIE JOHNSON
MATT KENSETH
BOBBY LABONTE

Cup Drivers

TERRY LABONTE

STERLING MARLIN

MARK MARTIN

JEREMY MAYFIELD

JAMIE MCMURRAY

CASEY MEARS

JERRY NADEAU

JOE NEMECHEK

RYAN NEWMAN

STEVE PARK

KYLE PETTY

RICKY RUDD

ELLIOTT SADLER

KEN SCHRADER

JIMMY SPENCER

TONY STEWART

RUSTY WALLACE

MICHAEL WALTRIP

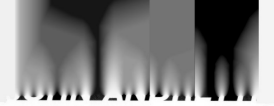

Current Team: Dale Earnhardt Incorporated
Residence: Mooresville, North Carolina
Hometown: Nazareth, Pennsylvania
Birthday: March 12, 1963
Height: 5 feet, 5 inches
Weight: 140

Races: 327
Running: 256 (78.3 percent)
Accidents: 43 (13.1 percent)
Mechanical Failures: 28 (8.6 percent)

John Andretti

2003	Dale Earnhardt Incorporated
	Haas CNC Racing
	Petty Enterprises
1998–2002	Petty Enterprises
1997	Cale Yarborough
1996	Cale Yarborough
	Michael Kranefuss
1995	Michael Kranefuss
1994	Petty Enterprises
	Billy Hagan
1993	Billy Hagan

Like many professional racers, John Andretti came from a racing family. As the son of Aldo Andretti and a nephew of Mario Andretti, John grew up around winning race teams, which presented him with early opportunities to begin his own racing career. As a youth, he competed in karts before climbing the ladder through different racing series. As he came from an "open-wheel" family, it is no surprise that that is where he started. He was, however, soon branching out into many different areas of racing, including SCCA (Sports Car Club of America), midget cars, sprint cars, IMSA GTP cars, and even drag racing.

In 1987 he entered his first CART race and finished in a very respectable 6th place. Over the next few years, John continued to drive Indy cars, but he also competed in some endurance events. In 1988 he finished 6th at the 24 Hours of Le Mans, sharing seat time with uncle and cousin Mario and Michael Andretti. A year later he won the 24-hour IMSA Daytona race. John won his first Indy car race in 1991, taking the top spot in Australia's Gold Coast Indy Car Grand Prix.

But even after winning, John was not completely taken with Indy car racing and began searching for another driving career. After a brief shot at drag racing in Top Fuel cars, John began racing Winston Cup cars in 1993, driving in four races. He liked it, and ran the entire season for the first time in 1994. John started his Winston Cup career with the Billy Hagan team and went on to drive for Petty Enterprises, the Kranefuss team, and Cale Yarborough's team.

In 1994 he pulled double duty on Memorial Day weekend, running the Indianapolis 500 and the Coca Cola 600 in the same day. He won his first race, the Pepsi 400 at Daytona in 1997 driving for Cale Yarborough. In 1998 he was named as the driver of the No. 43 STP Pontiac, which Richard Petty had made famous. In the pair's first season together, John had a decent year, finishing 11th in points for the championship. In 1999 he took the No. 43 back to victory lane with a win at Martinsville. The next year was not as kind, with John finishing in the top 10 only twice. Petty Enterprises switched from Pontiacs to Dodges in 2001, and the team struggled somewhat with the change. However, John did have some good runs, with a close 2nd at Bristol.

The 2002 season was disappointing, and with a poor start in 2003, John left Petty Enterprises after 14 races. He drove a few races for Haas CNC before being hired by Dale Earnhardt Incorporated to finish the 2003 season.

After a five-and-a-half-year run with Petty Enterprises, John moved to Dale Earnhardt Incorporated. Sponsorship problems, however, would mean a limited schedule in 2004. Here he tucks up the No. 90 car behind Jeremy Mayfield.

John Andretti got his first win at Talladega in 1997, behind the wheel of Cale Yarborough's Ford Thunderbird sponsored by RCA. John drove for Cale for only one full season before joining Petty Enterprises the following year.

Year-by-year Performance

	Races	Poles		Wins		Top 5		Top 10	
1993	4	0	0.0%	0	0.0%	0	0.0%	0	0.0%
1994	29	0	0.0%	0	0.0%	0	0.0%	0	0.0%
1995	31	1	3.2%	0	0.0%	1	3.2%	5	16.1%
1996	30	0	0.0%	0	0.0%	2	6.7%	3	10.0%
1997	32	1	3.1%	1	3.1%	3	9.4%	3	9.4%
1998	33	1	3.0%	0	0.0%	3	9.1%	10	30.3%
1999	34	1	2.9%	1	2.9%	3	8.8%	10	29.4%
2000	34	0	0.0%	0	0.0%	0	0.0%	2	5.9%
2001	35	0	0.0%	0	0.0%	1	2.9%	2	5.7%
2002	36	0	0.0%	0	0.0%	0	0.0%	1	2.8%
2003	29	0	0.0%	0	0.0%	0	0.0%	1	3.4%
Total	**327**	**4**	**1.2%**	**2**	**0.6%**	**13**	**4.0%**	**37**	**11.3%**

Track Performance

Less than 1 Mile

	Starts	1st	2nd	3rd	4th	5th	6th	7th	8th	9th	10th	11–20	21–43
Bristol	12	0	1	0	1	0	0	0	0	0	0	1	9
Martinsville	20	1	0	0	0	1	0	0	0	0	0	5	13
Richmond	20	0	0	0	0	1	0	1	0	1	1	6	10
N. Wilkes	7	0	0	0	0	0	0	0	0	0	0	3	4
Total	**59**	**1**	**1**	**0**	**1**	**2**	**0**	**1**	**0**	**1**	**1**	**15**	**36**
		1.7%	1.7%	0.0%	1.7%	3.4%	0.0%	1.7%	0.0%	1.7%	1.7%	25.4%	61.0%

1 Mile–1.49 Mile

	Starts	1st	2nd	3rd	4th	5th	6th	7th	8th	9th	10th	11–20	21–43
Dover	20	0	0	0	0	0	0	0	0	1	0	7	12
New Hamp.	17	0	0	1	0	0	1	1	0	0	0	4	10
N. Carolina	21	0	0	0	0	0	0	1	0	0	0	6	14
Phoenix	11	0	0	0	0	0	1	0	1	0	0	4	5
Darlington	19	0	0	0	0	1	1	0	0	1	1	6	9
Total	**88**	**0**	**0**	**1**	**0**	**1**	**3**	**2**	**1**	**2**	**1**	**27**	**50**
		0.0%	0.0%	1.1%	0.0%	1.1%	3.4%	2.3%	1.1%	2.3%	1.1%	30.7%	56.8%

1.5 mile

	Starts	1st	2nd	3rd	4th	5th	6th	7th	8th	9th	10th	11–20	21–43
Charlotte	20	0	0	0	0	0	0	1	0	0	0	7	12
Chicago	2	0	0	0	0	0	0	0	0	0	0	0	2
Homestead	5	0	0	0	0	0	0	0	0	0	0	1	4
Kansas	3	0	0	0	0	0	0	0	0	0	0	2	1
Las Vegas	6	0	0	0	0	0	0	0	0	0	0	2	4
Texas	7	0	0	0	0	0	0	0	0	0	0	2	5
Total	**43**	**0**	**0**	**0**	**0**	**0**	**0**	**1**	**0**	**0**	**0**	**14**	**28**
		0.0%	0.0%	0.0%	0.0%	0.0%	0.0%	2.3%	0.0%	0.0%	0.0%	32.6%	65.1%

Track Performance
1.51 Mile–2.5 Mile

	Starts	1st	2nd	3rd	4th	5th	6th	7th	8th	9th	10th	11–20	21–43
Atlanta	20	0	0	0	0	0	0	0	0	0	0	8	12
California	7	0	0	0	0	0	0	0	1	0	0	1	5
Michigan	18	0	0	0	1	0	0	0	1	2	1	3	10
Indianapolis	10	0	0	0	0	0	0	1	0	0	0	4	5
Pocono	20	0	0	0	0	0	0	0	0	0	0	3	17
Total	**75**	**0**	**0**	**0**	**1**	**0**	**0**	**1**	**2**	**2**	**1**	**19**	**49**
		0.0%	0.0%	0.0%	1.3%	0.0%	0.0%	1.3%	2.7%	2.7%	1.3%	25.3%	65.3%

Restrictor Plate

	Starts	1st	2nd	3rd	4th	5th	6th	7th	8th	9th	10th	11–20	21–43
Daytona	19	1	0	0	0	0	0	0	0	0	0	4	14
Talladega	20	0	0	1	1	0	0	0	0	2	0	5	11
Total	**39**	**1**	**0**	**1**	**1**	**0**	**0**	**0**	**0**	**2**	**0**	**9**	**25**
		2.6%	0.0%	2.6%	2.6%	0.0%	0.0%	0.0%	0.0%	5.1%	0.0%	23.1%	64.1%

Road Courses

	Starts	1st	2nd	3rd	4th	5th	6th	7th	8th	9th	10th	11–20	21–43
Sears Point	9	0	0	2	0	0	0	0	0	0	1	3	3
Watkins Glen	9	0	0	0	0	0	0	1	1	0	0	4	3
Total	**18**	**0**	**0**	**2**	**0**	**0**	**0**	**1**	**1**	**0**	**1**	**7**	**6**
		0.0%	0.0%	11.1%	0.0%	0.0%	0.0%	5.6%	5.6%	0.0%	5.6%	38.9%	33.3%

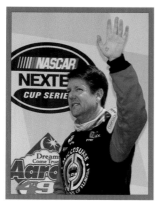

Johnny Benson

Current Team: none
Residence: Cornelius, North Carolina
Hometown: Grand Rapids, Michigan
Birthday: June 27, 1963
Height: 6 feet, 0 inches
Weight: 180

Races: 264
Running: 221 (84.7 percent)
Accidents: 25 (9.6 percent)
Mechanical Failures: 15 (5.7 percent)

2001–2003	MBV Motorsports
2000	MB2 Motorsports
	Tyler Jet Motorsports
1998–1999	Roush Racing
1996–1997	Bahari Racing

ohnny Benson Sr. retired from racing just as his son began his career. Johnny Jr. started driving on local dirt tracks in 1982 with his dad heavily involved in his career. In the mid 1980s he made the switch to paved tracks, first running at the Berlin Speedway where his father was a seven-time champion. By the late 1980s he was winning in late models, and in 1990 Benson signed up to drive on the ASA circuit in a Throop Motorsports Lumina. It was a great year for Johnny as he won the ASA Rookie of the Year finishing 8th in the overall points. He had five top 5s, eight top 10s, and led a lot of laps during the year. When he was driving in the ARCA Series, he was still racing his late model. In the 1991 ASA campaign, Johnny improved his consistency and finished 4th in the points, with 10 top fives and a couple of poles. In 1992 Johnny missed winning the ARCA Championship by only two points, although the year brought seven poles and four wins. In 1993 it was finally Johnny's year. He won five races and 10 poles, set seven track records, and was rewarded with the ASA Championship.

It was time for Johnny to move up, and his next stop was the Busch Grand National Series. Hired by BACE Motorsports to drive the 1994 schedule, Johnny drove to Rookie of the Year honors and finished 6th in overall points. His first win came at Dover in his 29th Busch Series start. In 1995, with new sponsorship, Johnny won two races, had 12 top fives and brought home the Busch Series Championship.

In 1996 Johnny made the move up to the Winston Cup Series and won the Rookie of the Year honors, driving for Chuck Rider's Bahari Racing team. He finished the year in a respectable 21st position in overall points. In 1997 with eight top-10 finishes, he improved to 11th position in points. In 1998 Benson moved to the Ford camp when he joined Jack Rousch's five-car operation, and in his first year with the team scored three top-5 and 10 top-10 finishes. After a tough 1999 season, Johnny left Rousch and began driving for Tim Beverley and the Tyler Jet Motorsports team, but at midyear, the team was bought out by MB2 Motorsports.

Even with all of the distractions, Johnny finished the year in 13th place in the Winston Cup Point standings. In 2001 Johnny was in command of the MBV Motorsports car, owned by Valvoline, and the year yielded another 11th place finish in points. In 2002 Johnny was injured early in the year and had to sit out a few races, but when he came back the team won its first race (at Rockingham). After a disappointing 2003 season, Johnny left the MBV team and entered 2004 looking for a full-time ride.

Currently, Johnny is driving a limited schedule behind the wheel of the Miccosukee Gaming and Resorts Dodge owned by James Finch while he looks for a full-time Nextel Cup ride.

Johnny Benson's first win came behind the wheel of Nelson Bower's Pontiac at Atlanta in 2002. Johnny was just ahead of ex-teammate and ex-Valvoline driver Mark Martin. Johnny spent two years with Jack Roush in the late 1990s, but the relationship never produced a win.

Year-by-year Performance

	Races	Poles		Wins		Top 5		Top 10	
1996	30	1	3.3%	0	0.0%	1	3.3%	6	20.0%
1997	32	1	3.1%	0	0.0%	0	0.0%	8	25.0%
1998	32	0	0.0%	0	0.0%	3	9.4%	10	31.3%
1999	34	0	0.0%	0	0.0%	0	0.0%	2	5.9%
2000	33	0	0.0%	0	0.0%	3	9.1%	7	21.2%
2001	36	0	0.0%	0	0.0%	6	16.7%	14	38.9%
2002	31	0	0.0%	1	3.2%	3	9.7%	7	22.6%
2003	36	0	0.0%	0	0.0%	2	5.6%	4	11.1%
Total	**264**	**2**	**0.8%**	**1**	**0.4%**	**18**	**6.8%**	**58**	**22.0%**

Track Performance

Less than 1 Mile

	Starts	1st	2nd	3rd	4th	5th	6th	7th	8th	9th	10th	11-20	21-43
Bristol	15	0	1	0	0	1	0	0	0	0	0	5	8
Martinsville	6	0	1	0	0	0	1	0	0	1	0	7	6
Richmond	5	0	0	0	0	0	1	1	0	2	2	3	6
N. Wilkes	2	0	0	0	0	0	0	0	0	0	0	1	1
Total	**48**	**0**	**2**	**0**	**0**	**1**	**2**	**1**	**0**	**3**	**2**	**16**	**21**
		0.0%	4.2%	0.0%	0.0%	2.1%	4.2%	2.1%	0.0%	6.3%	4.2%	33.3%	43.8%

1 Mile - 1.49 Mile

	Starts	1st	2nd	3rd	4th	5th	6th	7th	8th	9th	10th	11-20	21-43
Dover	15	0	1	0	0	1	0	1	0	0	1	4	7
New Hamp.	14	0	0	0	1	0	0	1	0	1	0	6	5
N. Carolina	16	1	0	1	0	0	1	0	0	0	0	5	8
Phoenix	8	0	0	0	0	0	0	1	0	1	1	2	3
Darlington	16	0	0	0	0	0	0	1	1	0	1	4	9
Total	**69**	**1**	**1**	**1**	**1**	**1**	**1**	**4**	**1**	**2**	**3**	**21**	**32**
		1.4%	1.4%	1.4%	1.4%	1.4%	1.4%	5.8%	1.4%	2.9%	4.3%	30.4%	46.4%

1.5 mile

	Starts	1st	2nd	3rd	4th	5th	6th	7th	8th	9th	10th	11-20	21-43
Charlotte	15	0	0	0	0	0	0	0	1	1	1	8	4
Chicago	2	0	0	0	0	0	0	0	0	0	0	1	1
Homestead	5	0	0	0	1	0	0	0	0	0	0	2	2
Kansas	3	0	0	0	0	0	0	0	0	0	0	0	3
Las Vegas	6	0	0	0	2	0	1	0	0	0	0	1	2
Texas	7	0	0	1	0	1	0	0	0	0	0	2	3
Total	**38**	**0**	**0**	**1**	**3**	**1**	**1**	**0**	**1**	**1**	**1**	**14**	**15**
		0.0%	0.0%	2.6%	7.9%	2.6%	2.6%	0.0%	2.6%	2.6%	2.6%	36.8%	39.5%

Track Performance

1.51 Mile - 2.5 Mile

Atlanta	15	0	0	0	0	0	0	1	0	1	2	1	10
California	7	0	0	0	0	0	0	0	1	0	0	3	3
Michigan	16	0	0	0	0	2	1	1	1	0	2	2	7
Indianapolis	8	0	0	1	0	0	0	1	1	0	0	2	3
Pocono	16	0	0	0	0	2	0	0	0	0	0	5	9
Total	**62**	**0**	**0**	**1**	**0**	**4**	**1**	**3**	**3**	**1**	**4**	**13**	**32**
		0.0%	0.0%	1.6%	0.0%	6.5%	1.6%	4.8%	4.8%	1.6%	6.5%	21.0%	51.6%

Restrictor Plate

Daytona	15	0	0	0	0	0	0	0	0	0	1	6	8
Talladega	16	0	0	0	0	0	0	1	0	1	1	3	10
Total	**31**	**0**	**0**	**0**	**0**	**0**	**0**	**1**	**0**	**1**	**2**	**9**	**18**
		0.0%	0.0%	0.0%	0.0%	0.0%	0.0%	3.2%	0.0%	3.2%	6.5%	29.0%	58.1%

Road Courses

Sears Point	8	0	0	0	0	0	0	0	0	0	0	3	5
Watkins Glen	8	0	0	0	0	0	0	0	0	1	0	3	4
Total	**16**	**0**	**0**	**0**	**0**	**0**	**0**	**0**	**0**	**1**	**0**	**6**	**9**
		0.0%	0.0%	0.0%	0.0%	0.0%	0.0%	0.0%	0.0%	6.3%	0.0%	37.5%	56.3%

Current Team: Roush Racing
Residence: Mooresville, North Carolina
Hometown: Vancouver, Washington
Birthday: December 23, 1969
Height: 5 feet, 9 inches
Weight: 170

Races: 42
Running: 35 (83.3 percent)
Accidents: 4 (9.5 percent)
Mechanical Failures: 3 (7.1 percent)

2003   Roush Racing

Greg Biffle

In the mid-1990s former racer Benny Parsons noticed Greg Biffle when he was driving in the NASCAR Winter Heat Series. Benny passed on his praise of the young driver to Jack Roush, who, like Parsons, liked what he saw and soon signed him to drive. While Biffle was coming on board with Roush racing, Grainger Industrial Supply was entering racing. Roush put the two together, and in 1998 both entered the Craftsman Truck Series. In their first year it was obvious that they were fast, as they won four poles. They finished the year winless but had eight top 5s and 12 top 10s. The team also led in 12 of the seasons races, and Greg won Rookie of the Year honors.

In the next year, 1999, the team showed steady improvement with its first win coming at Memphis. It was the first of nine wins that year, with the team finishing in 2nd place in the points race, only eight points shy of a Craftsman Truck Series Championship. The team was not daunted, and in the 2000 season Biffle and the team brought home something Jack Roush had never before possessed—a NASCAR Championship trophy. The team had an incredible 18 top-five finishes in 24 races, including five wins.

Biffle had proven his worth, and in 2001 he was moved to the Busch Series. He adjusted to the cars quickly and soon picked up where he left off in the trucks. In the season's 33 races, Greg won five times and had 16 top fives. He was named Rookie of the Year, finishing 4th in the points. In 2002 Greg's Busch team won another championship for Roush, this time in the Busch Series, with four wins and an impressive 20 top fives.

Greg started his next career in the 2002 season, when he drove in seven Winston Cup races. He qualified in the top five three times, although his best finish was 13th in his first race at California Speedway. It was decided that in 2003 both he and his sponsor would again graduate to the next level full-time. Greg's entry into the Winston Cup Series was not as dramatic as his first year in the Craftsman Trucks or Busch Series, but the team did have success. It won the summer race at Daytona, had three top 5s and six top 10s and finished in the top 20.

Greg scored 16 wins in the Craftsman Truck series and 12 wins in the Busch Series before moving up to the Nextel Cup Series in his No. 16 Jack Roush Ford.

Biffle's rookie year was full of ups and downs. He won one race, the summer race at Daytona, but also carded seven finishes of 13th place or worse.

Year-by-year Performance

	Races	Poles		Wins		Top 5		Top 10	
2003	42	0	0.0%	1	2.4%	3	7.1%	6	14.3%
Total	**42**	**0**	**0.0%**	**1**	**2.4%**	**3**	**7.1%**	**6**	**14.3%**

Track Performance

Less than 1 Mile

	Starts	1st	2nd	3rd	4th	5th	6th	7th	8th	9th	10th	11–20	21–43
Bristol	2	0	0	0	0	1	0	0	0	0	0	0	1
Martinsville	2	0	0	0	0	0	0	0	0	0	0	2	0
Richmond	3	0	0	0	0	0	0	0	0	0	0	2	1
Nashville	0	0	0	0	0	0	0	0	0	0	0	0	0
Total	**7**	**0**	**0**	**0**	**0**	**1**	**0**	**0**	**0**	**0**	**0**	**4**	**2**
		0.0%	0.0%	0.0%	0.0%	14.3%	0.0%	0.0%	0.0%	0.0%	0.0%	57.1%	28.6%

1 Mile–1.49 Mile

	Starts	1st	2nd	3rd	4th	5th	6th	7th	8th	9th	10th	11–20	21–43
Dover	3	0	0	0	0	0	0	1	0	0	0	0	2
New Hamp.	3	0	0	0	0	0	0	0	0	0	1	0	2
N. Carolina	3	0	0	0	0	0	0	0	0	0	0	1	2
Phoenix	1	0	0	0	0	0	0	0	0	0	0	1	0
Darlington	2	0	0	0	0	0	0	0	0	0	1	1	0
Total	**12**	**0**	**0**	**0**	**0**	**0**	**0**	**1**	**0**	**0**	**2**	**3**	**6**
		0.0%	0.0%	0.0%	0.0%	0.0%	0.0%	8.3%	0.0%	0.0%	16.7%	25.0%	50.0%

1.5 mile

	Starts	1st	2nd	3rd	4th	5th	6th	7th	8th	9th	10th	11–20	21–43
Charlotte	2	0	0	0	0	0	0	0	0	0	0	2	0
Chicago	1	0	0	0	0	0	0	0	0	0	0	1	0
Homestead	2	0	0	0	0	0	0	0	0	0	0	0	2
Kansas	2	0	0	0	0	0	0	0	0	0	0	1	1
Las Vegas	0	0	0	0	0	0	0	0	0	0	0	0	0
Texas	1	0	0	0	0	0	0	0	0	0	0	0	1
Total	**8**	**0**	**0**	**0**	**0**	**0**	**0**	**0**	**0**	**0**	**0**	**4**	**4**
		0.0%	0.0%	0.0%	0.0%	0.0%	0.0%	0.0%	0.0%	0.0%	0.0%	50.0%	50.0%

Track Performance
1.51 Mile–2.5 Mile

	Starts	1st	2nd	3rd	4th	5th	6th	7th	8th	9th	10th	11–20	21–43
Atlanta	2	0	0	0	0	0	0	0	0	0	0	1	1
California	2	0	0	0	0	0	0	0	0	0	0	2	0
Michigan	2	0	0	0	1	0	0	0	0	0	0	0	1
Indianapolis	1	0	0	0	0	0	0	0	0	0	0	0	1
Pocono	2	0	0	0	0	0	0	0	0	0	0	1	1
Total	**9**	**0**	**0**	**0**	**1**	**0**	**0**	**0**	**0**	**0**	**0**	**4**	**4**
		0.0%	0.0%	0.0%	11.1%	0.0%	0.0%	0.0%	0.0%	0.0%	0.0%	44.4%	44.4%

Restrictor Plate

	Starts	1st	2nd	3rd	4th	5th	6th	7th	8th	9th	10th	11–20	21–43
Daytona	2	1	0	0	0	0	0	0	0	0	0	0	1
Talladega	2	0	0	0	0	0	0	0	0	0	0	0	2
Total	**4**	**1**	**0**	**0**	**0**	**0**	**0**	**0**	**0**	**0**	**0**	**0**	**3**
		25.0%	0.0%	0.0%	0.0%	0.0%	0.0%	0.0%	0.0%	0.0%	0.0%	0.0%	75.0%

Road Courses

	Starts	1st	2nd	3rd	4th	5th	6th	7th	8th	9th	10th	11–20	21–43
Sears Point	1	0	0	0	0	0	0	0	0	0	0	0	1
Watkins Glen	1	0	0	0	0	0	0	0	0	0	0	0	1
Total	**2**	**0**	**0**	**0**	**0**	**0**	**0**	**0**	**0**	**0**	**0**	**0**	**2**
		0.0%	0.0%	0.0%	0.0%	0.0%	0.0%	0.0%	0.0%	0.0%	0.0%	0.0%	100.0%

Current Team: Roush Racing
Residence: Charlotte, North Carolina
Hometown: South Boston, Virginia
Birthday: June 29, 1967
Height: 5 feet, 7 inches
Weight: 160

Races: 331
Running: 295 (89.1 percent)
Accidents: 13 (3.9 percent)
Mechanical Failures: 23 (6.9 percent)

1996–2003	Roush Racing
1994–1995	Stavola Brothers Racing
1993	Filbert Martocci

Jeff Burton

Jeff Burton's racing career began in karts at the age of seven at South Boston Speedway in Virginia. From there he began his long march to the Winston Cup ranks, which he joined in 1993 in a one-race deal at New Hampshire for car owner Filbert Martocci. Burton qualified 6th but finished 37th after an accident in what was his only race of the year.

He found a more permanent home in 1994, when he signed on to drive for the Stavola Brothers in their No. 8 Raybestos Brakes Ford. Jeff performed well, starting 30 races, and won the Rookie of the Year award in 1994. In his best performances of the year, he finished 4th at both Atlanta and Pocono. He finished the year with two top 5s and three top 10s and a 24th position in the championship points race. His second year with the Stavolas was less successful, with only one top 5 and two top 10s.

In 1996 Burton left the Stavola team to drive a Ford for Roush Racing, and he has been there ever since. After this move, Jeff's finishing performance improved. In 1996 he had six top-5 and 12 top-10 finishes, and in half of the seasons 30 races, he finished in 11th place or better. His best finish of the year was a 3rd at Richmond. In 1997 Burton made it to victory lane for the first time, and a second time and a third. His first win came in the first race at the new Texas Motor Speedway, and he followed it with wins at New Hampshire and Martinsville. In the 1997 season, 32 races, Burton finished in the top five in 13 of them. He finished 4th in the points, a handful of bad finishes costing him a chance at the championship. Regardless, Jeff Burton had made the transition from a journeyman driver to a premier Winston Cup driver.

In the late 1990s his successes continued. He won twice in 1998 and had a banner year in 1999, when he won six races. Both seasons ended with a 5th place finish in the points race, and he made a better run at the championship in 2000, finishing 3rd with four wins. After joining the Roush organization, Burton was scoring about as many top 5s and top 10s as anyone in the business, but beginning in 2001 the percentages began to slip. In 2001 Jeff won two races, but he scored only eight top 5s. While this was lower than his norm, the team managed a top-10 finish in the points championship. In 2002 it was worse, with no wins and only five top-5 finishes. In 2003 the woes continued, with the team again going winless with only three top-5s. But Jeff Burton can never be counted out. When he and his team get back on course, they will always be a force to be reckoned with.

Jeff Burton came to Roush Racing in 1996 and has been a staple of the organization ever since. While sponsorship woes have put a damper on the team, they are still running. From 1996 to present Jeff has won 17 races in his Roush Ford.

Jeff's first two full years of racing were for the Stavola Brothers where he scored a handful of top five finishes and gained valuable seat time.

Year-by-year Performance

	Races	Poles		Wins		Top 5		Top 10	
1993	1	0	0.0%	0	0.0%	0	0.0%	0	0.0%
1994	30	0	0.0%	0	0.0%	2	6.7%	3	10.0%
1995	29	0	0.0%	0	0.0%	1	3.4%	2	6.9%
1996	30	1	3.3%	0	0.0%	6	20.0%	12	40.0%
1997	32	0	0.0%	3	9.4%	13	40.6%	18	56.3%
1998	33	1	3.0%	2	6.1%	18	54.5%	23	69.7%
1999	34	0	0.0%	6	17.6%	18	52.9%	23	67.6%
2000	34	1	2.9%	4	11.8%	15	44.1%	22	64.7%
2001	36	0	0.0%	2	5.6%	8	22.2%	16	44.4%
2002	36	0	0.0%	0	0.0%	5	13.9%	14	38.9%
2003	36	0	0.0%	0	0.0%	3	8.3%	11	30.6%
Total	**331**	**3**	**0.9%**	**17**	**5.1%**	**89**	**26.9%**	**144**	**43.5%**

Track Performance

Less than 1 Mile

	Starts	1st	2nd	3rd	4th	5th	6th	7th	8th	9th	10th	11–20	21–43
Bristol	20	0	1	0	2	1	1	0	0	2	0	5	8
Martinsville	19	1	2	2	1	2	0	0	0	2	1	3	5
Richmond	19	1	1	2	2	1	0	2	0	2	0	4	4
N. Wilkes	5	0	0	0	1	0	0	0	0	0	0	0	4
Total	**63**	**2**	**4**	**4**	**6**	**4**	**1**	**2**	**0**	**6**	**1**	**12**	**21**
		3.2%	6.3%	6.3%	9.5%	6.3%	1.6%	3.2%	0.0%	9.5%	1.6%	19.0%	33.3%

1 Mile–1.49 Mile

	Starts	1st	2nd	3rd	4th	5th	6th	7th	8th	9th	10th	11–20	21–43
Dover	20	0	1	2	0	0	2	0	1	1	0	4	9
New Hamp.	18	4	0	0	2	1	0	0	0	1	0	6	4
N. Carolina	20	1	0	1	3	3	1	1	0	0	0	7	3
Phoenix	10	2	0	0	2	0	0	0	1	0	0	2	3
Darlington	20	2	3	0	1	2	1	0	1	0	2	6	2
Total	**88**	**9**	**4**	**3**	**8**	**6**	**4**	**1**	**3**	**2**	**2**	**25**	**21**
		10.2%	4.5%	3.4%	9.1%	6.8%	4.5%	1.1%	3.4%	2.3%	2.3%	28.4%	23.9%

1.5 mile

	Starts	1st	2nd	3rd	4th	5th	6th	7th	8th	9th	10th	11–20	21–43
Charlotte	20	2	0	1	0	2	2	1	1	0	0	5	6
Chicago	3	0	0	0	0	0	1	0	0	0	0	1	1
Homestead	5	0	0	2	1	0	0	0	0	0	0	2	0
Kansas	3	0	0	0	0	0	0	0	0	0	0	2	1
Las Vegas	6	2	1	0	0	0	1	0	0	1	0	0	1
Texas	7	1	1	0	0	0	0	1	0	0	0	2	2
Total	**44**	**5**	**2**	**3**	**1**	**2**	**4**	**2**	**1**	**1**	**0**	**12**	**11**
		11.4%	4.5%	6.8%	2.3%	4.5%	9.1%	4.5%	2.3%	2.3%	0.0%	27.3%	25.0%

Track Performance

1.51 Mile–2.5 Mile

Atlanta	19	0	0	0	3	2	0	0	1	1	1	2	9
California	7	0	1	0	0	1	0	0	0	0	1	2	2
Michigan	20	0	0	1	2	1	0	1	1	1	1	6	6
Indianapolis	10	0	0	0	0	1	1	0	0	0	0	4	4
Pocono	20	0	2	2	2	0	2	1	0	1	1	2	7
Total	**76**	**0**	**3**	**3**	**7**	**5**	**3**	**2**	**2**	**3**	**4**	**16**	**28**
		0.0%	3.9%	3.9%	9.2%	6.6%	3.9%	2.6%	2.6%	3.9%	5.3%	21.1%	36.8%

Restrictor Plate

Daytona	19	1	2	1	0	1	0	0	1	0	0	7	6
Talladega	20	0	0	1	0	0	0	1	2	1	2	5	8
Total	**39**	**1**	**2**	**2**	**0**	**1**	**0**	**1**	**3**	**1**	**2**	**12**	**14**
		2.6%	5.1%	5.1%	0.0%	2.6%	0.0%	2.6%	7.7%	2.6%	5.1%	30.8%	35.9%

Road Courses

Riverside	0	0	0	0	0	0	0	0	0	0	0	0	0
Sears Point	10	0	0	0	0	0	0	0	1	1	0	3	5
Watkins Glen	10	0	1	1	0	0	0	1	0	0	0	1	6
Total	**20**	**0**	**1**	**1**	**0**	**0**	**0**	**1**	**1**	**1**	**0**	**4**	**11**
		0.0%	5.0%	5.0%	0.0%	0.0%	0.0%	5.0%	5.0%	5.0%	0.0%	20.0%	55.0%

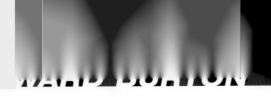

Current Team: Haas CNC Racing
Residence: Halifax, Virginia
Hometown: South Boston, Virginia
Birthday: October 25, 1961
Height: 5 feet, 6 inches
Weight: 150

Races: 322
Running: 252 (78.3 percent)
Accidents: 40 (12.4 percent)
Mechanical Failures: 30 (9.3 percent)

2003	Haas CNC Racing
	Bill Davis Racing
1996–2002	Bill Davis Racing
1995	Bill Davis Racing
	A. G. Dillard
1994	A. G. Dillard

Ward Burton

L ike so many others, Ward Burton drove karts competitively before his age reached double digits. Throughout his youth, he piloted his karts well, winning both poles and races. But unlike most other drivers, once he reached the age of 16, he was ready to take a break from racing. After graduating from a military academy where he was the best rifle shot in his class, he spent some time in college but spent more time in the woods hunting and fishing.

Ward was working in the family construction business when younger brother Jeff was beginning his racing career. Seeing Jeff race got Ward back to the track. Once he was back around the cars, it wasn't long before he was in one, this time in street stocks and late models. He continued running the short tracks through the 1980s until he joined the Busch Series in 1990, finishing second in the Rookie of the Year battle. He won his first Busch Series race in 1992 at Rockingham, and in 1993 won three times.

In 1994 he made the move to the Winston Cup Series. In his first year he again finished second in the Rookie battle, immediately behind his brother, Jeff. In late 1995 Ward joined the team of Bill Davis Racing, and in his first race for the team drove to an impressive 4th-place finish at the treacherous Darlington Raceway. Six races later, at the North Carolina Speedway in Rockingham, Burton and Davis both got their first win.

Ward stayed with Bill Davis racing for eight years, but the next few years were a struggle for the team. During the three seasons from 1996 to 1998, they carded only 16 top 10s and one top-5 finish. However, in 1999 the performance picked up. Although the team again went winless, it had six top-5 finishes. In 2000 it began to really come together for Ward. He won at Darlington and finished in the top 10 in half of the season's races.

In 2001 Ward found himself in one of the new Dodges, after the manufacturer decided to return to the sport. The Davis team had 10 top-10 finishes in its new car and won the prestigious Southern 500 at Darlington. The team entered 2002 with high hopes, and its dreams were realized when Ward drove his Dodge to a win in the Daytona 500. It was his first multi-win year, as he also won at New Hampshire. But in racing, the chemistry can change quickly. Ward and Davis parted ways in 2003 with Ward moving to Haas CNC Racing for the 2004 campaign.

Away from the track, Ward is also a driving force. His understanding of the concept of stewardship of the land has evolved into the Ward Burton Wildlife Foundation. The organization's purpose is "to promote an awareness of the need for wildlife conservation, enhancement, and proper stewardship of our natural resources through preservation and education."

Ward began driving the Net Zero Chevrolet owned by Gene Haas late in the 2003 season. While the relatively new team has yet to win, they have put together some good runs.

From 1999 to late in the 2003 season, Ward drove for Bill Davis Racing. He won five races with the team, including the 2002 Daytona 500.

Year-by-year Performance

	Races	Poles		Wins		Top 5		Top 10	
1994	26	1	3.8%	0	0.0%	1	3.8%	2	7.7%
1995	29	0	0.0%	1	3.4%	3	10.3%	6	20.7%
1996	27	1	3.7%	0	0.0%	0	0.0%	4	14.8%
1997	31	1	3.2%	0	0.0%	0	0.0%	7	22.6%
1998	33	2	6.1%	0	0.0%	1	3.0%	5	15.2%
1999	34	1	2.9%	0	0.0%	6	17.6%	16	47.1%
2000	34	0	0.0%	1	2.9%	4	11.8%	17	50.0%
2001	36	0	0.0%	1	2.8%	6	16.7%	10	27.8%
2002	36	1	2.8%	2	5.6%	3	8.3%	8	22.2%
2003	36	0	0.0%	0	0.0%	0	0.0%	4	11.1%
Total	**322**	**7**	**2.2%**	**5**	**1.6%**	**24**	**7.5%**	**79**	**24.5%**

Track Performance

Less than 1 Mile

	Starts	1st	2nd	3rd	4th	5th	6th	7th	8th	9th	10th	11-20	21-43
Bristol	20	0	0	1	0	1	0	0	1	2	0	6	9
Martinsville	17	0	0	1	0	1	0	1	0	0	0	6	8
Richmond	20	0	0	0	0	0	1	1	2	1	0	6	9
N. Wilkes	3	0	0	0	0	0	0	0	0	0	0	1	2
Total	**60**	**0**	**0**	**2**	**0**	**2**	**1**	**2**	**3**	**3**	**0**	**19**	**28**
		0.0%	0.0%	3.3%	0.0%	3.3%	1.7%	3.3%	5.0%	5.0%	0.0%	31.7%	46.7%

1 Mile–1.49 Mile

	Starts	1st	2nd	3rd	4th	5th	6th	7th	8th	9th	10th	11-20	21-43
Dover	20	0	0	0	0	0	0	1	1	0	0	3	15
New Hamp.	17	1	0	0	0	0	0	0	1	0	0	3	12
N. Carolina	18	1	1	1	0	0	1	1	2	0	0	6	5
Phoenix	10	0	0	0	0	0	0	0	0	0	0	5	5
Darlington	20	2	1	0	1	0	2	0	1	0	0	5	8
Total	**85**	**4**	**2**	**1**	**1**	**0**	**3**	**2**	**5**	**0**	**0**	**22**	**45**
		4.7%	2.4%	1.2%	1.2%	0.0%	3.5%	2.4%	5.9%	0.0%	0.0%	25.9%	52.9%

1.5 mile

	Starts	1st	2nd	3rd	4th	5th	6th	7th	8th	9th	10th	11-20	21-43
Charlotte	20	0	1	1	0	1	0	2	2	1	2	2	8
Chicago	3	0	0	0	0	0	0	0	0	0	0	2	1
Homestead	5	0	0	0	0	0	0	0	0	0	0	3	2
Kansas	3	0	0	0	0	0	0	0	0	0	0	0	3
Las Vegas	6	0	1	0	0	0	0	0	0	0	0	1	4
Texas	7	0	0	0	0	0	0	1	0	0	0	4	2
Total	**44**	**0**	**2**	**1**	**0**	**1**	**0**	**3**	**2**	**1**	**2**	**12**	**20**
		0.0%	4.5%	2.3%	0.0%	2.3%	0.0%	6.8%	4.5%	2.3%	4.5%	27.3%	45.5%

Track Performance
1.51 Mile–2.5 Mile

	Starts	1st	2nd	3rd	4th	5th	6th	7th	8th	9th	10th	11–20	21–43
Atlanta	19	0	0	1	0	2	0	1	2	1	0	9	3
California	7	0	0	0	0	0	2	0	0	0	0	2	3
Michigan	20	0	0	0	1	0	2	0	1	1	0	2	13
Indianapolis	10	0	0	0	0	0	2	0	0	0	0	1	7
Pocono	19	0	1	0	0	0	0	0	1	0	0	5	12
Total	**75**	**0**	**1**	**1**	**1**	**2**	**6**	**1**	**4**	**2**	**0**	**19**	**38**
		0.0%	1.3%	1.3%	1.3%	2.7%	8.0%	1.3%	5.3%	2.7%	0.0%	25.3%	50.7%

Restrictor Plate

	Starts	1st	2nd	3rd	4th	5th	6th	7th	8th	9th	10th	11–20	21–43
Daytona	19	1	0	0	1	0	0	3	2	1	0	1	10
Talladega	17	0	0	0	1	0	0	1	1	0	2	3	9
Total	**36**	**1**	**0**	**0**	**2**	**0**	**0**	**4**	**3**	**1**	**2**	**4**	**19**
		2.8%	0.0%	0.0%	5.6%	0.0%	0.0%	11.1%	8.3%	2.8%	5.6%	11.1%	52.8%

Road Courses

	Starts	1st	2nd	3rd	4th	5th	6th	7th	8th	9th	10th	11–20	21–43
Sears Point	10	0	0	0	0	0	1	0	0	0	2	1	6
Watkins Glen	10	0	0	0	0	0	1	0	0	0	0	2	7
Total	**20**	**0**	**0**	**0**	**0**	**0**	**2**	**0**	**0**	**0**	**2**	**3**	**13**
		0.0%	0.0%	0.0%	0.0%	0.0%	10.0%	0.0%	0.0%	0.0%	10.0%	15.0%	65.0%

Kurt Busch

Current Team: Roush Racing
Residence: Concord, North Carolina
Hometown: Las Vegas, Nevada
Birthday: August 4, 1978
Height: 5 feet, 11 inches
Weight: 155

Races: 114
Running: 95 (83.3 percent)
Accidents: 8 (7.9 percent)
Mechanical Failures: 11 (9.6 percent)

2003–2000   Roush Racing

Kurt Busch's first racing experiences came in the deserts of Nevada, far from the hills of North Carolina. At the age of 15, he began racing in the Dwarf Series, and like so many other drivers, was assisted by his father. He won the Rookie of the Year title for the Dwarf Series in 1994 and the championship in 1995. The next year he ran in the hobby stock division and again won a championship. As he won, his efforts were noticed, and he was propelled into new series.

In 1998 he again won Rookie of the Year honors, this time in the NASCAR Southwest Touring Series, a regional series that is managed, like the Nextel Cup, by NASCAR. He again followed rookie honors with a championship in the same series the next year. Once again, Kurt's success was noticed, this time by Jack Roush. Roush decided to put Kurt in the Craftsman Truck Series, and in his first year, Kurt proved the opportunity was merited. He won four races and finished 2nd in the points championship.

As Busch's stock was clearly rising, Roush again decided to give him another opportunity. In 2000, while he was still driving trucks, Roush allowed Busch to drive in seven Winston Cup events. While his best finish was a 13th at Charlotte, it was enough to convince Roush. In 2001 Kurt jumped directly from the Truck Series to Winston Cup, skipping the Busch Series. Many questioned the speed of Kurt's rise in the sport, but in 2001 he scored six top-10 finishes. He gained valuable experience, and he was usually able to keep the fenders on the car.

In 2002 this experience, coupled with his new veteran crew chief, Jimmy Fennig, propelled Kurt to the top ranks of the sport. Kurt recorded his first victory when he won the spring race at Bristol. By the end of the year, Busch had won four races and finished as a runner-up in three more. In all, Busch ran in 36 events, and he and his crew chief Fennig carded 20 top-10 finishes and finished 3rd in the points race. The team of Fennig and Busch had another good year in 2003, with four wins. Trouble and bad finishes, however, held them to an 11th-place finish in the final Winston Cup Championship.

While 2003 provided Kurt with more experience on the track, it also provided him with a few off-track lessons. Kurt perpetuated a running feud with Jimmy Spencer, and after it came to a head, Kurt's image was a bit tarnished. But his competitive edge did not suffer. At the height of the distractions, Kurt Busch continued to win.

Kurt Busch began his career in 2000 and has driven every one of his races in a Jack Roush Ford. He got his first win in 2002, and by the end of the 2003 season had a total of eight victories.

Kurt Busch's career took off when he was teamed up with veteran crew chief Jimmy Fennig.

Year-by-year Performance

	Races	Poles		Wins		Top 5		Top 10	
2000	7	0	0.0%	0	0.0%	0	0.0%	0	0.0%
2001	35	1	2.9%	0	0.0%	3	8.6%	6	17.1%
2002	36	1	2.8%	4	11.1%	12	33.3%	20	55.6%
2003	36	0	0.0%	4	11.1%	9	25.0%	14	38.9%
Total	**114**	**2**	**1.8%**	**8**	**7.0%**	**24**	**21.1%**	**40**	**35.1%**

Track Performance

Less than 1 Mile

Bristol	6	3	0	0	0	0	1	0	0	0	0	0	2
Martinsville	7	1	0	0	0	0	0	0	0	0	1	0	5
Richmond	6	0	0	0	0	0	0	0	1	0	0	2	3
Total	**19**	**4**	**0**	**0**	**0**	**0**	**1**	**0**	**1**	**0**	**1**	**2**	**10**
		21.1%	0.0%	0.0%	0.0%	0.0%	5.3%	0.0%	5.3%	0.0%	5.3%	10.5%	52.6%

1 Mile–1.49 Mile

Dover	7	0	0	0	0	0	0	1	0	0	0	3	3
New Hamp.	6	0	1	0	0	0	0	0	1	0	0	2	2
N. Carolina	7	0	1	1	0	0	0	0	0	0	0	2	3
Phoenix	4	0	0	0	1	0	1	0	0	0	0	0	2
Darlington	6	0	1	0	0	0	0	1	0	0	0	1	3
Total		**30**	**0**	**3**	**1**	**1**	**0**	**1**	**2**	**1**	**0**	**0**	**8**	**13**
		0.0%	10.0%	3.3%	3.3%	0.0%	3.3%	6.7%	3.3%	0.0%	0.0%	26.7%	43.3%

1.5 mile

Charlotte	14	0	0	0	0	0	0	0	0	0	0	11	3
Chicago	3	0	0	0	0	0	1	0	1	0	0	0	1
Homestead	4	1	0	0	0	0	0	0	0	0	0	1	2
Kansas	3	0	0	0	0	0	0	0	0	1	0	0	2
Las Vegas	3	0	0	0	0	0	0	0	0	0	0	2	1
Texas	3	0	0	0	1	0	0	0	0	1	0	0	1
Total	**30**	**1**	**0**	**0**	**1**	**0**	**1**	**0**	**1**	**2**	**0**	**14**	**10**
		3.3%	0.0%	0.0%	3.3%	0.0%	3.3%	0.0%	3.3%	6.7%	0.0%	46.7%	33.3%

Track Performance

1.51 Mile–2.5 Mile

Atlanta	6	1	0	0	0	0	0	0	1	0	1	1	2
California	3	1	1	0	0	0	0	0	0	0	0	1	0
Michigan	6	1	0	0	0	0	0	0	0	0	1	1	3
Indianapolis	3	0	0	0	0	1	0	1	0	0	0	0	1
Pocono	6	0	2	0	0	0	0	0	0	0	0	1	3
Total	**24**	**3**	**3**	**0**	**0**	**1**	**0**	**1**	**1**	**0**	**2**	**4**	**9**
		12.5%	12.5%	0.0%	0.0%	4.2%	0.0%	4.2%	4.2%	0.0%	8.3%	16.7%	37.5%

Restrictor Plate

Daytona	6	0	1	0	1	0	0	0	0	0	0	0	4
Talladega	6	0	0	2	1	0	1	0	0	0	0	1	1
Total	**12**	**0**	**1**	**2**	**2**	**0**	**1**	**0**	**0**	**0**	**0**	**1**	**5**
		0.0%	8.3%	16.7%	16.7%	0.0%	8.3%	0.0%	0.0%	0.0%	0.0%	8.3%	41.7%

Road Courses

Sears Point	3	0	0	0	1	0	0	0	0	0	0	0	2
Watkins Glen	3	0	0	0	0	0	0	0	0	0	0	1	2
Total	**6**	**0**	**0**	**0**	**1**	**0**	**0**	**0**	**0**	**0**	**0**	**1**	**4**
		0.0%	0.0%	0.0%	16.7%	0.0%	0.0%	0.0%	0.0%	0.0%	0.0%	16.7%	66.7%

Current Team: Arnold Motorsports
Residence: Charlotte, North Carolina
Hometown: Spanaway, Washington
Birthday: November 3, 1958
Height: 5 feet, 9 inches
Weight: 170

Races: 380
Running: 242 (63.7 percent)
Accidents: 51 (13.4 percent)
Mechanical Failures: 87 (22.9 percent)

Derrike Cope

2003	Quest Motor Racing	**1994**	Bobby Allison
2002	Warren Johnson		Motorsports
	Quest Motor Racing		T. W. Taylor
	BAM Racing		Cale Yarborough
2001	Ted Campbell		Motorsports
2000	Fenley-Moore Racing	**1990–1993**	Bob Whitcomb
1999	Fenley-Moore Racing	**1989**	Bob Whitcomb
	Chuck Rider		Jim Testa
1998	Chuck Rider	**1988**	Jim Testa
1997	Nelson Bowers	**1987**	Fred Stoke
1995–1996	Bobby Allison	**1986**	Rabanco Racing
	Motorsports	**1984–1985**	George Jefferson
		1982	George Jefferson

W hile Derrike Cope ended up as a race car driver, his first shot at a sports career was in baseball. But a knee injury ended his promising baseball career, and he switched to racing. In 1980 Derrike won the NASCAR Late Model Sportsman Rookie of the Year title, and in 1983 he won the series championship. In 1984 he moved up to the Winston West Series, won another Rookie of the Year award and made a good run at the championship.

While Derrike was running in these series, with some success, he was occasionally running a few Winston Cup events, most of them at the Riverside California Road Course. In 1984 and 1985 he drove to a couple of 15th-place finishes at the track. In 1986 and 1987 he began expanding his selection of tracks and ran more oval tracks. By the late 1980s his performance was improving; in 1989 he started 23 races and finished in the top 10 four times and in the top 20 nine times. Derrick's best year in the sport was 1990, when he raced in all 29 of the season's races and won twice. His first win came in the Daytona 500, and he backed it up later in the year at Dover.

By 1991 the team that had won two races the previous year was gone, and Derrike was searching for a good team. In 1994 he started the year in Cale Yarborough's car but had limited success. His career took an upswing later in 1994, when he drove for Bobby Allison Motorsports. Derrike started showing up in the top 10 again. The team barely missed a win at Phoenix late in the year, finishing a close second to Ricky Rudd. Lack of sponsorship was ultimately the demise of Bobby Allison Motorsports, and Derrike left the team to drive for Nelson Bowers in the Skittles Pontiac during the 1997 season. After one year with the team, Derrike joined Chuck Rider's team for a 1 1/2-year run. Derrike ran the entire 1998 schedule and started the 1999 campaign with No. 30, but left the team early in the year. He raced in a few more races later in 1999, but with little success. Since then Derrike has been without a full-time ride and has been forced to race in inferior equipment. He ran 18 races in 2003 but mechanical problems plagued him. In 2004 Derrike will again make an attempt to run the entire schedule with Arnold Motorsports—sponsorship willing.

After a few years of part-time racing on the circuit, Derrike is back to full-time racing behind the wheel of the Arnold Development Dodge.

In the mid 1990s Derrike drove Bobby Allison's Ford Thunderbird with the Mane and Tail sponsorship. The pair came close to a win at Phoenix in 1995, leading the race late and finishing a close second to Ricky Rudd.

Year-by-year Performance

	Races	Poles		Wins		Top 5		Top 10	
1982	1	0	0.0%	0	0.0%	0	0.0%	0	0.0%
1984	3	0	0.0%	0	0.0%	0	0.0%	0	0.0%
1985	2	0	0.0%	0	0.0%	0	0.0%	0	0.0%
1986	5	0	0.0%	0	0.0%	0	0.0%	1	20.0%
1987	11	0	0.0%	0	0.0%	0	0.0%	0	0.0%
1988	26	0	0.0%	0	0.0%	0	0.0%	0	0.0%
1989	23	0	0.0%	0	0.0%	0	0.0%	4	17.4%
1990	29	0	0.0%	2	6.9%	2	6.9%	6	20.7%
1991	28	0	0.0%	0	0.0%	1	3.6%	2	7.1%
1992	29	0	0.0%	0	0.0%	0	0.0%	3	10.3%
1993	30	0	0.0%	0	0.0%	0	0.0%	1	3.3%
1994	30	0	0.0%	0	0.0%	0	0.0%	2	6.7%
1995	31	0	0.0%	0	0.0%	2	6.5%	8	25.8%
1996	29	1	3.4%	0	0.0%	0	0.0%	3	10.3%
1997	31	0	0.0%	0	0.0%	1	3.2%	2	6.5%
1998	28	1	3.6%	0	0.0%	0	0.0%	0	0.0%
1999	15	0	0.0%	0	0.0%	0	0.0%	0	0.0%
2000	3	0	0.0%	0	0.0%	0	0.0%	0	0.0%
2001	1	0	0.0%	0	0.0%	0	0.0%	0	0.0%
2002	7	0	0.0%	0	0.0%	0	0.0%	0	0.0%
2003	18	0	0.0%	0	0.0%	0	0.0%	0	0.0%
Total	**380**	**2**	**0.5%**	**2**	**0.5%**	**6**	**1.6%**	**32**	**8.4%**

Track Performance

Less than 1 Mile

	Starts	1st	2nd	3rd	4th	5th	6th	7th	8th	9th	10th	11–20	21–43
Bristol	24	0	0	0	0	0	0	0	0	0	2	6	16
Martinsville	22	0	0	0	0	0	0	0	0	2	0	7	13
Richmond	23	0	0	0	0	0	1	0	1	0	0	5	16
N. Wilkes	16	0	0	0	0	0	0	0	0	0	0	6	10
Total	**85**	**0**	**0**	**0**	**0**	**0**	**1**	**0**	**1**	**2**	**2**	**24**	**55**
		0.0%	0.0%	0.0%	0.0%	0.0%	1.2%	0.0%	1.2%	2.4%	2.4%	28.2%	64.7%

1 Mile–1.49 Mile

	Starts	1st	2nd	3rd	4th	5th	6th	7th	8th	9th	10th	11–20	21–43
Dover	24	1	0	0	0	0	0	1	1	1	0	5	15
New Hamp.	8	0	0	0	0	0	0	1	0	0	0	2	5
N. Carolina	24	0	0	0	0	0	0	0	2	0	0	11	11
Phoenix	13	0	1	0	0	0	0	1	0	0	0	5	6
Darlington	23	0	0	0	1	1	0	0	0	1	0	8	12
Total	**92**	**1**	**1**	**0**	**1**	**1**	**0**	**3**	**3**	**2**	**0**	**31**	**49**
		1.1%	1.1%	0.0%	1.1%	1.1%	0.0%	3.3%	3.3%	2.2%	0.0%	33.7%	53.3%

1.5 mile

	Starts	1st	2nd	3rd	4th	5th	6th	7th	8th	9th	10th	11–20	21–43
Charlotte	27	0	0	0	0	0	1	1	1	1	0	11	12
Chicago	1	0	0	0	0	0	0	0	0	0	0	0	1
Homestead	1	0	0	0	0	0	0	0	0	0	0	0	1
Kansas	2	0	0	0	0	0	0	0	0	0	0	0	2
Las Vegas	4	0	0	0	0	0	0	0	0	0	0	0	4
Texas	2	0	0	0	0	0	0	0	0	0	0	0	2
Total	**37**	**0**	**0**	**0**	**0**	**0**	**1**	**1**	**1**	**1**	**0**	**11**	**22**
		0.0%	0.0%	0.0%	0.0%	0.0%	2.7%	2.7%	2.7%	2.7%	0.0%	29.7%	59.5%

Track Performance

1.51 Mile–2.5 Mile

	Starts	1st	2nd	3rd	4th	5th	6th	7th	8th	9th	10th	11–20	21–43
Atlanta	25	0	0	0	0	1	0	1	0	0	0	9	14
California	4	0	0	0	0	0	0	0	0	0	0	0	4
Michigan	28	0	0	0	0	0	1	0	1	1	0	5	20
Indianapolis	6	0	0	0	0	0	0	0	0	0	0	1	5
Pocono	26	0	0	0	0	0	0	0	0	0	2	8	16
Total	**89**	**0**	**0**	**0**	**0**	**1**	**1**	**1**	**1**	**1**	**2**	**23**	**59**
		0.0%	0.0%	0.0%	0.0%	1.1%	1.1%	1.1%	1.1%	1.1%	2.2%	25.8%	66.3%

Restrictor Plate

	Starts	1st	2nd	3rd	4th	5th	6th	7th	8th	9th	10th	11–20	21–43
Daytona	24	1	0	0	0	0	0	0	0	0	0	3	20
Talladega	22	0	0	0	0	0	0	1	1	0	0	5	15
Total	**46**	**1**	**0**	**0**	**0**	**0**	**0**	**1**	**1**	**0**	**0**	**8**	**35**
		2.2%	0.0%	0.0%	0.0%	0.0%	0.0%	2.2%	2.2%	0.0%	0.0%	17.4%	76.1%

Road Courses

	Starts	1st	2nd	3rd	4th	5th	6th	7th	8th	9th	10th	11–20	21–43
Riverside	9	0	0	0	0	0	0	0	0	0	0	6	3
Sears Point	10	0	0	0	0	0	0	0	0	0	0	5	5
Watkins Glen	12	0	0	0	0	0	0	0	0	0	0	4	8
Total	**31**	**0**	**0**	**0**	**0**	**0**	**0**	**0**	**0**	**0**	**0**	**15**	**16**
		0.0%	0.0%	0.0%	0.0%	0.0%	0.0%	0.0%	0.0%	0.0%	0.0%	48.4%	51.6%

Ricky Craven

Current Team: PPI Motorsports
Residence: Concord, North Carolina
Hometown: Newburgh, Maine
Birthday: May 24, 1966
Height: 5 feet, 9 inches
Weight: 165

Races: 252
Running: 194 (77.0 percent)
Accidents: 25 (9.4 percent)
Mechanical Failures: 33 (13.1 percent)

2001–2003	PPI Motorsports
2000	Hal Hicks
1999	Hal Hicks
	Scott Barbour
1998	Nelson Bowers
	Hendrick Motorsports
1997	Hendrick Motorsports
1995–1996	Hedrick Racing
1991	Dick Moroso

While many drivers hail from the South or Midwest, Ricky Craven was born and raised in Newburgh, Maine. By modern standards he got a late start with his racing career, beginning at the age of 15. After competing on local tracks throughout New England, he drove on the American Canadian Tour. In 1989 he began driving in NASCAR in the Grand National North division, and in 1990 he drove in the series full-time, winning Rookie of the Year honors.

He backed it up in 1991, winning the Busch Grand National North Championship. It was also in 1991 that Ricky got his first Winston Cup start. He started 34th in a race at Rockingham, and after a long day's drive, finished 34th. It was almost four years before Ricky got his second start. In 1992 Craven went from regional to national, when he began driving in NASCAR's Busch Grand National Series, and once again he won the Rookie of the Year honors. After a 1994 season that garnered two wins and 16 top 10s, some Winston Cup owners were taking a look at Ricky. In 1995 he signed on to drive the No. 41 Kodiak car owned by Larry Hedrick, and drove in all 31 Winston Cup events. The team finished the year with four top 10s and Ricky took home another Rookie of the Year trophy.

In 1996 Ricky had three top fives, including 3rd-place finishes at Darlington and Rockingham. The team also qualified in the top fives a total of seven times, including poles at Martinsville and New Hampshire. Ricky added seven more top-10 finishes (including another pair of 3rd-place finishes), but racing was about to become a more difficult proposition. A problem with post-concussion syndrome caused in a racing accident forced Ricky to leave the sport for a while. Perceived as a damaged commodity, he was forced to race a limited schedule, often in inferior equipment. That is, until the 2001 season.

Veteran car owner Cal Wells had decided to go NASCAR racing, and he choose a recovered Ricky Craven to drive for his new team. With Cal Wells as an owner, it took only 30 races to accomplish what Ricky had been trying to do for a decade—win a Winston Cup race. Ricky won at Martinsville, a good old-fashioned short track that rewards driving skill and a crew chief's setup. The team went winless in 2002 but became more consistent, with a finishing average of just over 19th position.

In 2003 Ricky got another win—one that ensured his place in every "greatest moments" highlight film until the end of time. Ricky won at Darlington, barely edging out Kurt Busch for the win. The two banged off each other throughout the last few laps; they came out of the last turn banging, and crossed the finish line welded together. The margin of victory, 0.002 second, was the closest ever recorded since timing equipment was introduced.

Ricky Craven is currently driving for Cal Wells, his seventh owner since 1991. When Cal began NASCAR racing in the 2001 season, he chose the winless Craven for his driver. He was rewarded for his choice that year when Ricky drove to a victory at Martinsville.

In 1997 and part of 1998 Ricky drove the No. 25 Budweiser Chevrolet for Rick Hendrick.

Year-by-year Performance

	Races	Poles		Wins		Top 5		Top 10	
1991	1	0	0.0%	0	0.0%	0	0.0%	0	0.0%
1995	31	0	0.0%	0	0.0%	0	0.0%	4	12.9%
1996	31	2	6.5%	0	0.0%	3	9.7%	5	16.1%
1997	30	0	0.0%	0	0.0%	4	13.3%	7	23.3%
1998	11	1	9.1%	0	0.0%	0	0.0%	1	9.1%
1999	24	0	0.0%	0	0.0%	0	0.0%	0	0.0%
2000	16	0	0.0%	0	0.0%	0	0.0%	0	0.0%
2001	36	1	2.8%	1	2.8%	4	11.1%	7	19.4%
2002	36	2	5.6%	0	0.0%	3	8.3%	9	25.0%
2003	36	0	0.0%	1	2.8%	3	8.3%	8	22.2%
Total	**252**	**6**	**2.4%**	**2**	**0.8%**	**17**	**6.7%**	**41**	**16.3%**

Track Performance

Less than 1 Mile

	Starts	1st	2nd	3rd	4th	5th	6th	7th	8th	9th	10th	11–20	21–43
Bristol	13	0	0	0	0	0	0	0	1	1	0	4	7
Martinsville	16	1	0	0	0	0	0	1	1	0	0	3	10
Richmond	15	0	0	0	0	0	0	0	0	1	0	5	9
N. Wilkes	4	0	0	0	0	0	0	1	0	0	0	0	3
Total	**48**	**1**	**0**	**0**	**0**	**0**	**0**	**2**	**2**	**2**	**0**	**12**	**29**
		2.1%	0.0%	0.0%	0.0%	0.0%	0.0%	4.2%	4.2%	4.2%	0.0%	25.0%	60.4%

1 Mile–1.49 Mile

	Starts	1st	2nd	3rd	4th	5th	6th	7th	8th	9th	10th	11–20	21–43
Dover	14	0	0	0	1	0	0	1	1	1	0	2	8
New Hamp.	15	0	0	0	0	1	1	0	0	0	0	3	10
N. Carolina	18	0	0	2	1	3	0	0	1	1	1	3	6
Phoenix	9	0	0	0	0	0	0	0	1	0	0	1	7
Darlington	13	1	0	1	0	0	0	0	1	0	0	3	7
Total	**69**	**1**	**0**	**3**	**2**	**4**	**1**	**1**	**4**	**2**	**1**	**12**	**38**
		1.4%	0.0%	4.3%	2.9%	5.8%	1.4%	1.4%	5.8%	2.9%	1.4%	17.4%	55.1%

1.5 mile

	Starts	1st	2nd	3rd	4th	5th	6th	7th	8th	9th	10th	11–20	21–43
Charlotte	14	0	0	1	0	1	0	0	0	0	1	1	10
Chicago	3	0	0	0	0	0	0	0	0	0	0	1	2
Homestead	4	0	0	0	0	0	0	0	0	0	0	0	4
Kansas	3	0	0	0	0	0	0	0	0	0	0	0	3
Las Vegas	6	0	0	0	0	0	0	0	0	0	0	0	6
Texas	4	0	0	0	0	0	0	0	0	0	0	1	3
Total	**34**	**0**	**0**	**1**	**0**	**1**	**0**	**0**	**0**	**0**	**1**	**3**	**28**
		0.0%	0.0%	2.9%	0.0%	2.9%	0.0%	0.0%	0.0%	0.0%	2.9%	8.8%	82.4%

Track Performance

1.51 Mile–2.5 Mile

Atlanta	16	0	0	0	0	1	0	0	0	0	0	4	11
California	5	0	0	0	0	0	0	0	0	1	0	1	3
Michigan	14	0	1	0	0	0	0	1	0	0	0	6	6
Indianapolis	9	0	0	0	0	0	0	0	0	1	0	3	5
Pocono	13	0	0	0	0	0	0	0	0	0	2	6	5
Total	**57**	**0**	**1**	**0**	**0**	**1**	**0**	**1**	**0**	**2**	**2**	**20**	**30**
		0.0%	1.8%	0.0%	0.0%	1.8%	0.0%	1.8%	0.0%	3.5%	3.5%	35.1%	52.6%

Restrictor Plate

Daytona	16	0	0	1	0	0	0	0	0	0	0	3	12
Talladega	15	0	0	0	1	0	1	0	1	0	0	5	7
Total	**31**	**0**	**0**	**1**	**1**	**0**	**1**	**0**	**1**	**0**	**0**	**8**	**19**
		0.0%	0.0%	3.2%	3.2%	0.0%	3.2%	0.0%	3.2%	0.0%	0.0%	25.8%	61.3%

Road Courses

Sears Point	6	0	0	0	0	0	0	0	0	0	0	2	4
Watkins Glen	7	0	0	0	0	0	0	0	0	0	1	1	5
Total	**13**	**0**	**0**	**0**	**0**	**0**	**0**	**0**	**0**	**0**	**1**	**3**	**9**
		0.0%	0.0%	0.0%	0.0%	0.0%	0.0%	0.0%	0.0%	0.0%	7.7%	23.1%	69.2%

Dale Earnhardt Jr.

Current Team: Dale Earnhardt Incorporated
Residence: Mooresville, North Carolina
Hometown: Concord, North Carolina
Birthday: October 10, 1974
Height: 6 feet, 0 inch
Weight: 170

Races: 147
Running: 129 (87.7 percent)
Accidents: 11 (7.5 percent)
Mechanical Failures: 7 (4.8 percent)

1999-2003   Dale Earnhardt Incorporated

Whether it is genetic or because of his mentors, Dale Earnhardt Jr. is well on his way to joining his grandfather and father as one of the sports all-time great drivers. Over his short career, he has proven himself to be a fast, versatile, and thoughtful driver. He has benefited from some of the best equipment in Winston Cup racing but, on the other hand, has had to deal with many distractions unknown to the typical driver entering the sport.

Some new drivers can slip in under the radar and race their first season without many distractions from the fans and media. Not so for Junior. His demeanor and words while the nation grieved for his father showed he was capable of leadership off the track as well as on. Like so many others, Dale Jr. began his driving career in the street stock and late model divisions at small speedways in North Carolina. By the late 1990s he was ready for the move up to the Busch Series, and his car owner would be a familiar figure—Dale Earnhardt. His father was not only his teacher but also his boss. He ran two full seasons in the series, in 1998 and 1999. With a fast car and competent team, he made the most of the opportunity, winning the Busch Series Championship in both years and racking up 13 wins.

While competing full-time on the Busch circuit in 1999, Dale Jr. also ran five Winston Cup races, with his best finish being a 10th at Richmond and his best qualifying effort an 8th at Charlotte. In 2000 Dale Jr., in his DEI

Chevrolet, entered his first full year on the Winston Cup Series. In the seventh race of the year on the 1 1/2-mile Texas Motor Speedway, Dale Jr. won his first race. He backed it up with a win at Richmond four races later. He also became the first rookie driver to win the Winston all-star event, and added two poles to his impressive rookie season.

In 2001 Earnhardt and his team upped the ante, winning three races, two poles, and an 8th-place finish in the Winston Cup Championship. Two of his wins came on restrictor plate tracks, including an emotional win in the summer race at Daytona. While the 2002 season yielded only two victories (both at Talladega), Earnhardt was becoming a force to be reckoned with. Of the seasons 36 races, he led at some point in 22 of them. Earnhardt earned his best finish in the Winston Cup Championship in 2003, when he finished 3rd. He had two wins, including his fourth consecutive victory at Talladega. A late-season win at Phoenix proved he could win at tracks other than superspeedways. In 2003 both press and fans heralded him when he was voted the sport's most popular driver.

Dale Jr. followed his famous father into NASCAR's highest division in 1999 after a successful stay in the Busch Series that yielded two Championships. Since he came into Cup racing he has driven the No. 8 Chevrolet for DEI.

While Dale Jr. has raced in good equipment, the team has shown it can win under difficult circumstances. Here a damaged front end could not keep them out of victory lane at Talladega.

Year-by-year Performance

	Races	Poles		Wins		Top 5		Top 10	
1999	5	0	0.0%	0	0.0%	0	0.0%	1	20.0%
2000	34	2	5.9%	2	5.9%	3	8.8%	5	14.7%
2001	36	2	5.6%	3	8.3%	9	25.0%	15	41.7%
2002	36	2	5.6%	2	5.6%	11	30.6%	16	44.4%
2003	36	0	0.0%	2	5.6%	13	36.1%	21	58.3%
Total	**147**	**6**	**4.1%**	**9**	**6.1%**	**36**	**24.5%**	**58**	**39.5%**

Track Performance

Less than 1 Mile

	Starts	1st	2nd	3rd	4th	5th	6th	7th	8th	9th	10th	11–20	21–43
Bristol	8	0	0	1	1	0	0	0	0	1	0	2	3
Martinsville	8	0	0	1	2	1	0	0	0	0	0	1	3
Richmond	9	1	0	2	1	0	0	1	0	0	1	2	1
Total	**25**	**1**	**0**	**4**	**4**	**1**	**0**	**1**	**0**	**1**	**1**	**5**	**7**
		4.0%	0.0%	16.0%	16.0%	4.0%	0.0%	4.0%	0.0%	4.0%	4.0%	20.0%	28.0%

1 Mile–1.49 Mile

	Starts	1st	2nd	3rd	4th	5th	6th	7th	8th	9th	10th	11–20	21–43
Dover	8	1	0	1	0	0	0	0	0	0	1	2	3
New Hamp.	9	0	0	0	0	1	1	0	0	1	0	1	5
N. Carolina	8	0	0	0	0	0	0	0	0	0	0	3	5
Phoenix	4	1	0	0	0	1	0	0	0	0	0	0	2
Darlington	8	0	0	0	1	0	1	0	0	0	0	3	3
Total	**37**	**2**	**0**	**1**	**1**	**2**	**2**	**0**	**0**	**1**	**1**	**9**	**18**
		5.4%	0.0%	2.7%	2.7%	5.4%	5.4%	0.0%	0.0%	2.7%	2.7%	24.3%	48.6%

1.5 mile

	Starts	1st	2nd	3rd	4th	5th	6th	7th	8th	9th	10th	11–20	21–43
Charlotte	9	0	0	0	2	0	0	0	0	2	0	2	3
Chicago	3	0	0	0	0	0	0	0	0	0	1	1	1
Homestead	4	0	0	0	0	0	0	0	0	0	0	2	2
Kansas	3	0	0	0	0	0	1	0	0	0	0	1	1
Las Vegas	4	0	1	0	0	0	0	0	0	0	1	1	1
Texas	4	1	1	0	0	0	0	0	1	0	0	0	1
Total	**27**	**1**	**2**	**0**	**2**	**0**	**1**	**0**	**1**	**2**	**2**	**7**	**9**
		3.7%	7.4%	0.0%	7.4%	0.0%	3.7%	0.0%	3.7%	7.4%	7.4%	25.9%	33.3%

Track Performance
1.51 Mile–2.5 Mile

	Starts	1st	2nd	3rd	4th	5th	6th	7th	8th	9th	10th	11–20	21–43
Atlanta	9	0	1	1	0	1	1	1	0	0	0	3	1
California	4	0	0	1	0	0	1	0	0	0	0	1	1
Michigan	9	0	0	0	0	0	0	1	0	0	1	2	5
Indianapolis	4	0	0	0	0	0	0	0	0	0	1	2	1
Pocono	8	0	1	1	1	0	0	0	0	0	0	4	1
Total	**34**	**0**	**2**	**3**	**1**	**1**	**2**	**2**	**0**	**0**	**2**	**12**	**9**
		0.0%	5.9%	8.8%	2.9%	2.9%	5.9%	5.9%	0.0%	0.0%	5.9%	35.3%	26.5%

Restrictor Plate

	Starts	1st	2nd	3rd	4th	5th	6th	7th	8th	9th	10th	11–20	21–43
Daytona	8	1	1	0	0	0	1	1	0	0	0	1	3
Talladega	8	4	1	0	0	0	0	0	1	0	0	1	1
Total	**16**	**5**	**2**	**0**	**0**	**0**	**1**	**1**	**1**	**0**	**0**	**2**	**4**
		31.3%	12.5%	0.0%	0.0%	0.0%	6.3%	6.3%	6.3%	0.0%	0.0%	12.5%	25.0%

Road Courses

	Starts	1st	2nd	3rd	4th	5th	6th	7th	8th	9th	10th	11–20	21–43
Sears Point	4	0	0	0	0	0	0	0	0	0	0	2	2
Watkins Glen	4	0	0	1	0	0	0	0	0	0	0	1	2
Total	**8**	**0**	**0**	**1**	**0**	**0**	**0**	**0**	**0**	**0**	**0**	**3**	**4**
		0.0%	0.0%	12.5%	0.0%	0.0%	0.0%	0.0%	0.0%	0.0%	0.0%	37.5%	50.0%

Bill Elliot

Current Team: Evernham Motorsports
Residence: Charlotte, North Carolina
Hometown: Dawsonville, Georgia
Birthday: October 8, 1955
Height: 6 feet, 1 inch
Weight: 180

Races: 731
Running: 627 (85.8 percent)
Accidents: 26 (3.6 percent)
Mechanical Failures: 78 (10.7 percent)

2001–2003	Evernham Motorsports
1995–2000	Bill Elliot Racing
1992–1994	Junior Johnson
1982–1991	Harry Melling
1980–1981	Elliot Racing
1979	Roger Hamby
	Elliot Racing
1976–1978	Elliot Racing

Like many other racers, Bill Elliot was introduced into racing by his father. Bill went to the track with his dad, George, who was both a racing vendor and a fan. By the mid-1970s he was driving at small tracks in Georgia. One of Bill's first cars was a 1963 Ford Fairlane, and he stayed a Ford man for many years. He was 20 years old when he made his debut in a Winston Cup race on February 29, 1976, at North Carolina Speedway. However, Elliot's desire to run the Winston Cup Circuit was tempered by a lack of funds.

He ended up with eight starts in 1976 and over the next six years ran a limited schedule ranging from 10 to 21 races each year. From 1976 to 1981 Elliot carded only two top-five finishes, but he began to come on strong in 1982. That year he ran in 21 races and was able to put together eight top-five finishes. Success usually leads to sponsorship, and in 1982 Harry Melling, a Michigan-based businessman, began to sponsor Elliott's team. It helped. Elliot won in his first race at Riverside International Raceway, a road course in California, and followed in 1984 with three wins. But Bill Elliot's success of 1983 and 1984 was just a taste of what was to come.

In 1985 Elliot had a year that drivers dream of. It started with a win in the Daytona 500. Elliot then swept both events at Atlanta, Darlington, Michigan, and Pocono. By the end off the year he had racked up 11 wins (and 11 poles). It was also in 1985 that Winston began the "Winston Million," which gave $1 million to any driver who won three of the four "crown jewel" races. By winning the Daytona 500, the Winston 500, and the Southern 500, Elliot won the million dollars in the program's first year. The only thing Bill Elliot did not win in 1985 was the championship. Darrell Waltrip, who did not win a race but was week in and week out more consistent, edged him out for the championship.

Throughout the rest of the 1980s and early 1990s Elliot was one of the sports most successful and well-liked drivers. He had another shot at the championship trophy in 1988. This time the total of six wins, six poles, 11 top-5, and 22 top-10 finishes was good enough to win it. Bill Elliot won from one to five races a year, until he finally went winless in 1993. In 1992 Elliott left Melling and began driving for Junior Johnson. The move nearly paid immediate dividends, with Elliott narrowly missing a second NASCAR Championship, losing to Alan Kulwicki by just 10 points. After the 1994 season Elliot left Junior Johnson's team to form his own. For the next few years, Elliot was both an owner and driver, although he never won a race as an owner-driver.

In 2001 the Ford faithful were rocked when Bill Elliot climbed into a Dodge and began driving for Evernham Motorsports, spearheading Dodge's return to Winston Cup racing. Although many had written Bill off as a possible winner, the move got him back into victory lane. The team won one race in 2001, two in 2002, and one in 2003. He was well on his way to another win in the last race of the year, dominating the field at Homestead, when he blew a tire on the last lap. Shortly thereafter, Bill announced that he would continue racing, but on a limited schedule.

At the conclusion of the 2003 season Bill Elliot elected to go into semi-retirement, driving in only a handful of races a year. His stay in Ray Evernham's Dodge revived Bill's career as he won a few races and came close to winning quite a few more.

Awesome Bill from Dawsonville was the man in the mid- and late-1980s in his Melling-owned Ford. Elliot won 32 races from 1983 to 1989, including 11 in 1985.

Year-by-year Performance

	Races	Poles		Wins		Top 5		Top 10	
1976	8	0	0.0%	0	0.0%	0	0.0%	0	0.0%
1977	10	0	0.0%	0	0.0%	0	0.0%	2	20.0%
1978	10	0	0.0%	0	0.0%	0	0.0%	5	50.0%
1979	13	0	0.0%	0	0.0%	1	7.7%	5	38.5%
1980	11	1	9.1%	0	0.0%	0	0.0%	4	36.4%
1981	13	0	0.0%	0	0.0%	1	7.7%	7	53.8%
1982	21	0	0.0%	0	0.0%	8	38.1%	9	42.9%
1983	30	4	13.3%	1	3.3%	12	40.0%	22	73.3%
1984	30	7	23.3%	3	10.0%	13	43.3%	24	80.0%
1985	28	0	0.0%	11	39.3%	16	57.1%	18	64.3%
1986	29	2	6.9%	2	6.9%	8	27.6%	16	55.2%
1987	29	3	10.3%	6	20.7%	16	55.2%	20	69.0%
1988	29	4	13.8%	6	20.7%	15	51.7%	22	75.9%
1989	29	2	6.9%	3	10.3%	8	27.6%	14	48.3%
1990	29	2	6.9%	1	3.4%	12	41.4%	16	55.2%
1991	29	2	6.9%	1	3.4%	6	20.7%	12	41.4%
1992	29	3	10.3%	5	17.2%	14	48.3%	17	58.6%
1993	30	1	3.3%	0	0.0%	6	20.0%	15	50.0%
1994	31	1	3.2%	1	3.2%	6	19.4%	12	38.7%
1995	31	1	3.2%	0	0.0%	4	12.9%	11	35.5%
1996	24	0	0.0%	0	0.0%	0	0.0%	6	25.0%
1997	32	1	3.1%	0	0.0%	5	15.6%	14	43.8%
1998	32	0	0.0%	0	0.0%	0	0.0%	5	15.6%
1999	34	0	0.0%	0	0.0%	1	2.9%	2	5.9%
2000	32	0	0.0%	0	0.0%	3	9.4%	7	21.9%
2001	36	2	5.6%	1	2.8%	5	13.9%	9	25.0%
2002	36	4	11.1%	2	5.6%	6	16.7%	13	36.1%
2003	36	0	0.0%	1	2.8%	9	25.0%	12	33.3%
Total	**731**	**40**	**5.5%**	**44**	**6.0%**	**175**	**23.9%**	**319**	**43.6%**

Track Performance

Less than 1 Mile

Bristol	41	1	1	0	1	3	2	1	1	3	1	15	12
Martinsville	42	0	0	2	0	1	3	2	2	2	2	17	11
Richmond	44	1	1	0	6	0	1	1	0	3	2	18	11
N. Wilkes	28	0	0	1	2	1	3	0	2	1	5	5	8
Nashville	7	0	0	0	0	1	0	2	0	0	0	3	1
Total	**162**	**2**	**2**	**3**	**9**	**6**	**9**	**6**	**5**	**9**	**10**	**58**	**43**
		1.2%	1.2%	1.9%	5.6%	3.7%	5.6%	3.7%	3.1%	5.6%	6.2%	35.8%	26.5%

1 Mile–1.49 Mile

Dover	41	4	3	1	4	0	0	1	5	0	1	13	9
New Hamp.	18	0	0	0	1	1	1	0	0	1	0	5	9
N. Carolina	48	4	2	1	4	1	3	2	2	0	2	11	16
Phoenix	16	1	0	0	1	2	0	0	0	0	0	3	9
Darlington	51	5	3	6	5	3	2	4	2	3	2	13	3
Total	**174**	**14**	**8**	**8**	**15**	**7**	**6**	**7**	**9**	**4**	**5**	**45**	**46**
		8.0%	4.6%	4.6%	8.6%	4.0%	3.4%	4.0%	5.2%	2.3%	2.9%	25.9%	26.4%

1.5 mile

Charlotte	54	2	4	0	4	1	3	3	1	1	3	15	17
Chicago	3	0	0	0	0	0	0	1	0	0	1	1	0
Homestead	5	1	0	0	0	0	0	1	1	0	0	0	2
Kansas	3	0	1	0	0	1	0	0	0	0	0	0	1
Las Vegas	6	0	0	0	1	0	0	0	1	1	0	2	1
Texas	7	0	0	0	0	0	0	0	0	1	0	3	3
Total	**78**	**3**	**5**	**0**	**5**	**2**	**3**	**5**	**3**	**3**	**4**	**21**	**24**
		3.8%	6.4%	0.0%	6.4%	2.6%	3.8%	6.4%	3.8%	3.8%	5.1%	26.9%	30.8%

Track Performance

1.51 Mile–2.5 Mile

Atlanta	54	5	2	2	3	1	2	0	0	2	2	14	21
California	7	0	0	0	2	0	0	0	0	0	0	3	2
Michigan	52	7	2	6	1	1	1	2	2	5	2	10	13
Indianapolis	10	1	0	2	1	1	0	0	2	0	1	1	1
Pocono	44	5	2	3	2	2	3	0	0	1	4	6	16
Total	**167**	**18**	**6**	**13**	**9**	**5**	**6**	**2**	**4**	**8**	**9**	**34**	**53**
		10.8%	3.6%	7.8%	5.4%	3.0%	3.6%	1.2%	2.4%	4.8%	5.4%	20.4%	31.7%

Restrictor Plate

Daytona	53	4	3	2	2	4	2	1	2	2	2	14	15
Talladega	54	2	4	0	1	3	4	2	3	1	2	18	14
Total	**107**	**6**	**7**	**2**	**3**	**7**	**6**	**3**	**5**	**3**	**4**	**32**	**29**
		5.6%	6.5%	1.9%	2.8%	6.5%	5.6%	2.8%	4.7%	2.8%	3.7%	29.9%	27.1%

Road Courses

Riverside	12	1	1	0	1	1	1	0	0	0	1	2	4
Sears Point	14	0	0	1	1	1	0	0	1	1	0	5	4
Watkins Glen	17	0	0	1	2	0	0	2	0	0	0	7	5
Total	**43**	**1**	**1**	**2**	**4**	**2**	**1**	**2**	**1**	**1**	**1**	**14**	**13**
		2.3%	2.3%	4.7%	9.3%	4.7%	2.3%	4.7%	2.3%	2.3%	2.3%	32.6%	30.2%

Current Team: Hendrick Motorsports
Residence: Charlotte, North Carolina
Birthplace: Vallejo, California
Birthday: August 4, 1971
Height: 5 feet, 8 inches
Weight: 150

Races: 365
Running: 312 (85.5 percent)
Accidents: 24 (6.6 percent)
Mechanical Failures: 29 (7.9 percent)

1992–2003   Hendrick Motorsports

Jeff Gordon

In 12 years of Winston Cup racing, Jeff Gordon has proven to be one of the greatest drivers in the history of the sport. He started racing in California, with the help of his stepfather, when he was five years old. He won his first national championship in quarter midgets at the age of eight. As he grew up, he was a force to be reckoned with in sprint cars and other open-wheel race cars. In 1989 he won the USAC Midget Rookie of the Year award, and followed it up the next year, winning the national championship. He was still just 19.

While visiting Buck Baker's driving school at the North Carolina Motor Speedway, Jeff found his calling to stock cars. The experience motivated him to immediately leave the open wheels and dirt tracks and make a move to the ranks of NASCAR. He made a short stop in the Busch Series and in 1991 won the Rookie of the Year award. In 1992 he drove Bill Davis' Ford to 11 poles and three wins in the Busch Series. Jeff had driven for Bill Davis in the Busch Series, but when he made the move to Winston Cup, it was with Rick Hendrick. He started his first Winston Cup race in November 1992 at Atlanta, which was by chance Richard Petty's last race. As one great driver left, another came along. But not quite yet.

Jeff qualified 21st and finished 31st after wrecking. Although his first outing was disappointing, an incredible career had begun. His first full year on the circuit was in 1993; he got out of the gate quickly, winning one of the 125-mile qualifying races at Daytona. He finished 5th in the Daytona 500, added a 6th two weeks later at Rockingham and a 4th at Atlanta the following week. Jeff Gordon finished the year with 11 top 10s and won the Rookie of the Year chase, although he recorded 11 DNFs.

In 1994 he got to the winner's circle for the first time with a victory at Charlotte. He also won the first Brickyard 400 at Indianapolis. His efforts resulted in an 8th-place finish in the Winston Cup points battle, his effort being hampered by another 10 DNFs. The next year, his third season, he became the youngest driver in the Modern Era to win the Winston Cup. He narrowly missed a second championship in 1996, losing it by only 37 points to his Hendrick Motorsport teammate, Terry Labonte; however, he did win 10 races. The next two years also yielded two more championships.

In 2000 he became the youngest driver ever to achieve 50 wins. Jeff Gordon won his fourth championship in 2001. By 2002 he earned his 60th career win with a victory at Darlington. As Jeff starts his second decade of NASCAR racing, his first decade credentials are impressive. He is a four-time Winston Cup Champion (1995, 1997, 1998, and 2001), a two-time Daytona 500 Winner (1997 and 1999), a three-time Brickyard 400 Winner (1994, 1998, and 2001), a five-time Southern 500 Winner (1995, 1996, 1997, 1998, and 2002), a four-time Winston No Bull 5 Winner, and a three-time winner of the Winston All Star race (1995, 1997, and 2001).

Jeff Gordon began his Winston Cup career with Rick Hendrick and remains in the same car to this day. From 1994 to the present Gordon has scored multiple wins every year.

Jeff has not taken long to prove that he is one of the sports all-time greats. He is currently ranked in fourth position in Modern Era wins behind Darrell Waltrip, Dale Earnhardt, and Cale Yarborough.

Year-by-year Performance

	Races	Poles		Wins		Top 5		Top 10	
1992	1	0	0.0%	0	0.0%	0	0.0%	0	0.0%
1993	30	1	3.3%	0	0.0%	7	23.3%	11	36.7%
1994	31	1	3.2%	2	6.5%	7	22.6%	14	45.2%
1995	31	8	25.8%	7	22.6%	17	54.8%	23	74.2%
1996	31	5	16.1%	10	32.3%	21	67.7%	24	77.4%
1997	32	1	3.1%	10	31.3%	22	68.8%	23	71.9%
1998	33	7	21.2%	13	39.4%	26	78.8%	28	84.8%
1999	34	8	23.5%	7	20.6%	18	52.9%	21	61.8%
2000	34	3	8.8%	3	8.8%	11	32.4%	22	64.7%
2001	36	6	16.7%	6	16.7%	18	50.0%	24	66.7%
2002	36	3	8.3%	3	8.3%	13	36.1%	20	55.6%
2003	36	4	11.1%	3	8.3%	15	41.7%	20	55.6%
Total	**365**	**47**	**12.9%**	**64**	**17.5%**	**175**	**47.9%**	**230**	**63.0%**

rack Performance

ess than 1 Mile

	Starts	1st	2nd	3rd	4th	5th	6th	7th	8th	9th	10th	11–20	21–43
ristol	22	6	0	1	2	1	2	0	1	1	0	2	6
artinsville	22	5	1	3	2	1	0	1	2	1	0	3	3
chmond	22	3	3	2	1	0	2	1	0	0	2	2	6
. Wilkes	8	0	2	1	0	0	0	0	1	0	0	1	3
otal	**74**	**14**	**6**	**7**	**5**	**2**	**4**	**2**	**4**	**2**	**2**	**8**	**18**
		18.9%	8.1%	9.5%	6.8%	2.7%	5.4%	2.7%	5.4%	2.7%	2.7%	10.8%	24.3%

Mile–1.49 Mile

	Starts	1st	2nd	3rd	4th	5th	6th	7th	8th	9th	10th	11–20	21–43
over	22	4	3	1	1	2	2	1	0	1	0	3	4
ew Hamp.	18	3	1	2	0	2	1	2	0	0	0	3	4
. Carolina	22	4	1	1	1	2	0	1	0	0	1	3	8
hoenix	11	0	0	1	1	2	1	3	0	0	1	1	1
arlington	22	5	3	2	1	0	1	0	1	1	0	1	7
otal	**95**	**16**	**8**	**7**	**4**	**8**	**5**	**7**	**1**	**2**	**2**	**11**	**24**
		16.8%	8.4%	7.4%	4.2%	8.4%	5.3%	7.4%	1.1%	2.1%	2.1%	11.6%	25.3%

.5 mile

	Starts	1st	2nd	3rd	4th	5th	6th	7th	8th	9th	10th	11–20	21–43
harlotte	22	4	1	0	2	5	0	0	1	0	1	2	6
nicago	3	0	1	0	1	0	0	0	0	0	0	1	0
omestead	5	0	0	0	0	2	0	1	0	0	1	0	1
ansas	3	2	0	0	0	1	0	0	0	0	0	0	0
as Vegas	6	1	0	1	0	0	0	0	0	0	0	2	2
exas	7	0	1	1	0	1	0	0	0	0	0	0	4
otal	**46**	**7**	**3**	**2**	**3**	**9**	**0**	**1**	**1**	**0**	**2**	**5**	**13**
		15.2%	6.5%	4.3%	6.5%	19.6%	0.0%	2.2%	2.2%	0.0%	4.3%	10.9%	28.3%

Track Performance

1.51 Mile–2.5 Mile

	Starts	1st	2nd	3rd	4th	5th	6th	7th	8th	9th	10th	11–20	21–43
Atlanta	23	4	2	2	2	0	2	0	1	1	0	4	5
California	7	2	1	0	1	0	0	0	0	0	0	3	0
Michigan	22	2	6	5	0	2	0	1	0	0	0	4	2
Indianapolis	10	3	0	1	3	0	2	0	0	0	0	0	1
Pocono	22	4	5	1	0	1	1	0	3	0	0	3	4
Total	**84**	**15**	**14**	**9**	**6**	**3**	**5**	**1**	**4**	**1**	**0**	**14**	**12**
		17.9%	16.7%	10.7%	7.1%	3.6%	6.0%	1.2%	4.8%	1.2%	0.0%	16.7%	14.3%

Restrictor Plate

	Starts	1st	2nd	3rd	4th	5th	6th	7th	8th	9th	10th	11–20	21–43
Daytona	22	4	0	0	1	2	0	0	1	1	1	3	9
Talladega	22	1	2	0	2	3	0	1	2	0	0	2	9
Total	**44**	**5**	**2**	**0**	**3**	**5**	**0**	**1**	**3**	**1**	**1**	**5**	**18**
		11.4%	4.5%	0.0%	6.8%	11.4%	0.0%	2.3%	6.8%	2.3%	2.3%	11.4%	40.9%

Road Courses

	Starts	1st	2nd	3rd	4th	5th	6th	7th	8th	9th	10th	11–20	21–43
Sears Point	11	3	2	2	0	0	1	0	0	0	0	1	2
Watkins Glen	11	4	0	1	0	1	0	0	0	1	0	0	4
Total	**22**	**7**	**2**	**3**	**0**	**1**	**1**	**0**	**0**	**1**	**0**	**1**	**6**
		31.8%	9.1%	13.6%	0.0%	4.5%	4.5%	0.0%	0.0%	4.5%	0.0%	4.5%	27.3%

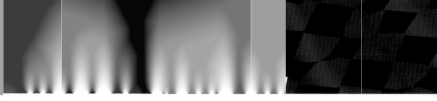

Current Team: Richard Childress Racing
Residence: Cornelius, North Carolina
Hometown: Bellflower, California
Birthday: January 2, 1969
Height: 5 feet, 10 inches
Weight: 180

Races: 134
Running: 106 (79.1 percent)
Accidents: 19 (14.2 percent)
Mechanical Failures: 9 (6.7 percent)

2002–2003	Richard Childress Racing
2001	Morgan McClure Motorsports
2000	Robby Gordon
1998	Buzz McCall
1997	SABCO
1996	SABCO
	Dale Earnhardt Incorporated
1994	Kranefuss-Hass
1993	Robert Yates
1991	Junie Donlavey

Robby Gordon

Robby Gordon is another driver who spent a lot of time racing without a track. He won a number of off-road championships before making the move to sports car racing in 1990. He had success in both GTO and Trans Am, and in 1993 he progressed to Indy cars to drive for A. J. Foyt. By 1995 he was up to speed in the series and won four poles and two races.

His Winston Cup career has been an up-and-down affair. He has been in the sport since the early 1990s, but his first successful full-time ride did not come until 2002. His first race in a Winston Cup car was in 1991, when he drove for Junie Donlavey in the Daytona, starting 35th and finishing 18th. He also raced in the next race, at Richmond, finishing 26th, but it wasn't until two years later that he drove his third race. On that occasion he had the difficult task of driving Robert Yates' No. 28 Ford at Talladega Superspeedway after Davey Allison's death in 1993. It was his only race of the year.

Over the next couple of years, he ran a few races here and there, and in 1996 began driving for Felix Sebates. They ran 20 races with little success in 1997, but then parted company. In 1998 Robby Gordon again ran only one race, and in 1999 was out of the series entirely. While he wasn't in a stock car he was still racing. He was leading the 1999 Indianapolis 500 when he ran out of gas on the last lap. In 2000 he was back in a stock car as an owner-driver. He did well on the road courses, but was only able to race in 17 events. His owner-driver days did not last long, as he was hired to drive the Kodak car for Morgan-McClure Motorsports in 2001. The union only lasted for five races, and Robby was again out of work. He was back in a car for the road race at Sears Point and finished second, but was without a ride for most of the first half of the season.

But Mike Skinner had knee problems, and his stay in Richard Childress' No. 31 car was coming to a close, so Robby got a shot driving for Richard Childress Racing. He soon proved that he could run well on tracks other than road courses, with a 7th-place finish at Phoenix and later a win at New Hampshire. In 2002 the Childress/Gordon duo scored only one top-5 finish, but in 2003 scored two wins, both on road courses, and had 10 top-10 finishes. At long last it looks like Robby Gordon has found a home.

Gordon's career was reborn when he was hired by Richard Childress in 2001. Since then he has won three races and become a much more consistent driver.

Until the 2002 season, Robby was a part-time Winston Cup racer. In 2000 he drove in 17 of the season's 34 races in the No. 13 Ford, owned by John Menard.

Year-by-year Performance

	Races	Poles		Wins		Top 5		Top 10	
1991	2	0	0.0%	0	0.0%	0	0.0%	0	0.0%
1993	1	0	0.0%	0	0.0%	0	0.0%	0	0.0%
1994	1	0	0.0%	0	0.0%	0	0.0%	0	0.0%
1996	3	0	0.0%	0	0.0%	0	0.0%	0	0.0%
1997	20	1	5.0%	0	0.0%	1	5.0%	1	5.0%
1998	1	0	0.0%	0	0.0%	0	0.0%	0	0.0%
2000	17	0	0.0%	0	0.0%	1	5.9%	2	11.8%
2001	17	0	0.0%	1	5.9%	2	11.8%	3	17.6%
2002	36	0	0.0%	0	0.0%	1	2.8%	5	13.9%
2003	36	0	0.0%	2	5.6%	4	11.1%	10	27.8%
Total	**134**	**1**	**0.7%**	**3**	**2.2%**	**9**	**6.7%**	**21**	**15.7%**

Track Performance

Less than 1 Mile

	Starts	1st	2nd	3rd	4th	5th	6th	7th	8th	9th	10th	11–20	21–43
Bristol	7	0	0	0	0	0	0	0	0	0	0	3	4
Martinsville	7	0	0	0	0	0	0	0	0	0	0	0	7
Richmond	8	0	0	0	1	0	0	0	0	0	0	0	7
Total	**22**	**0**	**0**	**0**	**1**	**0**	**0**	**0**	**0**	**0**	**0**	**3**	**18**
		0.0%	0.0%	0.0%	4.5%	0.0%	0.0%	0.0%	0.0%	0.0%	0.0%	13.6%	81.8%

1 Mile–1.49 Mile

	Starts	1st	2nd	3rd	4th	5th	6th	7th	8th	9th	10th	11–20	21–43
Dover	5	0	0	0	0	0	0	0	1	1	0	1	2
New Hamp.	8	1	0	0	0	1	0	1	0	0	0	1	4
N. Carolina	10	0	0	0	0	0	0	0	0	0	0	2	8
Phoenix	4	0	0	0	0	0	0	1	0	0	0	0	3
Darlington	8	0	0	0	0	0	0	0	0	0	0	1	7
Total	**35**	**1**	**0**	**0**	**0**	**1**	**0**	**2**	**1**	**1**	**0**	**5**	**24**
		2.9%	0.0%	0.0%	0.0%	2.9%	0.0%	5.7%	2.9%	2.9%	0.0%	14.3%	68.6%

1.5 mile

	Starts	1st	2nd	3rd	4th	5th	6th	7th	8th	9th	10th	11–20	21–43
Charlotte	7	0	0	0	0	0	0	0	0	0	0	2	5
Chicago	3	0	0	0	0	0	0	1	1	0	0	0	1
Homestead	2	0	0	0	0	0	0	0	0	0	0	0	2
Kansas	3	0	0	0	0	0	0	0	0	0	0	2	1
Las Vegas	4	0	0	0	0	0	0	0	0	0	0	1	3
Texas	3	0	0	0	0	0	0	0	0	0	0	1	2
Total	**22**	**0**	**0**	**0**	**0**	**0**	**0**	**1**	**1**	**0**	**0**	**6**	**14**
		0.0%	0.0%	0.0%	0.0%	0.0%	0.0%	4.5%	4.5%	0.0%	0.0%	27.3%	63.6%

Track Performance
1.51 Mile–2.5 Mile

Atlanta	7	0	0	0	0	0	0	0	0	0	0	5	2
California	3	0	0	0	0	0	0	0	0	0	0	1	2
Michigan	8	0	0	0	0	0	1	0	0	0	0	1	6
Indianapolis	4	0	0	0	0	0	1	0	1	0	0	0	2
Pocono	6	0	0	0	0	0	0	0	0	0	0	2	4
Total	**28**	**0**	**0**	**0**	**0**	**0**	**2**	**0**	**1**	**0**	**0**	**9**	**16**
		0.0%	0.0%	0.0%	0.0%	0.0%	7.1%	0.0%	3.6%	0.0%	0.0%	32.1%	57.1%

Restrictor Plate

Daytona	9	0	0	0	0	0	1	0	0	0	0	4	4
Talladega	7	0	0	0	0	0	0	0	0	0	1	3	3
Total	**16**	**0**	**0**	**0**	**0**	**0**	**1**	**0**	**0**	**0**	**1**	**7**	**7**
		0.0%	0.0%	0.0%	0.0%	0.0%	6.3%	0.0%	0.0%	0.0%	6.3%	43.8%	43.8%

Road Courses

Sears Point	6	1	1	0	0	0	0	0	0	1	0	1	2
Watkins Glen	5	1	0	1	2	0	0	0	0	0	0	0	1
Total	**11**	**2**	**1**	**1**	**2**	**0**	**0**	**0**	**0**	**1**	**0**	**1**	**3**
	0.0%	18.2%	9.1%	9.1%	18.2%	0.0%	0.0%	0.0%	0.0%	9.1%	0.0%	9.1%	27.3%

Jeff Green

Current Team: Petty Enterprises
Residence: Davidson, North Carolina
Hometown: Owensboro, Kentucky
Birthday: September 6, 1962
Height: 5 feet, 8 inches
Weight: 190

Races: 125
Running: 100 (80.0 percent)
Accidents: 10 (8.0 percent)
Mechanical Failures: 15 (12.0 percent)

2003	Petty Enterprises
	Dale Earnhardt Incorporated
	Richard Childress Racing
2001–2002	Richard Childress Racing
1999	SABCO
1998	SABCO
	Chuck Rider
	Gary Bechtel
1997	Gary Bechtel
1996	Gary Bechtel
	Dale Earnhardt Incorporated
1994	Sadler Brothers
	Junior Johnson

Jeff Green is another racer who spent a good bit of time in a kart. He always had competition, as he raced with his brothers David and Mark. He is also another who, not by his own choice, has been a journeyman driver. He has raced in the Craftsman Truck Series, the Busch Series, and off and on in the Winston Cup, now Nextel Cup Series. Green first raced in the Winston Cup in 1994. He ran in three races and scored a top five, a 5th-place finish at the half-mile North Wilkesboro track. In 1996 he ran four races, with a 26th being his best finish. He ran 20 races in 1997 and 22 in 1998 but only one race in 1999 and none in 2000.

In 2001 Green ran eight races and announced that in 2002 he would run full-time for Richard Childress Racing, as Childress was starting a third team. Green ran well at times, scoring four top-five finishes and a 17th-place finish in the final points standings, the highest for an RCR driver. The 2003 season started with great promise, as Jeff won the pole for the Daytona 500. An accident, however, relegated him to a 39th-place finish. The team's only top 10 was a 7th at Texas, and more often then not it ran outside the top 20.

When the season was still relatively young, Green left RCR and went to Dale Earnhardt Incorporated, when he and Steve Park exchanged seats. During his two-year stay with RCR, Jeff had driven to two poles, 11 top-5 and 25 top-10 finishes. He had run in the Busch Series in the mid-1990s with DEI, but it is difficult to arrive in midyear and achieve any degree of chemistry. Jeff's finishes were much the same as they had been earlier in the year, and as fall approached, Jeff left DEI and began driving for his third team of the year.

This time he was behind the wheel of Richard Petty's No. 43 Dodge, where he finished the 2003 season and signed for the 2004 campaign. While Jeff's best Winston Cup finish was a 2nd at New Hampshire International Speedway, he has been a big winner in the Busch Series. He won the 2000 Busch Championship, came in 2nd in the 1999 and 2001 campaigns, and ranks 10th in all-time Busch Series wins.

Jeff Green was hired by Petty Enterprises to drive the famous No. 43 late in the 2003 season. It was a busy year for Jeff as he started the year with Richard Childress Racing, was traded to Dale Earnhardt Incorporated, and later hired by the Pettys.

Year-by-year Performance

	Races	Poles		Wins		Top 5		Top 10	
1994	3	0	0.0%	0	0.0%	0	0.0%	0	0.0%
1996	4	0	0.0%	0	0.0%	0	0.0%	0	0.0%
1997	20	0	0.0%	0	0.0%	1	5.0%	2	10.0%
1998	22	0	0.0%	0	0.0%	0	0.0%	0	0.0%
1999	1	0	0.0%	0	0.0%	0	0.0%	0	0.0%
2001	8	1	12.5%	0	0.0%	0	0.0%	1	12.5%
2002	36	0	0.0%	0	0.0%	4	11.1%	6	16.7%
2003	31	1	3.2%	0	0.0%	0	0.0%	1	3.2%
Total	**125**	**2**	**1.6%**	**0**	**0.0%**	**5**	**4.0%**	**10**	**8.0%**

Track Performance

Less than 1 Mile

	Starts	1st	2nd	3rd	4th	5th	6th	7th	8th	9th	10th	11–20	21–43
Bristol	7	0	0	0	0	0	0	0	0	0	0	2	5
Martinsville	7	0	0	0	0	0	0	0	0	0	0	1	6
Richmond	8	0	0	1	0	0	0	0	0	0	0	2	5
N. Wilkes	2	0	0	0	0	1	0	0	0	0	0	0	1
Total	**24**	**0**	**0**	**1**	**0**	**1**	**0**	**0**	**0**	**0**	**0**	**5**	**17**
		0.0%	0.0%	4.2%	0.0%	4.2%	0.0%	0.0%	0.0%	0.0%	0.0%	20.8%	70.8%

1 Mile–1.49 Mile

	Starts	1st	2nd	3rd	4th	5th	6th	7th	8th	9th	10th	11–20	21–43
Dover	7	0	0	0	0	0	0	0	0	0	0	2	5
New Hamp.	7	0	1	0	0	0	0	0	0	0	0	1	5
N. Carolina	7	0	0	0	0	0	0	0	0	0	1	2	4
Phoenix	4	0	0	0	0	0	0	0	0	0	0	0	4
Darlington	7	0	0	0	0	0	0	0	0	0	0	4	3
Total	**32**	**0**	**1**	**0**	**0**	**0**	**0**	**0**	**0**	**0**	**1**	**9**	**21**
		0.0%	3.1%	0.0%	0.0%	0.0%	0.0%	0.0%	0.0%	0.0%	3.1%	28.1%	65.6%

1.5 mile

	Starts	1st	2nd	3rd	4th	5th	6th	7th	8th	9th	10th	11–20	21–43
Charlotte	7	0	0	0	0	0	0	0	0	0	0	2	5
Chicago	3	0	0	0	0	0	0	0	0	0	0	2	1
Homestead	3	0	0	0	0	0	0	0	0	1	0	0	2
Kansas	2	0	0	0	0	0	0	0	0	0	0	1	1
Las Vegas	3	0	0	0	0	0	0	0	0	0	0	0	3
Texas	2	0	0	0	0	0	0	1	0	0	0	1	0
Total	**20**	**0**	**0**	**0**	**0**	**0**	**0**	**1**	**0**	**1**	**0**	**6**	**12**
		0.0%	0.0%	0.0%	0.0%	0.0%	0.0%	5.0%	0.0%	5.0%	0.0%	30.0%	60.0%

Track Performance

1.51 Mile–2.5 Mile

	Starts	1st	2nd	3rd	4th	5th	6th	7th	8th	9th	10th	11–20	21–43
Atlanta	7	0	0	0	1	0	0	0	0	0	0	0	6
California	4	0	0	0	0	0	0	1	0	0	0	1	2
Michigan	9	0	0	0	0	0	0	0	0	1	0	3	5
Indianapolis	5	0	0	0	0	0	0	0	0	0	0	2	3
Pocono	11	0	0	0	0	0	0	0	0	0	0	0	11
Total	**36**	**0**	**0**	**0**	**1**	**0**	**0**	**1**	**0**	**1**	**0**	**6**	**27**
		0.0%	0.0%	0.0%	2.8%	0.0%	0.0%	2.8%	0.0%	2.8%	0.0%	16.7%	75.0%

Restrictor Plate

	Starts	1st	2nd	3rd	4th	5th	6th	7th	8th	9th	10th	11–20	21–43
Daytona	5	0	0	0	0	0	0	0	0	0	0	1	4
Talladega	5	0	0	0	0	1	0	0	0	0	0	2	2
Total	**10**	**0**	**0**	**0**	**0**	**1**	**0**	**0**	**0**	**0**	**0**	**3**	**6**
		0.0%	0.0%	0.0%	0.0%	10.0%	0.0%	0.0%	0.0%	0.0%	0.0%	30.0%	60.0%

Road Courses

	Starts	1st	2nd	3rd	4th	5th	6th	7th	8th	9th	10th	11–20	21–43
Sears Point	1	0	0	0	0	1	0	0	0	0	0	0	0
Watkins Glen	2	0	0	0	0	0	0	0	0	0	0	1	1
Total	**3**	**0**	**0**	**0**	**0**	**1**	**0**	**0**	**0**	**0**	**0**	**1**	**1**
		0.0%	0.0%	0.0%	0.0%	33.3%	0.0%	0.0%	0.0%	0.0%	0.0%	33.3%	33.3%

Kevin Harvick

Current Team: Richard Childress Racing
Residence: Winston Salem, North Carolina
Hometown: Bakersfield, California
Birthday: December 8, 1975
Height: 5 feet, 10 inches
Weight: 175

Races: 106
Running: 99 (93.4 percent)
Accidents: 3 (2.8 percent)
Mechanical Failures: 4 (3.8 percent)

2001–2003   Richard Childress Racing

Kevin Harvick began driving early—at age five—when his parents bought him a kart. He competed in karts for 10 years, and during that time won seven National Championships and two Grand National Championships. In 1992 he began running part-time in NASCAR's Featherlite Southwest Series while he completed high school. Kevin ran the full schedule in 1995, and his success resulted in the series' Rookie of the Year award. His next stop was the Winston West Series, where in 1998 he won five races and the Winston West Series Championship.

He moved from the Winston West Series into the Craftsman Truck Series at a time when many teams were looking for young, talented drivers. Richard Childress saw great potential in Harvick, and offered him a ride in the Busch Series. The team ran a full schedule in 2000 with the prestigious AC Delco sponsorship. In his rookie season Harvick won three races, which led to the Rookie of the Year award. Kevin intended to concentrate on being a full-time Busch driver in 2001, but when Dale Earnhardt was killed in the Daytona 500, Kevin took over the difficult task of driving the famed Goodwrench Chevrolet.

With a new No. 29 on the car, Harvick started the week after Daytona at Rockingham. He also kept his commitment to his Busch team and sponsor, making it a very busy year. The team that had faced such great hardship at the beginning of the season scored its first win in only its third start, with Harvick behind the wheel. While the year was a somber one for all of NASCAR, it should not distract from the accomplishment of the team and the driver. By the year's end, Kevin had won the Busch Series Championship and Rookie of the Year in Winston Cup, and had finished a strong 9th in the Winston Cup Championship, despite having not driven in the Daytona 500. He was the first driver in the history of NASCAR to win the Busch Series Championship and the Winston Cup Rookie of the Year award in the same year.

Kevin's success continued in 2002. The team won again, this time at Chicago, although there was some trouble along the way. NASCAR officials had warned Harvick about his aggressive driving and brash style, and after an early-season incident, Kevin was suspended and not allowed to compete in the eighth race of the season. Even so, Harvick finished the year with eight top-10 finishes and won the 2002 IROC Championship. Kevin came back for the 2003 campaign with even more focus, and the results showed. The highlight of the 2003 season was a win in the Brickyard 400 from the pole position. While the Brickyard 400 was the team's only win, consistency improved, and the team finished the year with 22 top-five finishes, including six 2nd-place finishes and a 5th-place finish in the last-ever Winston Cup Championship.

Kevin Harvick's entrance into NASCAR's highest division was accelerated when he was called up to drive Richard Childress's flagship car in 2001. Although the car would carry the No. 29 instead of 3, it would still continue its winning ways.

In his first three years in the Goodwrench Chevrolet, Kevin drove to four wins including an emotional win at Atlanta in his third start in the car.

Year-by-year Performance

	Races	Poles		Wins		Top 5		Top 10	
2001	35	0	0.0%	2	5.7%	6	17.1%	16	45.7%
2002	35	1	2.9%	1	2.9%	5	14.3%	8	22.9%
2003	36	1	2.8%	1	2.8%	11	30.6%	18	50.0%
Total	**106**	**2**	**1.9%**	**4**	**3.8%**	**22**	**20.8%**	**42**	**39.6%**

Track Performance

Less than 1 Mile

Bristol	6	0	2	0	1	0	0	1	0	0	1	0	1
Martinsville	5	0	0	0	0	0	0	1	0	0	0	1	3
Richmond	6	0	1	0	0	0	1	0	0	0	0	3	1
Total	**17**	**0**	**3**	**0**	**1**	**0**	**1**	**2**	**0**	**0**	**1**	**4**	**5**
		0.0%	17.6%	0.0%	5.9%	0.0%	5.9%	11.8%	0.0%	0.0%	5.9%	23.5%	29.4%

1 Mile–1.49 Mile

Dover	6	0	0	0	1	0	1	0	1	0	0	0	3
New Hamp.	6	0	1	0	0	0	0	0	1	1	0	1	2
N. Carolina	6	0	0	0	0	0	0	0	0	0	0	3	3
Phoenix	3	0	0	0	0	0	0	0	0	0	0	2	1
Darlington	6	0	1	1	0	0	0	0	1	0	0	1	2
Total	**27**	**0**	**2**	**1**	**1**	**0**	**1**	**0**	**3**	**1**	**0**	**7**	**11**
		0.0%	7.4%	3.7%	3.7%	0.0%	3.7%	0.0%	11.1%	3.7%	0.0%	25.9%	40.7%

1.5 mile

Charlotte	6	0	1	0	0	0	0	0	1	0	1	1	2
Chicago	3	2	0	0	0	0	0	0	0	0	0	1	0
Homestead	3	0	1	0	0	0	0	1	0	0	0	1	0
Kansas	3	0	0	0	0	0	1	0	0	0	0	2	0
Las Vegas	3	0	0	0	0	0	0	0	1	0	0	1	1
Texas	3	0	0	0	0	0	0	1	0	0	0	1	1
Total	**21**	**2**	**2**	**0**	**0**	**0**	**1**	**2**	**2**	**0**	**1**	**7**	**4**
		9.5%	9.5%	0.0%	0.0%	0.0%	4.8%	9.5%	9.5%	0.0%	4.8%	33.3%	19.0%

Track Performance

1.51 Mile–2.5 Mile

Atlanta	6	1	0	1	0	0	0	0	0	0	0	2	2
California	3	0	0	0	0	0	0	0	0	0	0	0	3
Michigan	6	0	1	1	0	0	0	0	0	0	1	1	2
Indianapolis	3	1	0	0	0	1	0	0	0	0	0	1	0
Pocono	6	0	0	0	0	0	1	0	0	0	0	3	2
Total	**24**	**2**	**1**	**2**	**0**	**1**	**1**	**0**	**0**	**0**	**1**	**7**	**9**
		8.3%	4.2%	8.3%	0.0%	4.2%	4.2%	0.0%	0.0%	0.0%	4.2%	29.2%	37.5%

Restrictor Plate

Daytona	5	0	0	0	1	0	0	0	0	1	0	1	2
Talladega	6	0	1	0	0	0	0	1	0	0	0	1	3
Total	**11**	**0**	**1**	**0**	**1**	**0**	**0**	**1**	**0**	**1**	**0**	**2**	**5**
		0.0%	9.1%	0.0%	9.1%	0.0%	0.0%	9.1%	0.0%	9.1%	0.0%	18.2%	45.5%

Road Courses

Sears Point	3	0	0	1	0	0	0	0	0	0	0	2	0
Watkins Glen	3	0	0	0	0	1	0	1	0	0	0	1	0
Total	**6**	**0**	**0**	**1**	**0**	**1**	**0**	**1**	**0**	**0**	**0**	**3**	**0**
		0.0%	0.0%	16.7%	0.0%	16.7%	0.0%	16.7%	0.0%	0.0%	0.0%	50.0%	0.0%

Dale Jarrett

Current Team: Robert Yates Racing
Residence: Hickory, North Carolina
Hometown: Hickory, North Carolina
Birthday: November 26, 1956
Height: 6 feet, 2 inches
Weight: 200

Races: 531
Running: 424 (79.8 percent)
Accidents: 40 (7.5 percent)
Mechanical Failures: 67 (12.6 percent)

1995–2003	Robert Yates Racing
1992–1994	Joe Gibbs Racing
1990–1991	Wood Brothers Racing
1989	Cale Yarborough
1988	Buddy Arrington
	Ralph Ball
	Hoss Ellington
	Cale Yarborough
1987	Eric Freedlander
1986	Mike Curb
1984	Jimmy Means
	Emanuel Zervakis

Dale Jarrett may be the only racer who is glad that the PGA started a Seniors Tour—it might give him another chance at the career he could have chosen. Growing up the son of a Winston Cup Champion meant that Dale Jarrett spent a good deal of time at the track, but as a youth he never got the racing bug. He was a quarterback on the football team, forward on the basketball team, and shortstop on the baseball team, but his real talent seemed to be golf. He was offered a golf scholarship to the University of South Carolina, but turned it down and began work at Hickory Motor Speedway.

When Dale was 20 years old, he helped work on a race car with some friends, and ended up in the driver's seat when his father loaned him the money to buy the motor. He finished 9th after starting 25th. One night in a race car had done what a lifetime of being around race cars could not do—it turned Dale Jarrett into a racer. By the early 1980s he was competing in the newly formed Busch Series, and in 1984 he started his Winston Cup career. He began to race the series full-time in 1987 and had limited success over the next three years. In 1990 he got what he acknowledges as the biggest break of his career when he was asked to drive the legendary No. 21 Ford of the Wood Brothers. His first win came the next year at Michigan.

Every year Jarrett garnered more top-5 and top-10 finishes, and in 1992 Joe Gibbs asked him to drive for his new team. In their second year, Jarrett and Gibbs got to victory lane in a memorable Daytona 500 win. They finished the year with 13 top-5 and 18 top-10 finishes. In 1994 their success continued with a win at Charlotte and a 2nd-place finish in Winston Cup points, loosing to Jeff Gordon by only 14 points. For the 1995 season, Jarrett was again faced with a choice of leaving one good team for another good team. Once again he said farewell to a top-line team in order to fill a vacancy somewhere else. This time it was the chance to get in a Robert Yates Ford after Ernie Irvan was injured.

During the 1995 season, the team had one win and 14 top 10s. The next year when Irvan returned, Yates formed a second team with Jarrett as the driver. The team started strong with a win in the 1996 Daytona 500, became the first Ford to win the Brickyard 400, and finished third in the Winston Cup Championship. In 1997 Jarrett raced to four wins, including another victory in the Daytona 500. The team carded seven wins in 1997 and three more in 1998. In 1999 the years of work paid off for the Yates-Jarrett combination with a Winston Cup Championship.

When Dale joined his father, Ned, on the list of champions, they became the second father and son to hold the honor. From 1996 to 2002, Jarrett won multiple Winston Cup races every year, making him one of the sports premier drivers. His 31 career victories rank him 19th in all-time wins and 11th in Modern Era wins.

Dale Jarrett joined Robert Yates Racing beginning with the 1995 season. They have combined for 28 wins over their nine seasons together including two Daytona 500 wins.

DALE JARRETT

One of Dale's dreams came true in 1999 when he and his Yates teammates won the
Winston Cup Championship with their Quality Care Ford.

Year-by-year Performance

	Races	Poles		Wins		Top 5		Top 10	
1984	3	0	0.0%	0	0.0%	0	0.0%	0	0.0%
1986	1	0	0.0%	0	0.0%	0	0.0%	0	0.0%
1987	24	0	0.0%	0	0.0%	0	0.0%	2	8.3%
1988	29	0	0.0%	0	0.0%	0	0.0%	1	3.4%
1989	29	0	0.0%	0	0.0%	2	6.9%	5	17.2%
1990	24	0	0.0%	0	0.0%	1	4.2%	7	29.2%
1991	29	0	0.0%	1	3.4%	3	10.3%	8	27.6%
1992	29	0	0.0%	0	0.0%	2	6.9%	8	27.6%
1993	30	0	0.0%	1	3.3%	13	43.3%	18	60.0%
1994	30	0	0.0%	1	3.3%	4	13.3%	9	30.0%
1995	31	1	3.2%	1	3.2%	9	29.0%	14	45.2%
1996	31	2	6.5%	4	12.9%	17	54.8%	21	67.7%
1997	32	3	9.4%	7	21.9%	20	62.5%	23	71.9%
1998	33	2	6.1%	3	9.1%	19	57.6%	22	66.7%
1999	34	0	0.0%	4	11.8%	24	70.6%	29	85.3%
2000	34	3	8.8%	2	5.9%	15	44.1%	24	70.6%
2001	36	4	11.1%	4	11.1%	12	33.3%	19	52.8%
2002	36	1	2.8%	2	5.6%	10	27.8%	28	77.8%
2003	36	0	0.0%	1	2.8%	1	2.8%	7	19.4%
Total	**531**	**16**	**3.0%**	**31**	**5.8%**	**152**	**28.6%**	**245**	**46.1%**

Track Performance

Less than 1 Mile

	Starts	1st	2nd	3rd	4th	5th	6th	7th	8th	9th	10th	11–20	21–43
Bristol	35	1	1	3	3	0	2	3	0	1	2	4	15
Martinsville	35	1	1	2	1	4	1	1	2	0	4	10	8
Richmond	27	2	2	3	4	0	0	0	0	0	1	7	8
N. Wilkes	19	0	0	1	0	0	0	1	0	2	1	8	6
Total	**116**	**4**	**4**	**9**	**8**	**4**	**3**	**5**	**2**	**3**	**8**	**29**	**37**
		3.4%	3.4%	7.8%	6.9%	3.4%	2.6%	4.3%	1.7%	2.6%	6.9%	25.0%	31.9%

1 Mile–1.49 Mile

	Starts	1st	2nd	3rd	4th	5th	6th	7th	8th	9th	10th	11–20	21–43
Dover	34	1	1	3	2	4	1	1	0	0	0	6	15
New Hamp.	18	1	1	1	4	0	1	4	0	0	1	2	3
N. Carolina	33	2	6	0	2	2	1	1	0	0	1	9	9
Phoenix	16	1	0	0	0	1	1	0	1	3	1	3	5
Darlington	32	3	1	3	2	2	1	0	0	1	0	8	11
Total	**133**	**8**	**9**	**7**	**10**	**9**	**5**	**6**	**1**	**4**	**3**	**28**	**43**
		6.0%	6.8%	5.3%	7.5%	6.8%	3.8%	4.5%	0.8%	3.0%	2.3%	21.1%	32.3%

1.5 mile

	Starts	1st	2nd	3rd	4th	5th	6th	7th	8th	9th	10th	11–20	21–43
Charlotte	34	3	0	2	1	5	1	1	1	1	1	3	15
Chicago	3	0	0	0	1	0	0	0	0	0	0	1	1
Homestead	5	0	0	0	0	1	0	0	0	0	0	2	2
Kansas	3	0	0	0	0	0	0	0	0	0	0	0	3
Las Vegas	6	0	1	0	0	0	0	2	0	0	0	1	2
Texas	7	1	2	0	0	0	0	0	0	0	0	2	2
Total	**58**	**4**	**3**	**2**	**2**	**6**	**1**	**3**	**1**	**1**	**1**	**9**	**25**
		6.9%	5.2%	3.4%	3.4%	10.3%	1.7%	5.2%	1.7%	1.7%	1.7%	15.5%	43.1%

Track Performance

1.51 Mile–2.5 Mile

	Starts	1st	2nd	3rd	4th	5th	6th	7th	8th	9th	10th	11–20	21–43
Atlanta	32	1	5	1	2	2	0	1	1	2	1	8	8
California	7	0	0	0	0	1	1	0	1	1	0	0	3
Michigan	34	4	2	1	5	1	2	0	1	0	2	4	12
Indianapolis	10	2	0	2	0	0	0	1	0	0	1	2	2
Pocono	34	3	2	5	2	1	1	1	1	0	2	7	9
Total	**117**	**10**	**9**	**9**	**9**	**5**	**4**	**3**	**4**	**3**	**6**	**21**	**34**
		8.5%	7.7%	7.7%	7.7%	4.3%	3.4%	2.6%	3.4%	2.6%	5.1%	17.9%	29.1%

Restrictor Plate

	Starts	1st	2nd	3rd	4th	5th	6th	7th	8th	9th	10th	11–20	21–43
Daytona	33	4	1	1	0	2	2	0	2	0	2	6	13
Talladega	34	1	5	2	0	1	1	1	1	1	0	7	14
Total	**67**	**5**	**6**	**3**	**0**	**3**	**3**	**1**	**3**	**1**	**2**	**13**	**27**
		7.5%	9.0%	4.5%	0.0%	4.5%	4.5%	1.5%	4.5%	1.5%	3.0%	19.4%	40.3%

Road Courses

	Starts	1st	2nd	3rd	4th	5th	6th	7th	8th	9th	10th	11–20	21–43
Riverside	3	0	0	0	0	0	0	0	1	0	0	2	0
Sears Point	15	0	0	0	1	0	1	1	0	0	0	6	6
Watkins Glen	17	0	0	0	1	2	0	2	0	0	0	5	7
Total	**35**	**0**	**0**	**0**	**2**	**2**	**1**	**3**	**1**	**0**	**0**	**13**	**13**
		0.0%	0.0%	0.0%	5.7%	5.7%	2.9%	8.6%	2.9%	0.0%	0.0%	37.1%	37.1%

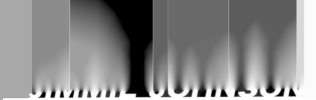

Jimmie Johnson

Current Team: Hendrick Motorsports
Residence: Mooresville, North Carolina
Hometown: El Cajon, California
Birthday: September 17, 1975
Height: 5 feet, 11 inches
Weight: 175

Races: 75
Running: 68 (90.7 percent)
Accidents: 2 (2.7 percent)
Mechanical Failures: 5 (6.7 percent)

2001–2003   Hendrick Motorsports

Jimmie learned to handle two wheels long before he drove on four. He began racing motorcycles at the age of four and by 15 was an accomplished racer. Before switching to cars, Jimmie won six motorcycling championships, including the 1996 and the 1997 SODA Winter Series Championship. He also raced in the Mickey Thompson Stadium Series and has 25 wins and more than 100 top-three finishes.

While most racers wait until the end of their career to move to the announcer's booth, Jimmie did so early. His presence and command of the language got him a job as a racing commentator for ESPN and a spokesperson for the Chevrolet Division of General Motors. In a day when sponsors are looking for both talent and personal presence, the skills he honed in these jobs made him a desirable commodity.

He began his automobile racing career at the age of 15. He raced in the ASA (American Speed Association) and won the Rookie of the Year trophy in 1998. In 1999 he scored two wins in ASA and finished 3rd in the final point standings. In 1999 he also made his Busch Series debut, finishing 7th at the Milwaukee Mile in his very first Busch Series start. He started four other Busch races that year before running the entire schedule the next year. The year 2000 was one of learning for Johnson. He finished 10th in the points, but mainly he got valuable seat time. In 2001 he won his first Busch Series at the first race at the new Chicagoland Speedway. He also ran three Winston Cup races in 2001 but never finished higher than 25th. After an 8th-place finish in the Busch Series points, Johnson was going to the Winston Cup Series full-time, and during the transition he was going to have some good advice.

None other than Jeff Gordon had partial ownership of his team and helped Johnson both on and off the track. His year in 2002 was better than anyone could have predicted. While Jimmie finished second to Ryan Newman in the Rookie of the Year competition, he could not have been disappointed by the performance of the team. It started with a pole at Daytona and, before it was over, Johnson had three wins (sweeping both races at Dover), five poles, and a 5th-place finish in the Winston Cup Championship. During 2003, he also garnered three wins, 14 top 5s and 20 top 10s, and a 2nd-place finish in points. As a rookie and a sophomore, Johnson had two seasons that many a seasoned veteran would be glad to have.

Jimmie was another of the new breed of rookies who won very early in their career. It took him only a handful of Winston Cup races before he visited victory lane. His first win was his 13th start in his home state of California.

Jimmie Johnson would win three times in his rookie season, ending the year with a fifth place finish in the points, and three more in his sophomore season, finishing second in the championship. He won four poles in 2002 including this one at Talladega.

Year-by-year Performance

	Races	Poles		Wins		Top 5		Top 10	
2001	3	0	0.0%	0	0.0%	0	0.0%	0	0.0%
2002	36	4	11.1%	3	8.3%	6	16.7%	21	58.3%
2003	36	2	5.6%	3	8.3%	14	38.9%	20	55.6%
Total	**75**	**6**	**8.0%**	**6**	**8.0%**	**20**	**26.7%**	**41**	**54.7%**

Track Performance

Less than 1 Mile

	Starts	1st	2nd	3rd	4th	5th	6th	7th	8th	9th	10th	11-20	21-43
Bristol	4	0	0	0	0	1	0	1	1	0	0	0	1
Martinsville	4	0	1	0	0	0	1	0	0	1	0	0	1
Richmond	4	0	0	0	0	0	0	0	0	0	0	3	1
Total	12	0	1	0	0	1	1	1	1	1	0	3	3
		0.0%	8.3%	0.0%	0.0%	8.3%	8.3%	8.3%	8.3%	8.3%	0.0%	25.0%	25.0%

1 Mile–1.49 Mile

	Starts	1st	2nd	3rd	4th	5th	6th	7th	8th	9th	10th	11-20	21-43
Dover	4	2	0	0	0	0	0	0	1	0	0	0	1
New Hamp.	4	2	0	0	0	0	0	0	0	1	0	1	0
N. Carolina	4	0	1	0	0	0	0	0	1	0	0	0	2
Phoenix	2	0	1	0	0	0	0	0	0	0	0	1	0
Darlington	4	0	0	1	0	0	1	0	0	1	0	0	1
Total	18	4	2	1	0	0	1	0	2	2	0	2	4
		22.2%	11.1%	5.6%	0.0%	0.0%	5.6%	0.0%	11.1%	11.1%	0.0%	11.1%	22.2%

1.5 mile

	Starts	1st	2nd	3rd	4th	5th	6th	7th	8th	9th	10th	11-20	21-43
Charlotte	5	1	0	1	0	0	1	1	0	0	0	0	1
Chicago	2	0	0	1	1	0	0	0	0	0	0	0	0
Homestead	3	0	0	1	0	0	0	0	1	0	0	0	1
Kansas	2	0	0	0	0	0	0	1	0	0	1	0	0
Las Vegas	2	0	0	0	0	0	1	0	0	0	0	1	0
Texas	2	0	0	0	0	0	1	0	1	0	0	0	0
Total	16	1	0	3	1	0	3	2	2	0	1	1	2
		6.3%	0.0%	18.8%	6.3%	0.0%	18.8%	12.5%	12.5%	0.0%	6.3%	6.3%	12.5%

Track Performance

1.51 Mile–2.5 Mile

Atlanta	5	0	0	2	0	0	0	0	0	0	0	0	3
California	2	1	0	0	0	0	0	0	0	0	0	1	0
Michigan	4	0	0	0	0	0	0	1	0	0	0	2	1
Indianapolis	2	0	0	0	0	0	0	0	0	1	0	1	0
Pocono	4	0	0	1	0	0	0	0	0	0	0	3	0
Total	**17**	**1**	**0**	**3**	**0**	**0**	**0**	**1**	**0**	**1**	**0**	**7**	**4**
		5.9%	0.0%	17.6%	0.0%	0.0%	0.0%	5.9%	0.0%	5.9%	0.0%	41.2%	23.5%

Restrictor Plate

Daytona	4	0	0	1	0	0	0	0	1	0	0	2	0
Talladega	4	0	0	0	0	0	0	1	0	0	0	1	2
Total	**8**	**0**	**0**	**1**	**0**	**0**	**0**	**1**	**1**	**0**	**0**	**3**	**2**
		0.0%	0.0%	12.5%	0.0%	0.0%	0.0%	12.5%	12.5%	0.0%	0.0%	37.5%	25.0%

Road Courses

Sears Point	2	0	0	0	0	0	0	0	0	0	0	1	1
Watkins Glen	2	0	0	0	1	0	0	0	0	0	0	1	0
Total	**4**	**0**	**0**	**0**	**1**	**0**	**0**	**0**	**0**	**0**	**0**	**2**	**1**
		0.0%	0.0%	0.0%	25.0%	0.0%	0.0%	0.0%	0.0%	0.0%	0.0%	50.0%	25.0%

Current Team: Roush Racing
Residence: Terrell, North Carolina
Hometown: Cambridge, Wisconsin
Birthday: March 10, 1972
Height: 5 feet, 9 inches
Weight: 152

Races: 148
Running: 131 (88.5 percent)
Accidents: 8 (5.4 percent)
Mechanical Failures: 9 (6.1 percent)

| **1999–2003** | Roush Racing |
| **1998** | Bill Elliot Racing |

Matt Kenseth

Matt Kenseth grew up competing in the fury of the Midwestern short tracks. The Wisconsin native began racing in the late 1980s at the age of 16. His father, also a racer, bought his first car for him but only allowed him to drive it if he worked on it. Matt agreed and won his first event in only his third outing. He raced in late models and ironically became the youngest winner of the ARTGO Challenge Series, a mark previously held by Mark Martin, his future teammate and mentor.

Matt scored 46 late-model wins while climbing his way to the elite divisions of NASCAR. He gained experience while driving in the NASCAR All Pro Series, the Hooter's Series, and the ASA Series. It was then that a former competitor, Robbie Reiser, called him to drive a car in the Busch Series in 1997. He was fast out of the box, and he scored seven top 10s in just 21 starts. The next year, going full-time racing in the Busch Series, Matt won three races and scored an impressive 17 top fives on his way to a 2nd-place finish in the points battle.

Like many other racers, Matt got an opportunity due to another driver's misfortune. He got his first Winston Cup start in 1998, at Dover, as a substitute driver for an injured Bill Elliot. Kenseth finished 6th, matching the team's best finish of the year and proving without a doubt that he would race at the next level. But before moving up, Matt stayed in the Busch

Series for another year. He won four times, finished 3rd in the points, and again amassed valuable seat time.

Toward the end of the 1999 season, Matt began showing up in select Winston Cup events, with his best being a 4th-place finish. In 2000 Kenseth was ready to run the Winston Cup circuit full-time in a Ford co-owned by Mark Martin and Jack Roush. In his 18th start, he visited victory lane for the first time and become the first rookie to win the prestigious Coca-Cola 600 at Charlotte. The new team finished in the top 10 in almost a third of the races and finished 14th in the Winston Cup Championship. While there were no wins in 2001, Matt once again gained more and more seat time and experience. The team still finished 13th in the point standings, with four top-5 finishes and nine top 10s. In 2002 Matt became one of the premier drivers in the sport. His 8th-place finish in points was somewhat disappointing, as he finished the year with five wins and 19 top 10s.

One of Kenseth's greatest assets was his fast pit crew, which won the World Pit Crew Competition. In 2003 it all paid off. Matt didn't even need the entire year to win the Winston Cup Championship. With one race to go, he had accumulated enough points to clinch the trophy, and he had led the point standings longer than any driver in NASCAR history. While the team had only one win, it did post 11 top 5s and an impressive 25 top 10s.

Matt Kenseth began driving for Jack Roush in the 2000 season. Three years later the consistent driver would bring Roush his first Winston Cup Champion.

Matt Kenseth has been a steady performer in the Busch Series, with 14 wins through 2003.

Year-by-year Performance

	Races	Poles		Wins		Top 5		Top 10	
1998	1	0	0.0%	0	0.0%	0	0.0%	1	100.0%
1999	5	0	0.0%	0	0.0%	1	20.0%	1	20.0%
2000	34	0	0.0%	1	2.9%	4	11.8%	11	32.4%
2001	36	0	0.0%	0	0.0%	4	11.1%	9	25.0%
2002	36	1	2.8%	5	13.9%	11	30.6%	19	52.8%
2003	36	0	0.0%	1	2.8%	11	30.6%	25	69.4%
Total	**148**	**1**	**0.7%**	**7**	**4.7%**	**31**	**20.9%**	**66**	**44.6%**

Track Performance

Less than 1 Mile

	Starts	1st	2nd	3rd	4th	5th	6th	7th	8th	9th	10th	11–20	21–43
Bristol	8	0	1	0	1	1	1	0	0	0	0	2	2
Martinsville	8	0	1	0	0	0	1	0	0	0	0	2	4
Richmond	8	1	0	0	0	0	1	2	1	0	0	1	2
Total	**24**	**1**	**2**	**0**	**1**	**1**	**3**	**2**	**1**	**0**	**0**	**5**	**8**
		4.2%	8.3%	0.0%	4.2%	4.2%	12.5%	8.3%	4.2%	0.0%	0.0%	20.8%	33.3%

1 Mile–1.49 Mile

	Starts	1st	2nd	3rd	4th	5th	6th	7th	8th	9th	10th	11–20	21–43
Dover	10	0	1	0	2	0	1	1	0	1	0	2	2
New Hamp.	8	0	0	1	1	0	0	1	0	0	1	3	1
N. Carolina	9	1	0	1	1	0	0	0	1	0	1	0	4
Phoenix	4	1	0	0	1	0	1	0	0	0	0	0	1
Darlington	9	0	0	0	0	0	1	0	2	0	0	2	4
Total	**40**	**2**	**1**	**2**	**5**	**0**	**3**	**2**	**3**	**1**	**2**	**7**	**12**
		5.0%	2.5%	5.0%	12.5%	0.0%	7.5%	5.0%	7.5%	2.5%	5.0%	17.5%	30.0%

1.5 mile

	Starts	1st	2nd	3rd	4th	5th	6th	7th	8th	9th	10th	11–20	21–43
Charlotte	9	1	2	0	0	0	0	0	1	1	0	2	2
Chicago	3	0	0	0	0	0	0	1	0	0	0	2	0
Homestead	4	0	0	0	0	0	0	0	0	0	0	0	4
Kansas	3	0	0	0	0	0	0	1	0	0	0	0	2
Las Vegas	4	1	0	0	0	0	0	0	0	0	0	3	0
Texas	4	1	0	0	0	0	1	0	0	0	0	1	1
Total	**27**	**3**	**2**	**0**	**0**	**0**	**1**	**2**	**1**	**1**	**0**	**8**	**9**
		11.1%	7.4%	0.0%	0.0%	0.0%	3.7%	7.4%	3.7%	3.7%	0.0%	29.6%	33.3%

Track Performance

1.51 Mile–2.5 Mile

	Starts	1st	2nd	3rd	4th	5th	6th	7th	8th	9th	10th	11–20	21–43
Atlanta	8	0	0	0	2	0	0	0	0	2	0	2	2
California	4	0	0	1	0	0	0	0	0	1	0	2	0
Michigan	9	1	0	0	2	0	0	0	1	1	0	4	0
Indianapolis	4	0	1	1	0	0	0	0	0	0	0	0	2
Pocono	8	0	0	1	0	1	1	0	1	0	0	3	1
Total	**33**	**1**	**1**	**3**	**4**	**1**	**1**	**0**	**2**	**4**	**0**	**11**	**5**
		3.0%	3.0%	9.1%	12.1%	3.0%	3.0%	0.0%	6.1%	12.1%	0.0%	33.3%	15.2%

Restrictor Plate

	Starts	1st	2nd	3rd	4th	5th	6th	7th	8th	9th	10th	11–20	21–43
Daytona	8	0	0	0	0	0	1	0	0	0	1	3	3
Talladega	8	0	0	0	1	0	0	0	0	1	1	3	2
Total	**16**	**0**	**0**	**0**	**1**	**0**	**1**	**0**	**0**	**1**	**2**	**6**	**5**
		0.0%	0.0%	0.0%	6.3%	0.0%	6.3%	0.0%	0.0%	6.3%	12.5%	37.5%	31.3%

Road Courses

	Starts	1st	2nd	3rd	4th	5th	6th	7th	8th	9th	10th	11–20	21–43
Sears Point	4	0	0	0	0	0	0	0	0	0	0	1	3
Watkins Glen	4	0	0	0	0	0	0	0	1	0	1	0	2
Total	**8**	**0**	**0**	**0**	**0**	**0**	**0**	**0**	**1**	**0**	**1**	**1**	**5**
		0.0%	0.0%	0.0%	0.0%	0.0%	0.0%	0.0%	12.5%	0.0%	12.5%	12.5%	62.5%

Bobby Labonte

Current Team: Joe Gibbs Racing
Residence: Trinity, North Carolina
Hometown: Corpus Christi, Texas
Birthday: May 8, 1964
Height: 5 feet, 9 inches
Weight: 175

Races: 366
Running: 317 (86.6 percent)
Accidents: 24 (6.6 percent)
Mechanical Failures: 25 (6.8 percent)

1995–2003	Joe Gibbs Racing
1993–1994	Bill Davis Racing
1991	Bobby Labonte

Like so many others, Bobby Labonte was driving and racing before he started school. As a five-year-old, he drove quarter midgets and in his teens switched to karts, competing in his home state of Texas. But Bobby had to quit racing the tracks of Texas when his family moved to North Carolina, where older brother Terry was coming on strong in the Winston Cup Series. After arriving in North Carolina, Bobby's first racing job was sweeping floors at Hagan Racing—his brother's team. A few years later, when Terry left to drive for Junior Johnson, Bobby was let go from the team.

While he worked on other people's Winston Cup cars during the day, Bobby worked on his own late-model car at night. He raced late models in the late 1980s, and in 1990 began a full-time Busch Series career. While his new team went winless in 1990, Bobby tended to take care of the equipment, and the team finished 4th in the points race. The following year, when the Busch Series rolled into Bristol, Labonte won his first Busch Series race, and he went on to win the 1991 NASCAR Busch Series Championship. It was also in 1991 that Bobby started his Winston Cup career, running (with little success) in races at Dover and Michigan. So, lacking a Winston Cup ride, Bobby stayed on the Busch circuit in 1992, winning three times and losing the championship by three points to Joe Nemechek.

Over the next few years, other driver's decisions began to benefit Bobby Labonte. Jeff Gordon decided to race his rookie year for Rick Hendrick instead of Bill Davis, so Labonte was offered the seat in Davis' car. Gordon edged him out for Rookie of the Year, although the team had six top-10 finishes. In 1994 Bobby broke into the top 5 once (at Michigan) but it was a mediocre season, with only two top 10s. Again, another driver's decision benefited Bobby. When Dale Jarrett left Joe Gibbs Racing to drive for Robert Yates, Gibbs called Bobby Labonte. The Gibbs Racing/Bobby Labonte combination yielded success right away. In the 11th race of the year, he qualified second at Charlotte and then won the race. Bobby also won both Michigan events. They finished the year with seven top 5s and 14 top 10s. That year Bobby also made it to the stage at the banquet to join his champion brother with a 10th-place finish in the Winston Cup championship. Over the next few years, Bobby consistently visited victory lane, usually on the circuit's longer tracks. In 2000 Bobby won four races and had 19 top-five finishes in 34 races. The result was the first Winston Cup Championship for him and Joe Gibbs. In winning NASCAR's ultimate trophy, he and Terry became the only brothers to have both won the coveted prize.

Bobby followed his brother into racing and has wound up in one of the newest and yet most prestigious rides on the circuit. In 1995 Bobby joined Joe Gibbs and the rest is history. To date the pair have racked up 21 wins and one Winston Cup Championship.

When Bobby came to Joe Gibbs Racing he had never won a race. That changed quickly in 1995 when he drove his Pontiac to three wins, two poles, and his first top-10 finish in the points.

Year-by-year Performance

	Races	Poles		Wins		Top 5		Top 10	
1991	2	0	0.0%	0	0.0%	0	0.0%	0	0.0%
1993	30	1	3.3%	0	0.0%	0	0.0%	6	20.0%
1994	31	0	0.0%	0	0.0%	1	3.2%	2	6.5%
1995	31	2	6.5%	3	9.7%	7	22.6%	14	45.2%
1996	31	4	12.9%	1	3.2%	5	16.1%	14	45.2%
1997	32	3	9.4%	1	3.1%	9	28.1%	18	56.3%
1998	33	3	9.1%	2	6.1%	11	33.3%	18	54.5%
1999	34	5	14.7%	5	14.7%	23	67.6%	26	76.5%
2000	34	2	5.9%	4	11.8%	19	55.9%	24	70.6%
2001	36	1	2.8%	2	5.6%	9	25.0%	20	55.6%
2002	36	0	0.0%	1	2.8%	5	13.9%	7	19.4%
2003	36	4	11.1%	2	5.6%	12	33.3%	17	47.2%
Total	**366**	**25**	**6.8%**	**21**	**5.7%**	**101**	**27.6%**	**166**	**45.4%**

Track Performance

Less than 1 Mile

Bristol	22	0	0	1	0	1	2	1	2	1	0	4	10
Martinsville	22	1	1	0	1	0	0	0	4	0	3	6	6
Richmond	22	0	2	1	0	0	2	0	2	0	1	4	10
N. Wilkes	8	0	0	0	0	0	0	0	0	0	1	5	2
Total	**74**	**1**	**3**	**2**	**1**	**1**	**4**	**1**	**8**	**1**	**5**	**19**	**28**
		1.4%	4.1%	2.7%	1.4%	1.4%	5.4%	1.4%	10.8%	1.4%	6.8%	25.7%	37.8%

1 Mile–1.49 Mile

Dover	23	1	1	2	4	3	0	1	0	1	0	5	5
New Hamp.	18	0	1	2	0	1	0	2	0	1	1	7	3
N. Carolina	22	1	2	3	0	0	1	1	1	1	0	6	6
Phoenix	11	0	0	1	0	1	0	0	1	1	0	2	5
Darlington	22	1	1	1	0	1	1	2	1	0	1	7	6
Total	**96**	**3**	**5**	**9**	**4**	**6**	**2**	**6**	**3**	**4**	**2**	**27**	**25**
		3.1%	5.2%	9.4%	4.2%	6.3%	2.1%	6.3%	3.1%	4.2%	2.1%	28.1%	26.0%

1.5 mile

Charlotte	22	2	5	2	0	1	2	0	2	0	1	1	6
Chicago	3	0	0	0	0	0	0	0	0	0	0	1	2
Homestead	5	1	1	0	1	0	0	0	1	0	0	0	1
Kansas	3	0	0	0	0	0	0	0	0	0	0	1	2
Las Vegas	6	0	0	0	1	2	0	0	0	0	0	2	1
Texas	7	0	0	3	0	0	0	0	1	0	0	0	3
Total	**46**	**3**	**6**	**5**	**2**	**3**	**2**	**0**	**4**	**0**	**1**	**5**	**15**
		6.5%	13.0%	10.9%	4.3%	6.5%	4.3%	0.0%	8.7%	0.0%	2.2%	10.9%	32.6%

Track Performance

1.51 Mile–2.5 Mile

Atlanta	22	6	3	0	1	2	0	0	1	0	0	4	5
California	7	0	2	1	0	0	1	0	0	0	0	0	3
Michigan	23	3	2	2	0	2	2	1	1	1	0	5	4
Indianapolis	10	1	2	1	0	0	0	0	0	1	0	3	2
Pocono	22	3	0	0	1	0	1	0	1	0	0	8	8
Total	**84**	**13**	**9**	**4**	**2**	**4**	**4**	**1**	**3**	**2**	**0**	**20**	**22**
		15.5%	10.7%	4.8%	2.4%	4.8%	4.8%	1.2%	3.6%	2.4%	0.0%	23.8%	26.2%

Restrictor Plate

Daytona	22	0	2	0	0	3	1	0	0	0	1	4	11
Talladega	22	1	1	1	1	2	1	1	1	0	0	4	9
Total	**44**	**1**	**3**	**1**	**1**	**5**	**2**	**1**	**1**	**0**	**1**	**8**	**20**
		2.3%	6.8%	2.3%	2.3%	11.4%	4.5%	2.3%	2.3%	0.0%	2.3%	18.2%	45.5%

Road Courses

Sears Point	11	0	0	0	2	0	0	1	0	2	0	5	1
Watkins Glen	11	0	0	0	0	2	1	1	0	1	1	2	3
Total	**22**	**0**	**0**	**0**	**2**	**2**	**1**	**2**	**0**	**3**	**1**	**7**	**4**
		0.0%	0.0%	0.0%	9.1%	9.1%	4.5%	9.1%	0.0%	13.6%	4.5%	31.8%	18.2%

Terry Labonte

Current Team: Hendrick Motorsports
Residence: Thomasville, North Carolina
Hometown: Corpus Christi, Texas
Birthday: November 16, 1956
Height: 5 feet, 10 inches
Weight: 165

Races: 780
Running: 635 (81.3 percent)
Accidents: 50 (6.4 percent)
Mechanical Failures: 96 (12.3 percent)

1994–2003	Hendrick Motorsports
1991–1993	Billy Hagan
1990	Richard Jackson
1987–1989	Junior Johnson
1978–1986	Billy Hagan

O nly one other current driver has been around the NASCAR circuit longer than Terry Labonte. Labonte's career has had its ups and downs, and through it all, Terry has always remained one of NASCAR's most admired and personable drivers. He began his racing career in quarter midget cars and later moved behind the wheel of a family-owned stock car. He raced throughout the mid-1970s until financial strains put an end to the team.

But Billy Hagan had noticed Terry and decided to put him in a Winston Cup car. Terry's first race of the 1978 season was late in the year at Darlington, where he qualified 19th and finished 4th. While the team was able to run only five races, it turned some heads with three top 10s, a 13th, and a 24th. Terry ran the entire 1979 season and was very competitive. But he had to wait until 1980 for his first win, which came at Darlington. While Terry often ran in the top 5, he had to wait until 1983 for his second win, which came at Rockingham. The next year Labonte won two races and scored an impressive 15 top 5s and 24 top 10s. Billy Hagan's confidence in Terry paid off as his driving consistency won him his first of two Winston Cup Championships. At 27, he was the youngest driver to have ever won the championship.

Terry won a race in every season from 1983 to 1989. He left Billy Hagan after the 1986 season to drive for Junior Johnson. Terry was a hot commodity, as he was known as a patient and calculating driver, at home on short tracks, superspeedways, or road courses. He could win on any of them. Terry left Junior Johnson's team after the 1989 season and drove one year for Richard Jackson, and in 1991 returned to Billy Hagan's team. But starting in 1990, Terry began a winless streak that lasted four years. Some were writing him off when Hendrick Motorsports hired him in 1994. Terry was finally back in good equipment with a united team. The result was a return to victory lane, with the team winning three times in 1994 and 1995. In 1996 Terry did everything right, and the result was his second Winston Cup Championship. The team won two races and had 21 top-five finishes, which means it was in the top five in almost 70 percent of the races that season.

Terry continued to win races throughout the late 1990s, but by 2000 the chemistry of the team had changed, and it went winless. It was also in 2000 that Terry did something he had not done for many years—he missed a race. His record of 655 consecutive starts came to an end when he had to sit out a race due to post-concussion syndrome. Over the next couple of years, Labonte was again shut out from the winner's circle, and again people quit talking about Terry as a possible winner. Terry proved them wrong once again, when in 2003 he won a race late in the year at—where else—Darlington.

Terry Labonte has been a fixture on the Winston and Nextel Cup circuit for over a quarter of a century. He has driven to two Championships with the first coming in 1984 and the second in 1996.

Year-by-year Performance

	Races	Poles		Wins		Top 5		Top 10	
1978	5	0	0.0%	0	0.0%	1	20.0%	3	60.0%
1979	31	0	0.0%	0	0.0%	2	6.5%	13	41.9%
1980	31	0	0.0%	1	3.2%	6	19.4%	16	51.6%
1981	31	2	6.5%	0	0.0%	8	25.8%	17	54.8%
1982	30	2	6.7%	0	0.0%	17	56.7%	21	70.0%
1983	30	3	10.0%	1	3.3%	11	36.7%	20	66.7%
1984	28	2	7.1%	2	7.1%	17	60.7%	24	85.7%
1985	29	4	13.8%	1	3.4%	8	27.6%	17	58.6%
1986	29	1	3.4%	1	3.4%	5	17.2%	10	34.5%
1987	29	4	13.8%	1	3.4%	13	44.8%	22	75.9%
1988	29	1	3.4%	1	3.4%	11	37.9%	18	62.1%
1989	29	0	0.0%	2	6.9%	9	31.0%	11	37.9%
1990	29	0	0.0%	0	0.0%	4	13.8%	9	31.0%
1991	29	1	3.4%	0	0.0%	1	3.4%	7	24.1%
1992	29	0	0.0%	0	0.0%	4	13.8%	16	55.2%
1993	30	0	0.0%	0	0.0%	0	0.0%	10	33.3%
1994	31	0	0.0%	3	9.7%	6	19.4%	14	45.2%
1995	31	1	3.2%	3	9.7%	14	45.2%	17	54.8%
1996	31	4	12.9%	2	6.5%	21	67.7%	24	77.4%
1997	32	0	0.0%	1	3.1%	8	25.0%	20	62.5%
1998	33	0	0.0%	1	3.0%	5	15.2%	15	45.5%
1999	34	0	0.0%	1	2.9%	1	2.9%	7	20.6%
2000	32	1	3.1%	0	0.0%	3	9.4%	6	18.8%
2001	36	0	0.0%	0	0.0%	1	2.8%	3	8.3%
2002	36	0	0.0%	0	0.0%	1	2.8%	4	11.1%
2003	36	1	2.8%	1	2.8%	4	11.1%	9	25.0%
Total	**780**	**27**	**3.5%**	**22**	**2.8%**	**181**	**23.2%**	**353**	**45.3%**

Track Performance

Less than 1 Mile

	Starts	1st	2nd	3rd	4th	5th	6th	7th	8th	9th	10th	11–20	21–43
Bristol	50	2	4	3	6	4	2	5	2	3	2	5	12
Martinsville	51	0	3	2	4	4	6	3	0	6	0	8	15
Richmond	51	3	2	2	1	4	2	2	8	2	0	10	15
N. Wilkes	36	4	2	3	3	3	3	4	2	2	1	4	5
Nashville	12	0	2	0	0	1	2	1	2	1	0	1	2
Total	200	9	13	10	14	16	15	15	14	14	3	28	49
		4.5%	6.5%	5.0%	7.0%	8.0%	7.5%	7.5%	7.0%	7.0%	1.5%	14.0%	24.5%

1 Mile–1.49 Mile

	Starts	1st	2nd	3rd	4th	5th	6th	7th	8th	9th	10th	11–20	21–43
Dover	50	0	2	2	3	1	1	2	2	0	2	17	18
New Hamp.	18	0	0	0	1	0	1	1	0	0	0	6	9
N. Carolina	50	2	2	4	4	1	0	5	3	2	2	12	13
Phoenix	16	1	2	1	0	0	0	0	0	0	1	8	3
Darlington	51	2	1	1	3	4	3	1	2	2	1	12	19
Total	185	5	7	8	11	6	5	9	7	4	6	55	62
		2.7%	3.8%	4.3%	5.9%	3.2%	2.7%	4.9%	3.8%	2.2%	3.2%	29.7%	33.5%

1.5 mile

	Starts	1st	2nd	3rd	4th	5th	6th	7th	8th	9th	10th	11–20	21–43
Charlotte	51	1	2	3	2	2	3	2	1	1	2	14	18
Chicago	3	0	0	0	0	0	0	0	0	0	0	2	1
Homestead	5	0	0	0	0	0	0	0	0	0	0	2	3
Kansas	3	0	0	0	0	0	0	0	0	0	0	2	1
Las Vegas	6	0	0	0	0	0	0	0	1	0	0	2	3
Texas	7	1	0	0	1	0	1	0	1	0	1	2	0
Total	78	2	2	3	3	4	4	2	3	1	3	24	27
		2.6%	2.6%	3.8%	3.8%	5.1%	5.1%	2.6%	3.8%	1.3%	3.8%	30.8%	34.6%

Track Performance
1.51 Mile–2.5 Mile

	Starts	1st	2nd	3rd	4th	5th	6th	7th	8th	9th	10th	11–20	21–43
Atlanta	51	0	1	2	3	4	2	3	7	2	0	13	14
California	7	0	1	1	0	0	0	1	0	1	0	1	2
Michigan	50	0	3	2	1	1	0	1	1	2	2	16	21
Indianapolis	9	0	0	1	0	0	0	0	0	1	0	6	1
Pocono	47	2	0	2	1	2	4	2	0	4	2	13	15
Ontario	2	0	0	0	0	0	0	0	1	0	0	1	0
Total	**166**	**2**	**5**	**8**	**5**	**7**	**6**	**7**	**9**	**10**	**4**	**50**	**53**
		1.2%	3.0%	4.8%	3.0%	4.2%	3.6%	4.2%	5.4%	6.0%	2.4%	30.1%	31.9%

Restrictor Plate

	Starts	1st	2nd	3rd	4th	5th	6th	7th	8th	9th	10th	11–20	21–43
Daytona	50	0	5	1	3	2	4	3	3	2	2	12	13
Talladega	50	2	3	3	3	2	4	2	0	1	1	6	23
Total	**100**	**2**	**8**	**4**	**6**	**4**	**8**	**5**	**3**	**3**	**3**	**18**	**36**
		2.0%	8.0%	4.0%	6.0%	4.0%	8.0%	5.0%	3.0%	3.0%	3.0%	18.0%	36.0%

Road Courses

	Starts	1st	2nd	3rd	4th	5th	6th	7th	8th	9th	10th	11–20	21–43
Riverside	20	2	4	2	1	0	0	2	1	0	1	2	5
Sears Point	15	0	1	2	0	2	1	0	0	1	0	2	6
Watkins Glen	17	0	2	0	0	1	1	0	2	0	0	5	6
Total	**52**	**2**	**7**	**4**	**1**	**3**	**2**	**2**	**3**	**1**	**1**	**9**	**17**
		3.8%	13.5%	7.7%	1.9%	5.8%	3.8%	3.8%	5.8%	1.9%	1.9%	17.3%	32.7%

STERLING MARLIN

Sterling Marlin

Current Team: Chip Ganassi Racing
Residence: Columbia, Tennessee
Hometown: Columbia, Tennessee
Birthday: June 30, 1957
Height: 6 feet, 0 inches
Weight: 185

Races: 607
Running: 486 (6.1 percent)
Accidents: 37 (13.8 percent)
Mechanical Failures: 84 (80.1 percent)

2001–2003	Chip Ganassi Racing
1998–2000	SABCO
1994–1997	Morgan-McClure
1993	Stavola Brothers Racing
1991–1992	Junior Johnson
1987–1990	Billy Hagan
1986	Hoss Ellington
1985	Helen Rae
	Earl Sadler
1984	Jimmy Means
	Dick Bahre
	Earl Sadler
1983	Roger Hamby
1982	Matthews Racing
1981	CooCoo Marlin
1980	D. K. Ulrich
	Jim Stacy
	CooCoo Marlin
1978–1980	CooCoo Marlin
1976	CooCoo Marlin

Sterling Marlin grew up in Tennessee, surrounded by the race cars that his father, CooCoo Marlin, drove. As a youth, he was good at both football and basketball, but, needless to say, racing was in his blood. Before becoming a driver, he learned to work on the race cars, and at the age of 16 was his father's crew chief. He drove in his first Winston Cup race in 1976 when he substituted for his injured father. He started 30th and over the course of the race gained one position to finish in 29th.

Over the next few years, Sterling competed at smaller tracks, especially in Tennessee, and won three consecutive track championships at Nashville Raceway in 1980, 1981, and 1982. From 1976 to 1983 Sterling drove in a handful of Winston Cup races each year, and in 1983 made the move to Winston Cup full-time and drove in 30 races. His best finish was a 10th at Dover, but he ran well enough throughout the year to win Rookie of the Year honors. Beginning the next year, Sterling again was a part-time Winston Cup Racer. From 1984 to 1986 Sterling only ran in 32 races, and for five different teams. Sterling's next full year on the circuit was 1987, when he began driving for Billy Hagan. He finished with eight top 10s, his best finish a 3rd at Charlotte. Over the next few years, Sterling ran well for Hagan and then with Junior Johnson, who hired him for the 1991 and 1992 seasons. He had a number of finishes in the top five but could not seem to put together a run good enough to win.

After a year with the Stavola Brothers, Sterling began driving for Morgan-McClure in 1994, and it proved to be a winning combination. In 1994 they won the Daytona 500, with Sterling's first win coming in his 279th race. The team repeated the performance in 1995, with Marlin joining Richard Petty and Cale Yarborough as the only drivers to win the Daytona 500 in consecutive years. The team finished the year with 3rd place in the Winston Cup points—the best of Marlin's career. Sterling drove for Morgan-McClure until the end of the 1997 season, when he began driving for owner Felix Sebates. Over the next couple of years, the team had limited success. Veteran race team owner Chip Ganassi threw in with the SABCO organization in 2000 and announced that their teams would run Dodge Intrepids, as the manufacturer was returning to Winston Cup racing. The team went winless in 2000, but in 2001 reached victory lane twice, with wins at Michigan and Charlotte. The team's excellent consistency paid off with a 3rd-place finish in the points. Expectations were high for 2002, but it turned into a bittersweet year for Marlin. He won two races and led the points race almost the entire year, only to be forced from the car with a neck injury he had suffered in a crash at Kansas. While the injury cost him a shot at the championship, his performance throughout his partial season left no doubt that Sterling could run with the best of them.

When Sterling Marlin drove his first race in 1976 it was a different sport. Since then he has driven in over 600 Winston Cup races, winning 10 of them. His best shot at a Championship came in 2002 when he led the points almost the entire year, only to have to sit out the final seven races due to a neck injury.

Sterling's first wins came in the mid-1990s when he was driving the Kodak Film Chevrolet for Morgan-McClure. The car was especially tough on superspeedways as the team won back to back Daytona 500s in 1994 and 1995.

Year-by-year Performance

	Races	Poles		Wins		Top 5		Top 10	
1976	1	0	0.0%	0	0.0%	0	0.0%	0	0.0%
1978	2	0	0.0%	0	0.0%	0	0.0%	1	50.0%
1979	1	0	0.0%	0	0.0%	0	0.0%	0	0.0%
1980	5	0	0.0%	0	0.0%	0	0.0%	2	40.0%
1981	2	0	0.0%	0	0.0%	0	0.0%	0	0.0%
1982	1	0	0.0%	0	0.0%	0	0.0%	0	0.0%
1983	30	0	0.0%	0	0.0%	0	0.0%	1	3.3%
1984	14	0	0.0%	0	0.0%	0	0.0%	2	14.3%
1985	8	0	0.0%	0	0.0%	0	0.0%	0	0.0%
1986	10	0	0.0%	0	0.0%	2	20.0%	4	40.0%
1987	29	0	0.0%	0	0.0%	4	13.8%	8	27.6%
1988	29	0	0.0%	0	0.0%	6	20.7%	13	44.8%
1989	29	0	0.0%	0	0.0%	4	13.8%	13	44.8%
1990	29	0	0.0%	0	0.0%	5	17.2%	10	34.5%
1991	29	2	6.9%	0	0.0%	7	24.1%	16	55.2%
1992	29	5	17.2%	0	0.0%	6	20.7%	13	44.8%
1993	30	0	0.0%	0	0.0%	1	3.3%	8	26.7%
1994	31	1	3.2%	1	3.2%	5	16.1%	11	35.5%
1995	31	1	3.2%	3	9.7%	9	29.0%	22	71.0%
1996	31	0	0.0%	2	6.5%	5	16.1%	10	32.3%
1997	32	0	0.0%	0	0.0%	2	6.3%	6	18.8%
1998	32	0	0.0%	0	0.0%	0	0.0%	6	18.8%
1999	34	1	2.9%	0	0.0%	2	5.9%	5	14.7%
2000	34	0	0.0%	0	0.0%	1	2.9%	7	20.6%
2001	39	1	2.6%	2	5.1%	12	30.8%	20	51.3%
2002	29	0	0.0%	2	6.9%	8	27.6%	14	48.3%
2003	36	0	0.0%	0	0.0%	0	0.0%	11	30.6%
Total	**607**	**11**	**1.8%**	**10**	**1.6%**	**79**	**13.0%**	**203**	**33.4%**

Track Performance

Less than 1 Mile

	Starts	1st	2nd	3rd	4th	5th	6th	7th	8th	9th	10th	11–20	21–43
Bristol	38	0	1	0	0	1	2	4	4	2	2	15	7
Martinsville	35	0	2	0	0	1	0	4	1	1	2	10	14
Richmond	36	0	0	0	1	2	0	1	1	1	2	13	15
N. Wilkes	22	0	0	0	0	2	0	1	1	1	0	12	5
Nashville	9	0	0	0	0	0	0	1	0	0	0	4	4
Total	**140**	**0**	**3**	**0**	**1**	**6**	**2**	**11**	**7**	**5**	**6**	**54**	**45**
		0.0%	2.1%	0.0%	0.7%	4.3%	1.4%	7.9%	5.0%	3.6%	4.3%	38.6%	32.1%

1 Mile–1.49 Mile

	Starts	1st	2nd	3rd	4th	5th	6th	7th	8th	9th	10th	11–20	21–43
Dover	36	0	0	0	0	2	2	1	2	0	3	12	14
New Hamp.	18	0	1	0	0	0	1	0	0	1	1	3	11
N. Carolina	36	0	2	1	1	1	3	1	3	1	1	13	9
Phoenix	15	0	0	2	0	0	0	0	0	1	1	5	6
Darlington	40	2	0	0	3	5	1	0	2	0	3	8	16
Total	**145**	**2**	**3**	**3**	**4**	**8**	**7**	**2**	**7**	**3**	**9**	**41**	**56**
		1.4%	2.1%	2.1%	2.8%	5.5%	4.8%	1.4%	4.8%	2.1%	6.2%	28.3%	38.6%

1.5 mile

	Starts	1st	2nd	3rd	4th	5th	6th	7th	8th	9th	10th	11–20	21–43
Charlotte	46	1	1	1	2	2	2	3	0	1	0	13	20
Chicago	3	0	0	0	0	0	0	0	0	1	0	1	1
Homestead	4	0	0	0	0	1	0	0	0	0	1	1	1
Kansas	3	0	0	0	0	1	0	0	0	0	0	0	2
Las Vegas	6	1	0	1	0	0	0	0	1	0	0	2	1
Texas	7	0	0	0	0	0	0	1	1	1	0	1	3
Total	**69**	**2**	**1**	**2**	**2**	**4**	**2**	**4**	**2**	**3**	**1**	**18**	**28**
		2.9%	1.4%	2.9%	2.9%	5.8%	2.9%	5.8%	2.9%	4.3%	1.4%	26.1%	40.6%

Track Performance

1.51 Mile–2.5 Mile

Atlanta	38	0	2	1	0	1	0	4	1	3	1	14	11
California	7	0	0	0	0	0	0	1	0	1	1	2	2
Michigan	37	1	0	2	1	0	2	2	2	0	1	15	11
Indianapolis	10	0	1	0	0	0	0	1	0	0	0	3	5
Pocono	37	0	0	1	4	1	3	2	2	2	1	11	10
Total	**129**	**1**	**3**	**4**	**5**	**2**	**5**	**10**	**5**	**6**	**4**	**45**	**39**
		0.8%	2.3%	3.1%	3.9%	1.6%	3.9%	7.8%	3.9%	4.7%	3.1%	34.9%	30.2%

Restrictor Plate

Daytona	43	3	5	2	0	2	0	2	4	2	0	10	13
Talladega	40	2	1	1	2	3	3	0	2	1	0	7	18
Total	**83**	**5**	**6**	**3**	**2**	**5**	**3**	**2**	**6**	**3**	**0**	**17**	**31**
		6.0%	7.2%	3.6%	2.4%	6.0%	3.6%	2.4%	7.2%	3.6%	0.0%	20.5%	37.3%

Road Courses

Riverside	4	0	0	0	0	0	0	0	0	2	0	1	1
Sears Point	15	0	1	0	0	0	1	2	0	0	0	4	7
Watkins Glen	17	0	0	0	0	0	1	2	1	0	0	5	8
Total	**36**	**0**	**1**	**0**	**0**	**0**	**2**	**4**	**1**	**2**	**0**	**10**	**16**
		0.0%	2.8%	0.0%	0.0%	0.0%	5.6%	11.1%	2.8%	5.6%	0.0%	27.8%	44.4%

Mark Martin

Current Team: Roush Racing
Residence: Daytona Beach, Florida
Birthplace: Batesville, Arkansas
Birthday: January 9, 1959
Height: 5 feet, 6 inches
Weight: 140

Races: 566
Running: 467 (82.5 percent)
Accidents: 30 (5.3 percent)
Mechanical Failures: 69 (12.2 percent)

1988–2003	Roush Racing
1987	Roger Hamby
1986	J. Gunderman
1983	J. D. Stacy
	D. K. Ulrich
	Emanuel Zerbakis
	Morgan-McClure
1982	Mark Martin
	Bob Rogers
1981	Mark Martin

Mark Martin began racing on the dirt tracks of Arkansas when he was 15 years old, and in his first year of racing won the Arkansas State Championship. A couple of years later he had left the dirt tracks and was racing on paved surfaces. In 1977 he began racing in the ASA, and won the ASA Rookie of the Year trophy. His racing skills were more finely honed competing with other ASA drivers, whose ranks included Rusty Wallace and Bobby Allison. Mark followed up his Rookie of the Year award impressively by winning the series championship in 1978, 1979, and 1980.

It was time for Mark to move on. As an owner/driver, he ran five Cup races in 1981, all on short tracks, and finished an impressive 3rd at Martinsville. He also drove to his first pole in 1981, at Nashville International Raceway, in his third start. In 1982 he raced the Cup circuit full-time, scoring eight top 10s. However, financial strains forced him to close his shop, and though he ran a few races, Mark did not return to the Winston Cup Series full-time until 1988. It was then that Jack Roush decided to go Winston Cup racing and hired Martin as his driver. Mark had finally found a stable racing home with the financial backing and engineering that could fund a winning effort.

In his first year with Roush Racing the team did not win, but scored 10 top-10 finishes. The next year at Rockingham, Martin and Roush got their first win. The team also finished second five times and had 14 top fives, proving it was a force on the Winston Cup circuit. In 1990 Mark had three wins and finished second in the points championship. Roush Racing would have won the championship, but received a questionable point subtracting penalty from NASCAR, which cost the championship. From 1989 to1995, Mark won at least one race a year for the No. 6 team. In 1993 Mark hit his stride and visited victory lane four times in a row, winning races at Watkins Glen, Michigan, Bristol, and then Darlington, tying Harry Gant's record.

Mark and his team always seemed to run well and were usually a factor in the points battle, but they have never been able to win the championship. Mark and company finished second in the point standings in 1990, 1994, 1998, and 2002. Mark is a steady racer and has been in the car for every race since February 18, 1988. His total of 33 career wins ranks him 17th on the all-time win list and 10th in Modern Era wins. He also has won a record 45 victories in the Busch Series. Mark is also one of the best ever in the International Race of Champions Series, with 11 victories and four IROC Championships, including three straight from 1996 to 1998.

Mark Martin is another of NASCAR's successful veteran drivers, racing on the circuit since 1981. His 33 wins rank him 10th on the total Modern Era win rankings.

Mark started his career in a self-owned car, spent two years driving for various owners, and in 1988 began driving for Roush Racing. He remains there to this day, making it one of the longest driver/owner relationships in the sport.

Year-by-year Performance

	Races	Poles		Wins		Top 5		Top 10	
1981	5	2	40.0%	0	0.0%	1	20.0%	2	40.0%
1982	30	0	0.0%	0	0.0%	2	6.7%	8	26.7%
1983	16	0	0.0%	0	0.0%	1	6.3%	3	18.8%
1986	5	0	0.0%	0	0.0%	0	0.0%	0	0.0%
1987	1	0	0.0%	0	0.0%	0	0.0%	0	0.0%
1988	29	1	3.4%	0	0.0%	3	10.3%	10	34.5%
1989	29	6	20.7%	1	3.4%	14	48.3%	18	62.1%
1990	29	3	10.3%	3	10.3%	16	55.2%	23	79.3%
1991	29	5	17.2%	1	3.4%	14	48.3%	17	58.6%
1992	29	1	3.4%	2	6.9%	10	34.5%	17	58.6%
1993	30	5	16.7%	5	16.7%	12	40.0%	19	63.3%
1994	31	1	3.2%	2	6.5%	15	48.4%	20	64.5%
1995	31	4	12.9%	4	12.9%	13	41.9%	22	71.0%
1996	31	4	12.9%	0	0.0%	14	45.2%	23	74.2%
1997	32	3	9.4%	4	12.5%	16	50.0%	24	75.0%
1998	33	3	9.1%	7	21.2%	22	66.7%	26	78.8%
1999	34	1	2.9%	2	5.9%	19	55.9%	26	76.5%
2000	34	0	0.0%	1	2.9%	13	38.2%	20	58.8%
2001	36	2	5.6%	0	0.0%	3	8.3%	15	41.7%
2002	36	0	0.0%	1	2.8%	12	33.3%	22	61.1%
2003	36	0	0.0%	0	0.0%	5	13.9%	10	27.8%
Total	566	41	7.2%	33	5.8%	205	36.2%	325	57.4%

Track Performance

Less than 1 Mile

	Starts	1st	2nd	3rd	4th	5th	6th	7th	8th	9th	10th	11–20	21–43
Bristol	34	2	5	4	2	2	2	1	2	0	0	5	9
Martinsville	36	2	0	5	0	3	1	3	1	2	1	10	8
Richmond	40	1	3	2	1	4	4	2	1	1	0	8	13
N. Wilkes	22	2	2	2	0	2	1	0	0	2	0	5	6
Nashville	5	0	0	0	0	0	0	0	0	0	0	3	2
Total	**137**	**7**	**10**	**13**	**3**	**11**	**8**	**6**	**4**	**5**	**1**	**31**	**38**
		5.1%	7.3%	9.5%	2.2%	8.0%	5.8%	4.4%	2.9%	3.6%	0.7%	22.6%	27.7%

1 Mile–1.49 Mile

	Starts	1st	2nd	3rd	4th	5th	6th	7th	8th	9th	10th	11–20	21–43
Dover	35	3	4	1	3	3	1	1	1	2	0	5	11
New Hamp.	18	0	3	2	1	1	1	0	1	2	0	4	3
N. Carolina	35	2	0	3	2	3	3	5	1	0	1	6	9
Phoenix	16	1	5	1	0	0	2	0	1	0	2	2	2
Darlington	36	1	5	3	5	1	3	2	1	1	0	4	10
Total	**140**	**7**	**17**	**10**	**11**	**8**	**10**	**8**	**5**	**5**	**3**	**21**	**35**
		5.0%	12.1%	7.1%	7.9%	5.7%	7.1%	5.7%	3.6%	3.6%	2.1%	15.0%	25.0%

1.5 mile

	Starts	1st	2nd	3rd	4th	5th	6th	7th	8th	9th	10th	11–20	21–43
Charlotte	38	3	2	4	4	1	1	1	0	2	0	4	16
Chicago	3	0	0	0	0	0	1	0	0	0	0	2	0
Homestead	5	0	0	1	1	0	0	0	0	0	0	0	3
Kansas	3	0	0	0	0	0	1	0	0	0	0	1	1
Las Vegas	6	1	0	1	0	0	1	0	0	0	1	0	2
Texas	7	1	0	0	0	2	0	0	0	1	0	1	2
Total	**62**	**5**	**2**	**6**	**5**	**3**	**4**	**1**	**0**	**3**	**1**	**8**	**24**
		8.1%	3.2%	9.7%	8.1%	4.8%	6.5%	1.6%	0.0%	4.8%	1.6%	12.9%	38.7%

Track Performance

1.51 Mile–2.5 Mile

	Starts	1st	2nd	3rd	4th	5th	6th	7th	8th	9th	10th	11–20	21–43
Atlanta	36	2	0	4	1	2	2	2	0	1	1	6	15
California	7	1	0	0	0	0	0	0	0	0	1	3	2
Michigan	36	4	2	3	3	0	2	2	2	4	1	7	6
Indianapolis	10	0	1	0	2	1	1	0	0	2	0	0	3
Pocono	34	0	5	3	3	6	2	3	0	1	1	4	6
Total	**123**	**7**	**8**	**10**	**9**	**9**	**7**	**7**	**2**	**8**	**4**	**20**	**32**
		5.7%	6.5%	8.1%	7.3%	7.3%	5.7%	5.7%	1.6%	6.5%	3.3%	16.3%	26.0%

Restrictor Plate

	Starts	1st	2nd	3rd	4th	5th	6th	7th	8th	9th	10th	11–20	21–43
Daytona	37	0	0	1	4	3	2	1	1	0	0	12	13
Talladega	36	2	0	7	1	0	2	3	1	2	2	6	10
Total	**73**	**2**	**0**	**8**	**5**	**3**	**4**	**4**	**2**	**2**	**2**	**18**	**23**
		2.7%	0.0%	11.0%	6.8%	4.1%	5.5%	5.5%	2.7%	2.7%	2.7%	24.7%	31.5%

Road Courses

	Starts	1st	2nd	3rd	4th	5th	6th	7th	8th	9th	10th	11–20	21–43
Sears Point	15	1	4	2	0	0	1	0	1	1	1	2	2
Watkins Glen	16	3	3	2	1	2	0	0	0	0	3	1	1
Total	**31**	**4**	**7**	**4**	**1**	**2**	**1**	**0**	**1**	**1**	**4**	**3**	**3**
		12.9%	22.6%	12.9%	3.2%	6.5%	3.2%	0.0%	3.2%	3.2%	12.9%	9.7%	9.7%

Jeremy Mayfield

Current Team: Evernham Motorsports
Residence: Mooresville, North Carolina
Hometown: Owensboro, Kentucky
Birthday: May 27, 1969
Height: 6 feet, 0 inches
Weight: 190

Races: 309
Running: 260 (84.1 percent)
Accidents: 22 (7.1 percent)
Mechanical Failures: 27 (8.7 percent)

2001–2003	Evernham Motorsports
2000	Roger Penske
	Penske-Kranefuss
1998–1999	Penske-Kranefuss
1997	Michael Kranefuss
1996	Michael Kranefuss
	Cale Yarborough
1995	Cale Yarborough
1994	Cale Yarborough
	T. W. Taylor
	Sadler Racing
1993	Sadler Racing

J eremy laid out his own track doing laps in his backyard long before he started school. Later he raced bikes before moving up to karts. Like other racers, as he grew he stair-stepped through different racing divisions. From karts he moved to street stocks. When he mastered street stocks, he moved up to the Sportsman division, and then on to late models. However, Jeremy did not have a silver spoon racing career. He often worked as a sign painter and at other odd jobs at race shops to help fund his driving effort.

At the age of 19, Jeremy moved to Nashville, where he went to work as a fabricator at Sadler Racing. The team later put Jeremy in a late-model car, and his success allowed him to compete on the ARCA Series in 1987. The next year Sadler and Mayfield raced their first Winston Cup race, finishing 29th at Charlotte. In 1994 Mayfield got the call to get in the driver's seat for racing legend and team owner Cale Yarborough. They ran 20 races in 1994, scoring only three top 20s, but Jeremy was gaining valuable seat time and learning how to compete in stock car racing's ultimate division. In 1995 the team ran the entire schedule, and its performance improved.

Every year the number of Jeremy's top 5s and top 10s grew. In 1996 he drove for both Cale Yarborough and Michael Kranefuss; in July of that year at Talladega, Jeremy managed his first career pole. He also broke into the top five twice with a 5th at Atlanta and a 4th at Martinsville. After being released from Cale Yarborough's team, Jeremy raced for Michael Kranefuss, who later joined forces with Roger Penske. It was good news for Mayfield, because it meant that he was gradually getting into better and better equipment. In 1998 he got his first win at Pocono, scored an additional 11 top-five finishes, and finished a career-high 7th in the points race.

In 2000 Jeremy won four poles and had his first multiple-win year, with victories at Pocono and California. In 2001 Jeremy had the honor of being selected by Ray Evernham to drive one of the "factory" Dodges in Dodge's return to racing. With Bill Elliot as his teammate, Jeremy was in one of the best cars on the circuit. In 2001 and 2002, the team had some good runs but was not able to win. By midseason in 2003, rumors of Jeremy's demise were circulating. In the last 10 races, however, the team came together and posted two 2nd-place finishes, two 3rds, two 6ths, and one 7th-place finish. The Evernham team finished with four top 5s and seven top 10s in the last 10 races (they also had an 11th-place finish and blew up twice). Jeremy kept his seat in Evernham's Dodge, and he headed into the 2004 season ready for success.

When Ray Evernham began his Dodge team in 2002, he selected Jeremy Mayfield as one of his two drivers. The team got off to an understandable slow start but by the end of the 2003 season was consistently finishing in the top 5 and top 10.

Jeremy's first big-time ride came when he was hired to drive for Cale Yarborough in the mid 1990s. His first win came in 1998 when he was driving the No. 12 Ford for Michael Kranefuss and Roger Penske.

Year-by-year Performance

	Races	Poles		Wins		Top 5		Top 10	
1993	1	0	0.0%	0	0.0%	0	0.0%	0	0.0%
1994	20	0	0.0%	0	0.0%	0	0.0%	0	0.0%
1995	27	0	0.0%	0	0.0%	0	0.0%	1	3.7%
1996	30	1	3.3%	0	0.0%	2	6.7%	2	6.7%
1997	32	0	0.0%	0	0.0%	3	9.4%	8	25.0%
1998	33	1	3.0%	1	3.0%	12	36.4%	16	48.5%
1999	34	0	0.0%	0	0.0%	5	14.7%	12	35.3%
2000	32	4	12.5%	2	6.3%	6	18.8%	12	37.5%
2001	28	0	0.0%	0	0.0%	5	17.9%	7	25.0%
2002	36	0	0.0%	0	0.0%	2	5.6%	4	11.1%
2003	36	1	2.8%	0	0.0%	4	11.1%	12	33.3%
Total	**309**	**7**	**2.3%**	**3**	**1.0%**	**39**	**12.6%**	**74**	**23.9%**

Track Performance

Less than 1 Mile

Bristol	18	0	0	1	1	0	0	0	1	1	1	4	9
Martinsville	17	0	0	0	1	0	0	3	0	0	0	5	8
Richmond	20	0	1	0	0	1	1	0	0	0	2	2	13
N. Wilkes	4	0	0	0	0	0	0	0	0	0	0	1	3
Total	**59**	**0**	**1**	**1**	**2**	**1**	**1**	**3**	**1**	**1**	**3**	**12**	**33**
		0.0%	1.7%	1.7%	3.4%	1.7%	1.7%	5.1%	1.7%	1.7%	5.1%	20.3%	55.9%

1 Mile–1.49 Mile

Dover	19	0	1	1	1	1	0	0	0	1	0	5	9
New Hamp.	16	0	0	0	0	0	0	0	1	0	0	4	11
N. Carolina	18	0	0	1	0	1	0	1	0	1	0	7	7
Phoenix	9	0	1	0	0	0	0	0	0	0	0	3	5
Darlington	19	0	1	2	1	1	1	0	0	0	0	6	7
Total	**81**	**0**	**3**	**4**	**2**	**3**	**1**	**1**	**1**	**2**	**0**	**25**	**39**
		0.0%	3.7%	4.9%	2.5%	3.7%	1.2%	1.2%	1.2%	2.5%	0.0%	30.9%	48.1%

1.5 mile

Charlotte	20	0	1	0	0	0	2	0	0	0	2	3	12
Chicago	3	0	0	0	0	0	0	0	0	0	1	0	2
Homestead	4	0	1	0	0	0	1	0	0	0	0	1	1
Kansas	3	0	0	1	0	0	0	0	0	1	0	0	1
Las Vegas	6	0	1	0	0	1	0	0	0	0	0	2	2
Texas	7	0	0	0	0	1	1	0	0	0	0	1	4
Total	**43**	**0**	**3**	**1**	**0**	**2**	**4**	**0**	**0**	**1**	**3**	**7**	**22**
		0.0%	7.0%	2.3%	0.0%	4.7%	9.3%	0.0%	0.0%	2.3%	7.0%	16.3%	51.2%

Track Performance

1.51 Mile–2.5 Mile

Atlanta	16	0	0	2	0	1	0	1	0	0	0	3	9
California	7	1	1	0	0	1	0	1	0	0	0	1	2
Michigan	20	0	0	0	1	1	0	1	0	0	0	9	8
Indianapolis	9	0	0	0	0	1	0	0	0	0	0	1	7
Pocono	19	2	0	0	0	1	0	0	1	2	1	5	7
Total	**71**	**3**	**1**	**2**	**1**	**5**	**0**	**3**	**1**	**2**	**1**	**19**	**33**
		4.2%	1.4%	2.8%	1.4%	7.0%	0.0%	4.2%	1.4%	2.8%	1.4%	26.8%	46.5%

Restrictor Plate

Daytona	20	0	0	1	1	0	1	0	2	1	0	6	8
Talladega	19	0	0	0	0	1	0	0	0	0	0	9	9
Total	**39**	**0**	**0**	**1**	**1**	**1**	**1**	**0**	**2**	**1**	**0**	**15**	**17**
		0.0%	0.0%	2.6%	2.6%	2.6%	2.6%	0.0%	5.1%	2.6%	0.0%	38.5%	43.6%

Road Courses

Sears Point	8	0	0	0	0	0	0	1	0	0	1	1	5
Watkins Glen	8	0	0	1	0	0	0	0	0	0	0	3	4
Total	**16**	**0**	**0**	**1**	**0**	**0**	**0**	**1**	**0**	**0**	**1**	**4**	**9**
		0.0%	0.0%	6.3%	0.0%	0.0%	0.0%	6.3%	0.0%	0.0%	6.3%	25.0%	56.3%

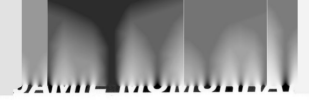

Jamie McMurray

Current Team: Chip Ganassi Racing
Residence: Statesville, North Carolina
Hometown: Joplin, Missouri
Birthday: June 3, 1976
Height: 5 feet, 8 inches
Weight: 150

Races: 42
Running: 36 (85.7 percent)
Accidents: 4 (9.5 percent)
Mechanical Failures: 2 (4.8 percent)

2002–2003   Chip Ganassi Racing

J amie McMurray had a grand beginning in his Winston Cup racing career. Late in 2002, a neck injury forced Sterling Marlin out of his race car. Jamie got the call to sub for Marlin for the final six races of the year. His first race was at Talladega, where he qualified a respectable 5th and finished 27th. The next week he again qualified 5th, but this time he did not have to rely on drafting help, and he took the checkered flag. In only his second start, he had beaten the best stock car racers in the world in their own back-yard. The feat made him the quickest winner in the history of NASCAR, and unless someone wins in their first outing it is a record he will keep.

Jamie first competed in karts, which he began racing at the age of eight. He won his first kart title at the age of 10 in 1986. By the early 1990s, when he had four U.S. kart titles and one world championship, he began his stock car career, driving late models. By the end of the decade, he was racing on the NASCAR RE/MAX Series, and he also ran in five Craftsman Truck Series races. Jamie raced in 15 NASCAR Craftsman Truck Series races in 2000, finishing with one top-5 and three top-10 finishes. In 2000 he also started a couple of Busch Series races, and in 2001 Brewco Motorsports chose him to run the entire Busch Series season. He competed in all 33 races in 2001, finishing the year with three top 10s and a 3rd-place finish in the Rookie of the Year battle.

By 2002 Jamie had gained the experience it takes to be competitive—and competitive he was. He won twice (at Atlanta and Rockingham), had six top-5 finishes and 14 top 10s. After his impressive entrance into the Winston Cup, he was rewarded with a full-time ride with Chip Ganassi Racing with long-time sponsor Texaco-Havoline on the car. In his rookie year, he made the most of the opportunity, with 13 top 10s and a 13th-place finish in the points battle. He also added another Rookie of the Year trophy to his shelf. While having this excellent rookie season in the Winston Cup, he also ran in 19 Busch races, winning two and finishing with nine top 10s.

Jamie McMurray carries some old colors on a new car. His Ganassi Racing Dodge began carrying the legendary Texaco Havoline colors in 2003 when Jamie began his full-time Winston Cup/Nextel Cup career.

Jamie got an early start when he replaced an injured Sterling Marlin for the last six races of 2002. He made the most of the opportunity, winning at Charlotte in only his second Winston Cup start and seemed to take no time learning to make his way through the crowds on the track.

Year-by-year Performance

	Races	Poles		Wins		Top 5		Top 10	
2002	6	0	0.0%	1	16.7%	1	16.7%	2	33.3%
2003	36	1	2.8%	0	0.0%	5	13.9%	13	36.1%
Total	**42**	**1**	**2.4%**	**1**	**2.4%**	**6**	**14.3%**	**15**	**35.7%**

rack Performance

ess than 1 Mile

	Starts	1st	2nd	3rd	4th	5th	6th	7th	8th	9th	10th	11–20	21–43
ristol	2	0	0	1	0	0	0	0	0	0	0	1	0
artinsville	2	0	0	0	0	0	0	0	1	0	0	0	1
ichmond	2	0	0	0	0	0	0	0	0	0	0	1	1
otal	**6**	**0**	**0**	**1**	**0**	**0**	**0**	**0**	**1**	**0**	**0**	**2**	**2**
		0.0%	0.0%	16.7%	0.0%	0.0%	0.0%	0.0%	16.7%	0.0%	0.0%	33.3%	33.3%

Mile–1.49 Mile

	Starts	1st	2nd	3rd	4th	5th	6th	7th	8th	9th	10th	11–20	21–43
over	2	0	0	0	0	0	1	0	0	0	0	1	0
ew Hamp.	2	0	0	0	0	0	0	0	0	0	1	0	1
. Carolina	3	0	0	0	0	1	0	0	0	0	0	1	1
hoenix	2	0	0	0	0	0	0	0	0	0	0	1	1
arlington	2	0	0	0	1	0	0	0	0	0	0	0	1
otal	**11**	**0**	**0**	**0**	**1**	**1**	**1**	**0**	**0**	**0**	**1**	**3**	**4**
		0.0%	0.0%	0.0%	9.1%	9.1%	9.1%	0.0%	0.0%	0.0%	9.1%	27.3%	36.4%

5 mile

	Starts	1st	2nd	3rd	4th	5th	6th	7th	8th	9th	10th	11–20	21–43
harlotte	3	1	0	0	0	0	0	1	0	0	0	0	1
hicago	1	0	0	0	0	0	0	0	1	0	0	0	0
omestead	2	0	0	0	0	0	0	0	0	1	0	0	1
ansas	1	0	0	0	0	0	0	0	1	0	0	0	0
s Vegas	1	0	0	0	0	0	0	0	0	0	0	0	1
xas	1	0	0	0	0	0	0	0	0	0	1	0	0
otal	**9**	**1**	**0**	**0**	**0**	**0**	**0**	**1**	**2**	**1**	**1**	**0**	**3**
		11.1%	0.0%	0.0%	0.0%	0.0%	0.0%	11.1%	22.2%	11.1%	11.1%	0.0%	33.3%

Track Performance

1.51 Mile–2.5 Mile

	Starts	1st	2nd	3rd	4th	5th	6th	7th	8th	9th	10th	11–20	21–43
Atlanta	3	0	0	0	0	0	0	1	0	0	0	1	1
California	1	0	0	0	0	1	0	0	0	0	0	0	0
Michigan	2	0	0	0	0	0	0	0	0	0	0	1	1
Indianapolis	1	0	0	1	0	0	0	0	0	0	0	0	0
Pocono	2	0	0	0	0	0	0	0	0	0	0	0	2
Total	**9**	**0**	**0**	**1**	**0**	**1**	**0**	**1**	**0**	**0**	**0**	**2**	**4**
		0.0%	0.0%	11.1%	0.0%	11.1%	0.0%	11.1%	0.0%	0.0%	0.0%	22.2%	44.4%

Restrictor Plate

	Starts	1st	2nd	3rd	4th	5th	6th	7th	8th	9th	10th	11–20	21–43
Daytona	2	0	0	0	0	0	0	0	0	0	0	0	2
Talladega	3	0	0	0	0	0	0	0	0	0	0	1	2
Total	**5**	**0**	**0**	**0**	**0**	**0**	**0**	**0**	**0**	**0**	**0**	**1**	**4**
		0.0%	0.0%	0.0%	0.0%	0.0%	0.0%	0.0%	0.0%	0.0%	0.0%	20.0%	80.0%

Road Courses

	Starts	1st	2nd	3rd	4th	5th	6th	7th	8th	9th	10th	11–20	21–43
Sears Point	1	0	0	0	0	0	0	0	0	0	0	1	0
Watkins Glen	1	0	0	0	0	0	0	0	0	0	0	0	1
Total	**2**	**0**	**0**	**0**	**0**	**0**	**0**	**0**	**0**	**0**	**0**	**1**	**1**
		0.0%	0.0%	0.0%	0.0%	0.0%	0.0%	0.0%	0.0%	0.0%	0.0%	50.0%	50.0%

Current Team: Chip Ganassi Racing
Residence: Mooresville, North Carolina
Hometown: Bakersfield, California
Birthday: March 12, 1978
Height: 5 feet, 8 inches
Weight: 160

Races: 36
Running: 26 (72.2 percent)
Accidents: 6 (16.7 percent)
Mechanical Failures: 4 (11.1 percent)

2003   Chip Ganassi Racing

Casey Mears

Casey Mears follows his father and uncle into racing, but has elected to run a different course. At the age of four, Casey was competing on BMX bicycles and by the time he was six years old he was racing ATVs. His father, Roger Mears, who competed in both Indy cars and off-road racing, supported him. Casey's uncle, Rick Mears, was also an inspiration, being a four-time winner of the Indianapolis 500. It is little wonder that as Casey's driving skills developed, he gravitated toward open-wheel cars.

In his teens, he raced karts and then super lites and, following in his father's footsteps, he also raced in some off-road events. Casey then moved to USAC, where in 1994 he won a feature race at the age of 16. In 1995 he won the Jim Russell USAC Triple Crown Championship, and in 1996 he again changed programs, graduating to the Indy Lights Series. Over the next couple of years he gained experience, and in 1999 he finished second in the Indy Lights points race, losing the championship by only 14 points. He took care of his car that year, completing every lap of every race of the entire season.

In 2000 Casey did some driving in the CART Series as well as the Indy Lights, and he finished a very respectable 4th in the CART race at California. It was in 2001 that Casey began leaning toward cars with fenders, although he still ran a handful of CART races, finishing in the top 10 twice. But he also ran a race in a Busch Series race (finishing 21st) and an ARCA race (finishing 9th). The experience was enough to make Casey decide to race stock cars full-time. In November 2001 Mears decided to race in the Busch Series full-time in the 2002 season, driving a Dodge fielded by Welliver-Jesel Motorsports.

In the first year of his new career, Mears had some rough days but also had a few good runs. In his first full season running stock cars, Casey had one top 5 and two top 10s and finished 21st in driver points. In 2003 Casey drove one of Chip Ganassi's Winston Cup Dodges. It was a year of learning, with Casey posting only five top-20 finishes but gaining valuable experience.

Casey Mears' first year was in 2003, behind the wheel of one of Chip Ganassi's Dodges. While the team did not score a top-10 finish, Casey gained valuable seat time which should pay off in the near future.

Casey drove open-wheel cars before making the move to the heavier, full-bodied stock-cars. Here he negotiates the superspeedway crowd in his rookie year.

Year-by-year Performance

	Races	Poles		Wins		Top 5		Top 10	
2003	36	0	0.0%	0	0.0%	0	0.0%	0	0.0%
Total	**36**	**0**	**0.0%**	**0**	**0.0%**	**0**	**0.0%**	**0**	**0.0%**

Track Performance

Less than 1 Mile

	Starts	1st	2nd	3rd	4th	5th	6th	7th	8th	9th	10th	11–20	21–43
Bristol	2	0	0	0	0	0	0	0	0	0	0	0	2
Martinsville	2	0	0	0	0	0	0	0	0	0	0	1	1
Richmond	2	0	0	0	0	0	0	0	0	0	0	0	2
Total	**6**	**0**	**0**	**0**	**0**	**0**	**0**	**0**	**0**	**0**	**0**	**1**	**5**
		0.0%	0.0%	0.0%	0.0%	0.0%	0.0%	0.0%	0.0%	0.0%	0.0%	16.7%	83.3%

1 Mile–1.49 Mile

	Starts	1st	2nd	3rd	4th	5th	6th	7th	8th	9th	10th	11–20	21–43
Dover	2	0	0	0	0	0	0	0	0	0	0	0	2
New Hamp.	2	0	0	0	0	0	0	0	0	0	0	2	0
N. Carolina	2	0	0	0	0	0	0	0	0	0	0	0	2
Phoenix	1	0	0	0	0	0	0	0	0	0	0	0	1
Darlington	2	0	0	0	0	0	0	0	0	0	0	0	2
Total	**9**	**0**	**0**	**0**	**0**	**0**	**0**	**0**	**0**	**0**	**0**	**2**	**7**
		0.0%	0.0%	0.0%	0.0%	0.0%	0.0%	0.0%	0.0%	0.0%	0.0%	22.2%	77.8%

1.5 mile

	Starts	1st	2nd	3rd	4th	5th	6th	7th	8th	9th	10th	11–20	21–43
Charlotte	2	0	0	0	0	0	0	0	0	0	0	0	2
Chicago	1	0	0	0	0	0	0	0	0	0	0	0	
Homestead	1	0	0	0	0	0	0	0	0	0	0	0	1
Kansas	1	0	0	0	0	0	0	0	0	0	0	0	
Las Vegas	1	0	0	0	0	0	0	0	0	0	0	1	
Texas	1	0	0	0	0	0	0	0	0	0	0	0	
Total	**7**	**0**	**0**	**0**	**0**	**0**	**0**	**0**	**0**	**0**	**0**	**1**	
		0.0%	0.0%	0.0%	0.0%	0.0%	0.0%	0.0%	0.0%	0.0%	0.0%	14.3%	85.7%

Track Performance

1.51 Mile–2.5 Mile

Atlanta	2	0	0	0	0	0	0	0	0	0	0	0	2
California	1	0	0	0	0	0	0	0	0	0	0	0	1
Michigan	2	0	0	0	0	0	0	0	0	0	0	1	1
Indianapolis	1	0	0	0	0	0	0	0	0	0	0	0	1
Pocono	2	0	0	0	0	0	0	0	0	0	0	0	2
Total	**8**	**0**	**0**	**0**	**0**	**0**	**0**	**0**	**0**	**0**	**0**	**1**	**7**
		0.0%	0.0%	0.0%	0.0%	0.0%	0.0%	0.0%	0.0%	0.0%	0.0%	12.5%	87.5%

Restrictor Plate

Daytona	2	0	0	0	0	0	0	0	0	0	0	0	2
Talladega	2	0	0	0	0	0	0	0	0	0	0	0	2
Total	**4**	**0**	**0**	**0**	**0**	**0**	**0**	**0**	**0**	**0**	**0**	**0**	**4**
		0.0%	0.0%	0.0%	0.0%	0.0%	0.0%	0.0%	0.0%	0.0%	0.0%	0.0%	100.0%

Road Courses

Sears Point	1	0	0	0	0	0	0	0	0	0	0	0	1
Watkins Glen	1	0	0	0	0	0	0	0	0	0	0	0	1
Total	**2**	**0**	**0**	**0**	**0**	**0**	**0**	**0**	**0**	**0**	**0**	**0**	**2**
		0.0%	0.0%	0.0%	0.0%	0.0%	0.0%	0.0%	0.0%	0.0%	0.0%	0.0%	100.0%

Jerry Nadeau

Current Team: MB2 Motorsports
Residence: Mooresville, North Carolina
Hometown: Danbury, Connecticut
Birthday: September 9, 1970
Height: 5 feet, 6 inches
Weight: 150

Races: 177
Running: 134 (75.7 percent)
Accidents: 25 (14.1 percent)
Mechanical Failures: 18 (10.2 percent)

2003	MB2 Motorsports
2002	Petty Enterprises
	Michael Waltrip Racing
	MBV Motorsports
	Hendrick Motorsports
2000–2001	Hendrick Motorsports
1999	MB2 Motorsports
	Melling Racing
1998	Melling Racing
	Elliott/Marino Motorsports
1997	Richard Jackson

Jerry Nadeau, like many other racers, began his drive to NASCAR's highest level in karts. He began driving them at the age of four, and from 1988 to 1990 won three consecutive World Karting Association Gold Cup Championships. In 1991 he won a WKA Grand National Championship, and he even drove a kart race in Russia—on ice—finishing in 2nd place. In all, from 1984 to 1990 Jerry racked up 11 WKA Championships and International Karting Federation Championships.

In 1991 he drove in the Skip Barber Eastern Series, driving open-wheel cars, winning eight times during the season and taking the Rookie of the Year award. He then ran in the Skip Barber Pro Series from 1993 to 1995, winning five races. In 1995 he began his Busch Series career, running in five events. In 1996 he drove in two more Busch Series races, and went overseas to drive in 13 races in the Formula Opel European Series. He made it back to America, and the next year Jerry made his first Winston Cup race, qualifying 32nd at Michigan and finishing 36th. He drove in a total of five races that year with his best being a 30th-place finish at

Daytona. He also drove in a couple of ARCA races, finishing in the top five in both of them; when he wasn't driving for Richard Jackson, he was working as a spotter.

In 1998 ex-Miami quarterback Dan Marino decided to form a racing team in conjunction with Bill Elliot. They hired Jerry Nadeau to drive for the new and inexperienced team. The team never cracked the top 10, but Jerry was gaining that all-important seat time. In 1999 he drove for two teams and scored a 5th-place finish at the Watkins Glen road course while driving for Melling Racing. In 2000 Jerry moved to Hendrick Motorsports, and while his first year netted only five top 10s, one of them was a win. At Atlanta, in the last race of the year, Jerry drove away from the competition in his Chevrolet, taking the checkered flag in his 103rd start.

The next year Jerry drove to a 17th-place finish in the points, his best ever, but after 11 races into the 2002 season, Jerry and Hendrick parted ways. For the remainder of the 2002 season, Jerry drove for three other teams, making it difficult to gain any degree of chemistry. His best finish that year came at Bristol, where he finished 8th. He also missed five races after breaking some ribs when he crashed his kart at a friend's house. In 2003 Jerry gained a full-time ride with MB2 Motorsports, with the U.S. Army as a steady sponsor. After 10 races, Jerry was again injured and forced out of the car for the remainder of the 2003 season and the beginning of the 2004 campaign.

Jerry's first and only win came in 2000 behind the wheel of a Rick Hendrick Chevrolet sponsored by Michael Holigan.com.

Jerry Nadeau began driving for Nelson Bowers beginning in the 2003 season but was injured after just 10 races. His career started behind the wheel of the No. 13 Ford owned by Bill Elliot and Dan Marino.

Year-by-year Performance

	Races	Poles		Wins		Top 5		Top 10	
1997	5	0	0.0%	0	0.0%	0	0.0%	0	0.0%
1998	30	0	0.0%	0	0.0%	0	0.0%	0	0.0%
1999	34	0	0.0%	0	0.0%	1	2.9%	2	5.9%
2000	34	0	0.0%	1	2.9%	3	8.8%	5	14.7%
2001	36	0	0.0%	0	0.0%	4	11.1%	10	27.8%
2002	28	0	0.0%	0	0.0%	0	0.0%	1	3.6%
2003	10	0	0.0%	0	0.0%	1	10.0%	1	10.0%
Total	**177**	**0**	**0.0%**	**1**	**0.6%**	**9**	**5.1%**	**19**	**10.7%**

rack Performance

ss than 1 Mile

	Starts	1st	2nd	3rd	4th	5th	6th	7th	8th	9th	10th	11–20	21–43
istol	11	0	0	0	0	0	0	0	1	0	0	3	7
artinsville	10	0	0	0	0	0	0	0	0	0	1	2	7
chmond	10	0	0	0	0	0	0	0	0	0	1	2	7
tal	31	0	0	0	0	0	0	0	1	0	2	7	21
		0.0%	0.0%	0.0%	0.0%	0.0%	0.0%	0.0%	3.2%	0.0%	6.5%	22.6%	67.7%

Mile–1.49 Mile

	Starts	1st	2nd	3rd	4th	5th	6th	7th	8th	9th	10th	11–20	21–43
ver	9	0	1	0	0	0	0	0	0	0	0	1	7
w Hamp.	11	0	0	0	1	0	1	0	0	0	0	1	8
Carolina	10	0	0	0	0	1	0	0	0	0	0	1	8
oenix	4	0	0	0	0	0	0	0	0	0	0	0	4
rlington	11	0	0	0	0	0	0	0	0	1	0	2	8
tal	45	0	1	0	1	1	1	0	0	1	0	5	35
		0.0%	2.2%	0.0%	2.2%	2.2%	2.2%	0.0%	0.0%	2.2%	0.0%	11.1%	77.8%

5 mile

	Starts	1st	2nd	3rd	4th	5th	6th	7th	8th	9th	10th	11–20	21–43
arlotte	10	0	0	0	0	0	0	0	0	0	0	3	7
icago	2	0	0	0	0	0	0	0	0	0	0	0	2
mestead	3	0	0	0	0	0	0	0	0	0	0	1	2
nsas	2	0	0	0	0	0	0	0	0	0	0	1	1
s Vegas	5	0	0	0	0	0	0	0	0	0	0	3	2
xas	5	0	0	0	1	0	0	0	0	0	0	0	4
tal	27	0	0	0	1	0	0	0	0	0	0	8	18
		0.0%	0.0%	0.0%	3.7%	0.0%	0.0%	0.0%	0.0%	0.0%	0.0%	29.6%	66.7%

Track Performance

1.51 Mile–2.5 Mile

	Starts	1st	2nd	3rd	4th	5th	6th	7th	8th	9th	10th	11–20	21–43
Atlanta	10	1	0	1	1	0	0	0	0	0	0	1	6
California	7	0	0	0	0	0	0	0	1	0	0	3	3
Michigan	10	0	0	0	0	0	0	0	0	0	0	1	9
Indianapolis	5	0	0	0	1	0	0	0	0	0	0	0	4
Pocono	10	0	0	0	0	0	0	0	0	0	0	2	8
Total	**42**	**1**	**0**	**1**	**2**	**0**	**0**	**0**	**1**	**0**	**0**	**7**	**30**
		2.4%	0.0%	2.4%	4.8%	0.0%	0.0%	0.0%	2.4%	0.0%	0.0%	16.7%	71.4%

Restrictor Plate

	Starts	1st	2nd	3rd	4th	5th	6th	7th	8th	9th	10th	11–20	21–43
Daytona	11	0	0	0	0	0	1	0	0	0	0	3	7
Talladega	11	0	0	0	0	0	0	0	1	0	0	2	8
Total	**22**	**0**	**0**	**0**	**0**	**0**	**1**	**0**	**1**	**0**	**0**	**5**	**15**
		0.0%	0.0%	0.0%	0.0%	0.0%	4.5%	0.0%	4.5%	0.0%	0.0%	22.7%	68.2%

Road Courses

	Starts	1st	2nd	3rd	4th	5th	6th	7th	8th	9th	10th	11–20	21–43
Sears Point	5	0	0	0	0	0	0	0	1	0	0	0	4
Watkins Glen	5	0	0	0	0	1	1	0	0	0	0	1	2
Total	**10**	**0**	**0**	**0**	**0**	**1**	**1**	**0**	**1**	**0**	**0**	**1**	**6**
		0.0%	0.0%	0.0%	0.0%	10.0%	10.0%	0.0%	10.0%	0.0%	0.0%	10.0%	60.0%

Joe Nemechek

Current Team: MB2 Motorsports
Residence: Mooresville, North Carolina
Hometown: Lakeland, Florida
Birthday: September 26, 1963
Height: 5 feet, 9 inches
Weight: 180

Races: 322
Running: 255 (79.2 percent)
Accidents: 33 (10.2 percent)
Mechanical Failures: 34 (10.6 percent)

2003	MB2 Motorsports
	Hendrick Motorsports
2002	Hendrick Motorsports
	Carl Haas
2000–2001	Andy Petree
1997–1999	SABCO
1995–1996	Joe Nemechek
1994	Larry Hedrick
1993	Morgan-McClure
	Joe Nemechek

oe Nemechek is another racer who started out on two wheels instead of four. In his youth, the motocross racer turned stock car racer was very successful, and in six years was able to take home hundreds of trophies. Joe began racing in 1986, and he did not stop until he was at the sport's highest level. Every time he entered a new racing series, he tended to win the Rookie of the Year award. In 1987 it was at the Lakeland Interstate Speedway. In 1988 it was the United Stock Car Alliance Series (he also won the championship). In 1989 he was named Rookie of the Year in the All-Pro Late Model Stock Car Challenge Series (once again, he also won the championship).

In 1990 Joe again headed to the next level, but this time the stakes were higher. With a natural engineering talent that was honed at the Florida Institute of Technology where he studied, Joe decided to go racing on the Busch Series and formed a family team to do so. In 1990 NEMCO Motorsports was formed in Mooresville, North Carolina. He ran the entire Busch season in 1990 and once again ended up as the series' Rookie of the Year. In 1991 he stayed in the Busch Series and drove to 13 top-10 finishes in 31 starts. In 1992 Joe drove the family car to the series' ultimate prize—the NASCAR Busch Series Championship.

Joe began his Winston Cup career in 1993, driving in five races but never finishing in the top 20. Joe joined the Winston Cup circuit full-time in 1994, driving a Larry Hedrick Chevrolet. At times he had difficulty competing with the top-line teams. Joe left Hedrick after one year and spent the next two years running a car from the family team, before joining Felix Sebates in 1997. The team had limited success, but in 1999 Joe finally made it to victory lane at New Hampshire. Joe left SABCO, and his next ride was an Andy Petree Chevrolet. Nemechek's second 2001 win came when he dominated the Pop Secret 400 at North Carolina Motor Speedway, leading 196 of 393 laps—including the all-important last one.

In 2002 Nemechek joined the Haas Carter team, but sponsor problems caused the team to fold in midseason. Joe then moved into the No. 25 Hendrick Motorsports Chevrolet. Joe won his third race in the Hendrick car, but again had a midseason move. Before 2003 was over, Joe was in a Pontiac fielded by MB2 Motorsports with U.S. Army sponsorship, where he would stay for the 2004 season.

Joe Nemechek left Hendrick Motorsports during the 2003 season despite a win earlier in the year at Richmond. By the end of the year he was driving the Nelson Bowers Pontiac filling in for an injured Jerry Nadeau.

Joe began his career in a self-owned car and in 1995 and 1996 drove the car with Burger King sponsorship.

Year-by-year Performance

	Races	Poles		Wins		Top 5		Top 10	
1993	5	0	0.0%	0	0.0%	0	0.0%	0	0.0%
1994	29	0	0.0%	0	0.0%	1	3.4%	3	10.3%
1995	29	0	0.0%	0	0.0%	1	3.4%	4	13.8%
1996	29	0	0.0%	0	0.0%	0	0.0%	2	6.9%
1997	30	2	6.7%	0	0.0%	0	0.0%	3	10.0%
1998	32	0	0.0%	0	0.0%	1	3.1%	4	12.5%
1999	34	3	8.8%	1	2.9%	1	2.9%	3	8.8%
2000	34	1	2.9%	0	0.0%	3	8.8%	9	26.5%
2001	31	0	0.0%	1	3.2%	1	3.2%	4	12.9%
2002	33	0	0.0%	0	0.0%	3	9.1%	3	9.1%
2003	36	0	0.0%	1	2.8%	2	5.6%	6	16.7%
Total	**322**	**6**	**1.9%**	**3**	**0.9%**	**13**	**4.0%**	**41**	**12.7%**

Track Performance

Less than 1 Mile

Track													
Bristol	18	0	0	0	0	0	0	0	0	0	0	5	13
Martinsville	19	0	0	0	0	0	0	0	0	0	0	7	12
Richmond	20	1	0	0	0	0	2	0	0	0	0	5	12
N. Wilkes	5	0	0	0	0	0	0	0	0	0	0	1	4
Total	**62**	**1**	**0**	**0**	**0**	**0**	**2**	**0**	**0**	**0**	**0**	**18**	**41**
		1.6%	0.0%	0.0%	0.0%	0.0%	3.2%	0.0%	0.0%	0.0%	0.0%	29.0%	66.1%

1 Mile–1.49 Mile

Track													
Dover	19	0	0	0	1	0	0	3	0	0	1	3	11
New Hamp.	18	1	1	1	0	0	0	0	0	1	0	5	9
N. Carolina	20	1	0	0	0	0	0	0	0	2	2	2	13
Phoenix	10	0	0	0	0	0	0	0	0	0	0	3	7
Darlington	18	0	0	0	0	0	1	0	0	0	0	4	13
Total	**85**	**2**	**1**	**1**	**1**	**0**	**1**	**3**	**0**	**3**	**3**	**17**	**53**
		2.4%	1.2%	1.2%	1.2%	0.0%	1.2%	3.5%	0.0%	3.5%	3.5%	20.0%	62.4%

1.5 mile

Track													
Charlotte	19	0	0	0	0	0	1	1	0	0	0	8	9
Chicago	3	0	0	0	0	0	0	0	0	0	0	1	2
Homestead	5	0	1	0	0	0	0	0	0	0	0	2	2
Kansas	3	0	0	0	1	0	0	0	0	0	0	1	1
Las Vegas	6	0	0	0	0	0	0	0	0	2	0	1	3
Texas	6	0	0	0	1	0	0	0	0	0	0	0	5
Total	**42**	**0**	**1**	**0**	**2**	**0**	**1**	**1**	**0**	**2**	**0**	**13**	**2**
		0.0%	2.4%	0.0%	4.8%	0.0%	2.4%	2.4%	0.0%	4.8%	0.0%	31.0%	52.4%

.51 Mile–2.5 Mile

lanta	20	0	1	0	0	1	0	0	1	1	1	6	9
alifornia	7	0	0	0	0	0	0	0	0	0	0	3	4
ichigan	20	0	0	0	0	0	0	1	0	1	0	3	15
dianapolis	10	0	0	0	0	0	0	0	0	0	0	4	6
ocono	19	0	0	1	0	0	0	1	0	1	0	2	14
tal	**76**	**0**	**1**	**1**	**0**	**1**	**0**	**2**	**1**	**3**	**1**	**18**	**48**
		0.0%	1.3%	1.3%	0.0%	1.3%	0.0%	2.6%	1.3%	3.9%	1.3%	23.7%	63.2%

estrictor Plate

aytona	19	0	0	0	0	0	0	0	0	0	0	5	14
lladega	18	0	0	1	0	0	1	0	1	0	0	3	12
tal	**37**	**0**	**0**	**1**	**0**	**0**	**1**	**0**	**1**	**0**	**0**	**8**	**26**
		0.0%	0.0%	2.7%	0.0%	0.0%	2.7%	0.0%	2.7%	0.0%	0.0%	21.6%	70.3%

oad Courses

ears Point	8	0	0	0	0	0	0	0	0	0	0	3	5
atkins Glen	11	0	0	0	0	0	0	0	3	0	0	3	5
tal	**19**	**0**	**0**	**0**	**0**	**0**	**0**	**0**	**3**	**0**	**0**	**6**	**10**
		0.0%	0.0%	0.0%	0.0%	0.0%	0.0%	0.0%	15.8%	0.0%	0.0%	31.6%	52.6%

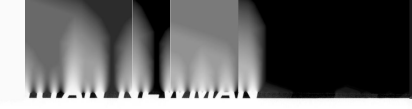

Ryan Newman

Current Team: Penske Racing
Residence: Charlotte, North Carolina
Hometown: South Bend, Indiana
Birthday: December 8, 1977
Height: 5 feet, 10 inches
Weight: 200

Races: 80
Running: 65 (81.3 percent)
Accidents: 8 (10.0 percent)
Mechanical Failures: 7 (8.8 percent)

2000–2003   Penske Racing

Ryan Newman grew up racing. He started his career in quarter midgets, moved up to midgets, and graduated to sprint cars. From the beginning, Ryan was a winner, chalking up more than 100 quarter midget wins. He made a habit of moving into a series and becoming Rookie of the Year. He took that honor in the All American Midget Series in 1993, winning the championship as well; the USAC National Midget Series in 1995; and the USAC Silver Crown in 1996. He was also the 1999 Sprint Car Rookie of the Year.

When Ryan was not racing, he was studying. It paid off with his graduation from Purdue University with a degree in structural engineering for vehicles. By 2000 Ryan's talent had been noticed by many, but most importantly, by Roger Penske. In 2000 he ran a very limited schedule in the ARCA Series to get seat time on longer tracks. While his number of starts was small, his winning percentage was not. In just five starts, he won two races and three pole positions. He also ran a Winston Cup race late in the year at Phoenix. He qualified a very respectable 10th in his first attempt, but finished the race in 41st position after having engine problems.

The year 2001 was another one dedicated to gaining experience. Instead of running in one racing series full-time, Ryan ran a partial schedule in three separate series. In all, he ran in 26 races, split between ARCA, the Busch Series, and the Winston Cup Series. In 15 Busch races he had one win and six poles. In seven Winston Cup races he captured one pole and had two top fives, his best finish was a 2nd at Kansas. In 2002 Newman drove a Penske Racing Ford for the entire Winston Cup schedule for the first time. In 36 races he had 22 top 10s and 14 top 5s. Ryan claimed his first win after a hard days racing at New Hampshire. He also walked away with a win in the Winston All Star race, and took Rookie of the Year honors. Ryan's first full year of Winston Cup racing had been a smashing success.

Heading into 2003, if there was anything to be nervous about it was a change of equipment, as the Penske organizations switched from Fords to Dodges. There was no need to worry. In one year, Ryan was able to accomplish what few dream of. Although wrecks and mechanical failures kept him out of championship contention, he and his team won eight races and 11 poles. (Ryan is quickly proving to be a qualifying master.) To put this in perspective, only 52 drivers in the history of the sport have eight or more career wins—Ryan Newman's total for his sophomore season.

With less than a hundred starts under his belt, Ryan Newman finds himself one of the sport's hottest commodities. In his first two years of racing he racked up nine wins and 17 poles.

Ryan went full time on the Winston Cup Series in 2002 driving a Ford, winning once and finishing sixth in the points. His sophomore season would again yield a sixth place finish in the points, but this time there were eight wins in a Dodge backing it up.

Year-by-year Performance

	Races	Poles		Wins		Top 5		Top 10	
2000	1	0	0.0%	0	0.0%	0	0.0%	0	0.0%
2001	7	1	14.3%	0	0.0%	2	28.6%	2	28.6%
2002	36	6	16.7%	1	2.8%	14	38.9%	22	61.1%
2003	36	11	30.6%	8	22.2%	17	47.2%	22	61.1%
Total	**80**	**18**	**22.5%**	**9**	**11.3%**	**33**	**41.3%**	**46**	**57.5%**

rack Performance

ess than 1 Mile

	Starts	1st	2nd	3rd	4th	5th	6th	7th	8th	9th	10th	11–20	21–43
ristol	4	0	0	0	0	0	1	0	0	0	0	0	3
lartinsville	4	0	0	0	0	1	0	0	0	0	0	1	2
ichmond	4	1	2	0	0	0	0	0	0	0	0	0	1
otal	12	1	2	0	0	1	1	0	0	0	0	1	6
		8.3%	16.7%	0.0%	0.0%	8.3%	8.3%	0.0%	0.0%	0.0%	0.0%	8.3%	50.0%

Mile–1.49 Mile

	Starts	1st	2nd	3rd	4th	5th	6th	7th	8th	9th	10th	11–20	21–43
over	4	2	0	0	1	0	0	0	1	0	0	0	0
ew Hamp.	4	1	0	0	1	1	0	0	0	1	0	0	0
. Carolina	4	0	0	0	0	1	0	0	0	0	0	2	1
noenix	4	0	0	1	0	0	0	0	0	0	0	1	2
arlington	4	0	1	0	0	1	0	0	0	0	0	1	1
otal	20	3	1	1	2	3	0	0	1	1	0	4	4
		15.0%	5.0%	5.0%	10.0%	15.0%	0.0%	0.0%	5.0%	5.0%	0.0%	20.0%	20.0%

.5 mile

	Starts	1st	2nd	3rd	4th	5th	6th	7th	8th	9th	10th	11–20	21–43
harlotte	6	0	1	0	0	1	0	0	1	0	0	1	2
hicago	2	1	0	0	0	1	0	0	0	0	0	0	0
omestead	2	0	0	0	0	0	1	0	0	0	0	0	1
ansas	3	1	2	0	0	0	0	0	0	0	0	0	0
as Vegas	3	0	0	0	1	0	0	1	0	0	0	0	1
exas	2	1	0	0	0	0	0	0	0	0	0	0	1
otal	18	3	3	0	1	2	1	1	1	0	0	1	5
		16.7%	16.7%	0.0%	5.6%	11.1%	5.6%	5.6%	5.6%	0.0%	0.0%	5.6%	27.8%

Track Performance
1.51 Mile–2.5 Mile

	Starts	1st	2nd	3rd	4th	5th	6th	7th	8th	9th	10th	11-20	21-43
Atlanta	4	0	0	0	0	0	0	0	0	0	3	0	1
California	2	0	0	0	0	0	0	0	0	0	0	1	1
Michigan	5	1	0	1	0	1	0	0	0	0	0	0	2
Indianapolis	3	0	0	0	1	0	0	0	0	0	0	1	1
Pocono	4	1	0	0	0	2	0	0	0	0	0	0	1
Total	**18**	**2**	**0**	**1**	**1**	**3**	**0**	**0**	**0**	**0**	**3**	**2**	**6**
		11.1%	0.0%	5.6%	5.6%	16.7%	0.0%	0.0%	0.0%	0.0%	16.7%	11.1%	33.3%

Restrictor Plate

	Starts	1st	2nd	3rd	4th	5th	6th	7th	8th	9th	10th	11-20	21-43
Daytona	4	0	0	0	0	0	0	1	0	0	0	0	3
Talladega	4	0	0	0	1	0	0	1	0	0	0	0	2
Total	**8**	**0**	**0**	**0**	**1**	**0**	**0**	**2**	**0**	**0**	**0**	**0**	**5**
		0.0%	0.0%	0.0%	12.5%	0.0%	0.0%	25.0%	0.0%	0.0%	0.0%	0.0%	62.5%

Road Courses

	Starts	1st	2nd	3rd	4th	5th	6th	7th	8th	9th	10th	11-20	21-43
Sears Point	2	0	0	0	0	1	0	0	0	1	0	0	0
Watkins Glen	3	0	2	0	0	0	0	0	0	1	0	0	0
Total	**5**	**0**	**2**	**0**	**0**	**1**	**0**	**0**	**0**	**2**	**0**	**0**	**0**
		0.0%	40.0%	0.0%	0.0%	20.0%	0.0%	0.0%	0.0%	40.0%	0.0%	0.0%	0.0%

Steve Park

Current Team: Richard Childress Racing
Residence: Mooresville, North Carolina
Hometown: Islip, New York
Birthday: August 23, 1967
Height: 6 feet, 2 inches
Weight: 195

Races: 181
Running: 153 (84.5 percent)
Accidents: 16 (8.8 percent)
Mechanical Failures: 12 (6.6 percent)

2003	Richard Childress Racing, Dale Earnhardt Incorporated
1998–2002	Dale Earnhardt Incorporated
1997	Dale Earnhardt Incorporated SABCO

Steve Park followed his father, Bob, into racing. Before he was a teenager he was driving a kart, and he was racing cars by the time he was 16. In one ARCA event, he ran a qualifying heat when the driver, his father, could not make it to the track. Despite starting in the rear of the field, Steve took the last qualifying spot for the main event; this delighted his father, who made it to the track in time to replace Steve for the actual race.

In the late 1980s he ran modifieds, winning his first race in 1988. In 1989 he won five modified races and was ready to move on. He sold his stock of modified equipment and bought a well-used Busch car, which he and his father got ready for racing. In their first attempt, they missed qualifying for the Busch race at Daytona by one spot and headed home. Despite a noble attempt to land a sponsor, they had to park the Busch car, and Steve went back to the modified ranks. Steve spent most of the 1990s driving anything he could. He won the February Goody's Dash Series at Daytona five times in a row from 1990 to1994. In 1994 he also claimed the New England Pro-Four Modified Championship, and in 1995 he graduated to the NASCAR Featherlite Modified Tour. Steve had 17 wins and 24 poles in the open-wheel series and finished second in the series championship in 1996.

Over the next few years, Steve was a very successful modified driver, often winning but not satisfied to stay in the lower ranks of racing. In 1996 he raced in 11 races in the Busch North Series, winning twice, and drove in the Craftsman Truck Series. He finished 11th at Indianapolis Raceway Park, and was once again helped by a driver who could not get to the track for qualifying. Joe Nemechek, who was at Bristol, asked Steve to "just get his truck in the field" at Riverhead Speedway. Steve promptly climbed in the truck and took the pole.

Major racing owners who were beginning to take a look at Steve included Richard Childress and Dale Earnhardt. It was hard for Steve to believe, and when Dale Earnhardt left him a message, Steve thought it was a joke and ignored the call. But Dale called back, and this time Steve returned the call. The two got together and Steve began driving a Busch car for Dale Earnhardt Incorporated. Steve was the Rookie of the Year in the Busch Series in 1998, finishing the year with three wins and 20 top 10s. In 1997 Steve drove in five Cup races: four for DEI and one for SABCO. In 1998 his schedule expanded to 17 races (all for DEI) with his best finishes being a pair of 11ths at Michigan and Dover.

In 1999 Steve raced full-time on the Winston Cup circuit. In 2000 he drove to two poles, 13 top 10s, and his first win (at Watkins Glen). He followed in 2001 with another win, this time taking the checkered flag at Rockingham. After the first 24 races of 2001, Steve had won once and finished in the top 10 in half of them. But his year ended when he was injured in a Busch car. He also missed a few races at the beginning of the 2002 season, and ran only 32 of the season's 36 races.

He started the 2003 campaign with DEI but made a midyear move to Richard Childress Racing. For the season, he ran 35 races, scoring one top 5 and three top 10s. In 2002 and 2003, Steve was not able to achieve the chemistry with his team that he had in the 2001 campaign. He entered 2004 still looking for a full-time Nextel Cup ride, and will drive a Dodge in the Craftsman Truck Series.

Steve drove for Dale Earnhardt Incorporated from 1997 to 2003, winning twice.

Year-by-year Performance

	Races	Poles		Wins		Top 5		Top 10	
1997	5	0	0.0%	0	0.0%	0	0.0%	0	0.0%
1998	17	0	0.0%	0	0.0%	0	0.0%	0	0.0%
1999	34	0	0.0%	0	0.0%	0	0.0%	5	14.7%
2000	34	2	5.9%	1	2.9%	6	17.6%	13	38.2%
2001	24	0	0.0%	1	4.2%	5	20.8%	12	50.0%
2002	32	0	0.0%	0	0.0%	0	0.0%	2	6.3%
2003	35	2	5.7%	0	0.0%	1	2.9%	3	8.6%
Total	**181**	**4**	**2.2%**	**2**	**1.1%**	**12**	**6.6%**	**35**	**19.3%**

Track Performance

Less than 1 Mile

	Starts	1st	2nd	3rd	4th	5th	6th	7th	8th	9th	10th	11–20	21–4
Bristol	11	0	0	0	0	1	0	2	0	1	0	0	7
Martinsville	11	0	0	0	0	0	0	0	0	0	0	5	6
Richmond	10	0	0	0	2	0	0	0	0	0	0	3	5
Total	**32**	**0**	**0**	**0**	**2**	**1**	**0**	**2**	**0**	**1**	**0**	**8**	**18**
		0.0%	0.0%	0.0%	6.3%	3.1%	0.0%	6.3%	0.0%	3.1%	0.0%	25.0%	56.3%

1 Mile–1.49 Mile

	Starts	1st	2nd	3rd	4th	5th	6th	7th	8th	9th	10th	11–20	21–4
Dover	10	0	1	0	1	0	0	0	0	1	0	3	4
New Hamp.	10	0	0	0	0	0	1	0	1	0	0	2	6
N. Carolina	11	1	0	0	0	0	1	0	0	1	0	1	7
Phoenix	6	0	0	1	0	0	0	0	0	0	0	1	4
Darlington	10	0	1	0	0	0	0	0	0	0	2	3	4
Total	**47**	**1**	**2**	**1**	**1**	**0**	**2**	**0**	**1**	**2**	**2**	**10**	**25**
		2.1%	4.3%	2.1%	2.1%	0.0%	4.3%	0.0%	2.1%	4.3%	4.3%	21.3%	53.2%

1.5 mile

	Starts	1st	2nd	3rd	4th	5th	6th	7th	8th	9th	10th	11–20	21–4
Charlotte	10	0	0	0	0	0	0	1	0	1	1	1	6
Chicago	3	0	0	0	0	0	0	0	0	0	0	0	3
Homestead	4	0	0	0	0	0	0	0	1	0	0	3	0
Kansas	2	0	0	0	0	0	0	0	0	0	0	0	2
Las Vegas	4	0	0	0	0	0	0	1	0	0	1	1	1
Texas	5	0	1	0	0	0	0	0	0	0	0	2	2
Total	**28**	**0**	**1**	**0**	**0**	**0**	**0**	**2**	**1**	**1**	**2**	**7**	**14**
		0.0%	3.6%	0.0%	0.0%	0.0%	0.0%	7.1%	3.6%	3.6%	7.1%	25.0%	50.0%

Track Performance

.51 Mile–2.5 Mile

Atlanta	10	0	0	0	1	0	0	0	0	0	0	5	4
California	5	0	0	0	0	0	0	0	0	0	0	2	3
Michigan	11	0	0	0	0	1	1	0	0	1	0	2	6
Indianapolis	6	0	0	0	0	0	0	2	0	0	0	3	1
Pocono	10	0	0	0	0	0	0	0	1	0	0	4	5
Total	**42**	**0**	**0**	**0**	**1**	**1**	**1**	**2**	**1**	**1**	**0**	**16**	**19**
		0.0%	0.0%	0.0%	2.4%	2.4%	2.4%	4.8%	2.4%	2.4%	0.0%	38.1%	45.2%

Restrictor Plate

Daytona	11	0	0	0	0	0	0	0	0	0	0	1	10
Talladega	9	0	0	0	0	0	1	0	0	0	0	3	5
Total	**20**	**0**	**0**	**0**	**0**	**0**	**1**	**0**	**0**	**0**	**0**	**4**	**15**
		0.0%	0.0%	0.0%	0.0%	0.0%	5.0%	0.0%	0.0%	0.0%	0.0%	20.0%	75.0%

Road Courses

Sears Point	5	0	0	0	0	0	0	0	0	0	0	1	4
Watkins Glen	7	1	0	0	0	0	0	0	0	0	1	2	3
Total	**12**	**1**	**0**	**0**	**0**	**0**	**0**	**0**	**0**	**0**	**1**	**3**	**7**
		8.3%	0.0%	0.0%	0.0%	0.0%	0.0%	0.0%	0.0%	0.0%	8.3%	25.0%	58.3%

Kyle Petty

Current Team: Petty Enterprises
Residence: Trinity, North Carolina
Hometown: Randleman, North Carolina
Birthday: June 2, 1960
Height: 6 feet, 2 inches
Weight: 195

Races: 678
Running: 523 (77.1 percent)
Accidents: 42 (6.2 percent)
Mechanical Failures: 113 (16.7)

1997-2003	Petty Enterprises
1989–1996	SABCO
1985–1988	Wood Brothers Racing
1983–1984	Petty Enterprises
1982	Petty Enterprises
	Hoss Ellington
1981	Petty Enterprises
1980	Petty Enterprises
	Rah Moc
1979	Petty Enterprises

Kyle Petty has had both the benefits and the difficulties of starting a racing career as the son and grandson of two racing legends. His father and grandfather—Richard and Lee Petty, respectively—were instrumental in building the sport of NASCAR. Kyle has added to their legacy in the sport while always being his own man. His gentlemanly manner and dignity under difficult circumstances have been an example to the entire NASCAR family.

But early on, it was not certain that Kyle would be in NASCAR. Before he went to full-time racing, there was talk of football and baseball scholarships, and even a country music career. But some things are just meant to be, and in the late 1970s Kyle began his long racing career. In 1979 he drove in his first major race, a 200-mile ARCA event, and he won it. He also drove in five Winston Cup events in a second Petty Enterprises car. Although he did not qualify well, in every race he finished better than he started. He retired with engine failure in his last race of the year, but finished the other four in the top 20, with his best finish a 9th at Talladega.

In 1980 he ran 15 races and finished six of them in the top 10. It was clear that Kyle could run with the best of them, and in 1981 he went Winston Cup racing full-time. Over the next few years, when Kyle was running at the end of the race he finished well, but mechanical failures and accidents plagued him. In 1982 at Dover, he was close to winning his first race, but finished a close second to Darrell Waltrip.

When Kyle moved from a Petty car to a seat in the Wood Brothers car in 1985, to many it was like a Hatfield driving a McCoy car. Kyle stayed with the Wood Brothers for four years and ran well. In their first year they had seven top fives and almost won at Talladega. In 1986 they made it to victory lane at Richmond. They won again the next year but not in 1988, and Kyle changed seats again. This time he landed in a Felix Sebates car, where he stayed for eight years. Kyle resumed his trips to victory lane in 1991, and before leaving SABCO won six races. Kyle returned in 1997 and started a second Petty team, which merged with his father's team in 1999. The two have been together ever since.

While Kyle has had some good runs since being back with Petty Enterprises, his team has not been able to put together a win. Off the track, Kyle is a tireless benefactor to the community, with charitable work that is legendary in and out of racing circles.

Kyle Petty has driven the No. 45 Petty Enterprises Dodge since 2001.

Kyle came from one of the most successful racing families in the sport. He proved himself in smaller venues before he came to the Winston Cup Series on a full-time basis in 1981.

Year-by-year Performance

	Races	Poles		Wins		Top 5		Top 10	
1979	5	0	0.0%	0	0.0%	0	0.0%	1	20.0%
1980	15	0	0.0%	0	0.0%	0	0.0%	6	40.0%
1981	31	0	0.0%	0	0.0%	1	3.2%	10	32.3%
1982	29	0	0.0%	0	0.0%	2	6.9%	4	13.8%
1983	30	0	0.0%	0	0.0%	0	0.0%	2	6.7%
1984	30	0	0.0%	0	0.0%	1	0.0%	6	20.0%
1985	28	0	0.0%	0	0.0%	7	3.6%	12	42.9%
1986	29	0	0.0%	1	3.4%	4	24.1%	14	48.3%
1987	29	0	0.0%	1	3.4%	6	13.8%	14	48.3%
1988	29	0	0.0%	0	0.0%	2	20.7%	8	27.6%
1989	19	0	0.0%	0	0.0%	1	10.5%	5	26.3%
1990	29	2	6.9%	1	3.4%	2	3.4%	14	48.3%
1991	18	2	11.1%	1	5.6%	2	11.1%	4	22.2%
1992	29	3	10.3%	2	6.9%	9	6.9%	17	58.6%
1993	30	1	3.3%	1	3.3%	9	30.0%	15	50.0%
1994	31	0	0.0%	0	0.0%	2	29.0%	7	22.6%
1995	30	0	0.0%	1	3.3%	1	6.7%	5	16.7%
1996	28	0	0.0%	0	0.0%	0	3.6%	2	7.1%
1997	32	0	0.0%	0	0.0%	2	0.0%	9	28.1%
1998	33	0	0.0%	0	0.0%	0	6.1%	2	6.1%
1999	32	0	0.0%	0	0.0%	0	0.0%	9	28.1%
2000	19	0	0.0%	0	0.0%	0	0.0%	1	5.3%
2001	24	0	0.0%	0	0.0%	0	0.0%	0	0.0%
2002	36	0	0.0%	0	0.0%	0	0.0%	1	2.8%
2003	33	0	0.0%	0	0.0%	0	0.0%	0	0.0%
Total	**678**	**8**	**1.2%**	**8**	**1.2%**	**51**	**7.5%**	**168**	**24.8%**

Track Performance

Less than 1 Mile

	Starts	1st	2nd	3rd	4th	5th	6th	7th	8th	9th	10th	11–20	21–43
Bristol	42	0	0	1	1	0	1	2	1	1	1	14	20
Martinsville	46	0	1	0	1	3	1	1	1	2	3	13	20
Richmond	44	1	0	0	0	2	3	3	2	1	1	15	16
N. Wilkes	32	0	2	1	2	2	1	0	2	0	3	9	10
Nashville	8	0	0	0	0	0	1	1	0	0	0	4	2
Total	172	1	3	2	4	7	7	7	6	4	8	55	68
		0.6%	1.7%	1.2%	2.3%	4.1%	4.1%	4.1%	3.5%	2.3%	4.7%	32.0%	39.5%

1 Mile–1.49 Mile

	Starts	1st	2nd	3rd	4th	5th	6th	7th	8th	9th	10th	11–20	21–43
Dover	43	1	1	4	0	1	2	1	1	1	0	14	17
New Hamp.	16	0	0	0	0	0	0	0	3	0	0	2	11
N. Carolina	44	3	0	0	0	1	1	0	2	2	3	7	25
Phoenix	14	0	0	1	0	0	1	1	0	1	0	3	7
Darlington	45	0	0	0	0	0	1	2	1	1	1	14	25
Total	162	4	1	5	0	2	5	4	7	5	4	40	85
		2.5%	0.6%	3.1%	0.0%	1.2%	3.1%	2.5%	4.3%	3.1%	2.5%	24.7%	52.5%

1.5 mile

	Starts	1st	2nd	3rd	4th	5th	6th	7th	8th	9th	10th	11–20	21–43
Charlotte	44	1	0	2	1	1	0	2	1	2	1	19	14
Chicago	2	0	0	0	0	0	0	0	0	0	0	0	2
Homestead	3	0	0	0	0	0	0	1	0	0	0	1	1
Kansas	2	0	0	0	0	0	0	0	0	0	0	1	1
Las Vegas	4	0	0	0	0	0	0	0	0	0	0	0	4
Texas	3	0	0	0	0	0	0	0	0	0	0	1	2
Total	59	1	0	2	1	1	0	3	1	2	1	22	25
		1.7%	0.0%	3.4%	1.7%	1.7%	0.0%	5.1%	1.7%	3.4%	1.7%	37.3%	42.4%

Track Performance

1.51 Mile–2.5 Mile

	Starts	1st	2nd	3rd	4th	5th	6th	7th	8th	9th	10th	11–20	21–43
Atlanta	46	0	0	0	1	1	3	2	2	1	0	12	24
California	7	0	0	0	0	0	0	0	0	0	0	1	6
Michigan	46	0	0	1	2	0	3	1	2	0	1	17	19
Indianapolis	9	0	0	0	0	0	0	0	0	0	0	2	7
Pocono	43	1	0	1	0	0	1	3	5	0	1	16	15
Ontario	2	0	0	0	0	0	0	0	0	0	0	1	1
Total	**153**	**1**	**0**	**2**	**3**	**1**	**7**	**6**	**9**	**1**	**2**	**49**	**72**
		0.7%	0.0%	1.3%	2.0%	0.7%	4.6%	3.9%	5.9%	0.7%	1.3%	32.0%	47.1%

Restrictor Plate

	Starts	1st	2nd	3rd	4th	5th	6th	7th	8th	9th	10th	11–20	21–43
Daytona	44	0	0	0	0	2	2	3	0	0	1	13	23
Talladega	44	0	1	1	2	0	2	4	2	5	2	13	12
Total	**88**	**0**	**1**	**1**	**2**	**2**	**4**	**7**	**2**	**5**	**3**	**26**	**35**
		0.0%	1.1%	1.1%	2.3%	2.3%	4.5%	8.0%	2.3%	5.7%	3.4%	29.5%	39.8%

Road Courses

	Starts	1st	2nd	3rd	4th	5th	6th	7th	8th	9th	10th	11–20	21–43
Riverside	15	0	0	1	0	1	2	0	1	0	0	5	5
Sears Point	13	0	0	0	0	1	0	0	1	0	0	6	5
Watkins Glen	16	1	0	0	0	0	1	0	1	1	0	2	10
Total	**44**	**1**	**0**	**1**	**0**	**2**	**3**	**0**	**3**	**1**	**0**	**13**	**20**
		2.3%	0.0%	2.3%	0.0%	4.5%	6.8%	0.0%	6.8%	2.3%	0.0%	29.5%	45.5%

Ricky Rudd

Current Team: Wood Brothers Racing
Residence: Charlotte, North Carolina
Hometown: Chesapeake, Virginia
Birthday: September 12, 1956
Height: 5 feet, 8 inches
Weight: 160

Races: 803
Running: 632 (78.7 percent)
Accidents: 54 (6.7 percent)
Mechanical Failures: 117 (14.6 percent)

2003	Wood Brothers Racing
2000–2002	Robert Yates Racing
1994–1999	Rudd Performance Motorsports
1990–1993	Hendrick Motorsports
1988–1989	Kenny Bernstein
1984–1987	Bud Moore
1982–1983	Richard Childress
1981	DiGard Racing
1980	Al Rudd
1979	Junie Donlavey
1976–1978	Al Rudd
1975	Bill Champion

Ricky Rudd is somewhat unique in Nextel Cup racing. While all the other drivers spent time running some form of stock car before entering NASCAR's highest division, Ricky skipped all that. The first time he drove a stock car was in Winston Cup practice at Rockingham in 1975. Since he practiced well, they let him attempt to qualify, and he secured a 26th-place starting position. He started the race on March 2, 1975, in a Ford and drove to an 11th place. At 18, Ricky had his first Winston Cup start behind him. One week later he raced again, this time at Bristol, and scored his first top 10.

By the end of the 2003 season, Rudd was NASCAR's start leader, having competed in 803 races, and he held a record with 716 consecutive starts.

Ricky started driving karts at the age of nine and raced motocross in his teens, but his path to NASCAR was a one-step process. He drove in four races in 1975 for car owner Bill Champion. He then drove in a car owned by his father, Al Rudd. From 1975 until 1980, Ricky drove only partial schedules of 4 to 25 events on the Winston Cup circuit.

Although he did not drive for top teams in his early years, Ricky ran well. In 1977 he got his first top five, a 4th at Talladega. It was a big year for Ricky. He raced in 25 of the seasons 30 races, scored 10 top 10s, finished

17th in points, and won the Winston Cup Rookie of the Year award. Two years later, driving for Junie Donlavey and again running a partial schedule, he finished 9th in points. In 1981 Ricky joined the DiGard Racing team and after six partial seasons finally ran every race. Rudd did not win a race, but he finished the year with 14 top-five finishes and a strong 6th-place finish in the Winston Cup points battle.

Rudd left DiGard Racing after the 1981 season and drove for Richard Childress the next two seasons. In 1983 he finally broke into the winner's circle, taking home wins at Riverside and Martinsville. At the end of the season, Rudd and Dale Earnhardt swapped rides, and in 1984 he piloted Bud Moore's Ford. Rudd began a streak in 1984. He won again, and for the next 16 years won at least one race every year. In 1988 Ricky moved to King Motorsports, with Quaker State sponsorship, and in 1990 began driving for Hendrick Motorsports.

In 1994 Rudd became a driver-owner. The difference between Ricky and many other driver-owners of the time was that Ricky continued to win races every year, the biggest being the 1997 Brickyard 400 at Indianapolis Motor Speedway. Ricky's record winning streak came to an end in 1999, and in 2000 it was announced he would come out from behind the desk and drive the famous Robert Yates No. 28 Ford. Success was immediate, and Rudd drove to a 5th-place finish in the points in the team's first year with Rudd driving. In 2001 the team won twice and finished 4th in points. Things were going well in 2002 until, for some reason, it all seemed to unravel. By 2003 there was no No. 28 car, and Ricky was driving for the Wood Brothers. In its first year together, the team put together four top fives and a 23rd-place finish in the points.

Ricky Rudd now has the dubious honor of being around longer than anybody driving these days. He came to the Wood Brothers for the 2003 season after a successful three year run with Robert Yates Racing.

From 1983 to 1998, Ricky won at least one race per year and after a two year shutout was back in victory lane in 2001 and 2002. From 1994 to 1999 he won six races as an owner/driver.

Year-by-year Performance

	Races	Poles		Wins		Top 5		Top 10	
1975	4	0	0.0%	0	0.0%	0	0.0%	1	25.0%
1976	4	0	0.0%	0	0.0%	0	0.0%	1	25.0%
1977	25	0	0.0%	0	0.0%	1	4.0%	10	40.0%
1978	13	0	0.0%	0	0.0%	0	0.0%	4	30.8%
1979	28	0	0.0%	0	0.0%	4	14.3%	17	60.7%
1980	13	0	0.0%	0	0.0%	1	7.7%	3	23.1%
1981	31	3	9.7%	0	0.0%	14	45.2%	17	54.8%
1982	30	2	6.7%	0	0.0%	6	20.0%	13	43.3%
1983	30	4	13.3%	2	6.7%	7	23.3%	14	46.7%
1984	30	4	13.3%	1	3.3%	7	23.3%	16	53.3%
1985	28	0	0.0%	1	3.6%	13	46.4%	19	67.9%
1986	29	1	3.4%	2	6.9%	11	37.9%	17	58.6%
1987	29	0	0.0%	2	6.9%	10	34.5%	13	44.8%
1988	29	2	6.9%	1	3.4%	6	20.7%	11	37.9%
1989	29	0	0.0%	1	3.4%	7	24.1%	15	51.7%
1990	29	2	6.9%	1	3.4%	8	27.6%	15	51.7%
1991	29	1	3.4%	1	3.4%	9	31.0%	17	58.6%
1992	29	1	3.4%	1	3.4%	9	31.0%	28	96.6%
1993	30	0	0.0%	1	3.3%	9	30.0%	14	46.7%
1994	31	1	3.2%	1	3.2%	6	19.4%	15	48.4%
1995	31	2	6.5%	1	3.2%	10	32.3%	16	51.6%
1996	31	0	0.0%	1	3.2%	5	16.1%	16	51.6%
1997	32	0	0.0%	2	6.3%	6	18.8%	11	34.4%
1998	33	0	0.0%	1	3.0%	1	3.0%	5	15.2%
1999	34	1	2.9%	0	0.0%	3	8.8%	5	14.7%
2000	34	2	5.9%	0	0.0%	12	35.3%	19	55.9%
2001	36	1	2.8%	2	5.6%	14	38.9%	22	61.1%
2002	36	1	2.8%	1	2.8%	8	22.2%	12	33.3%
2003	36	0	0.0%	0	0.0%	4	11.1%	5	13.9%
Total	**803**	**28**	**3.5%**	**23**	**2.9%**	**191**	**23.8%**	**371**	**46.2%**

Track Performance

Less than 1 Mile

Bristol	52	0	4	6	2	3	2	1	2	4	6	9	1:
Martinsville	49	3	3	2	4	1	1	1	3	0	1	12	1
Richmond	50	2	5	4	5	4	3	1	2	2	0	7	1
N. Wilkes	36	0	2	2	2	5	5	5	0	2	0	8	
Nashville	12	0	0	0	3	2	0	0	0	0	3	3	
Total	**199**	**5**	**14**	**14**	**16**	**15**	**11**	**8**	**7**	**8**	**10**	**39**	**5:**
		2.5%	7.0%	7.0%	8.0%	7.5%	5.5%	4.0%	3.5%	4.0%	5.0%	19.6%	26.1

1 Mile–1.49 Mile

Dover	51	4	0	4	2	4	4	1	3	0	4	14	1
New Hamp.	18	1	1	3	0	2	0	0	0	1	2	5	
N. Carolina	53	1	3	3	5	0	2	3	1	0	1	16	1
Phoenix	16	1	0	1	0	1	1	1	0	0	0	4	
Darlington	54	1	0	1	2	3	4	4	4	3	3	10	1
Total	**192**	**8**	**4**	**12**	**9**	**10**	**11**	**9**	**8**	**4**	**10**	**49**	**5**
		4.2%	2.1%	6.3%	4.7%	5.2%	5.7%	4.7%	4.2%	2.1%	5.2%	25.5%	30.2

1.5 mile

Charlotte	55	0	0	2	5	2	3	3	4	4	2	10	2
Chicago	3	0	0	1	0	0	0	0	0	0	0	2	
Homestead	5	0	0	0	0	0	1	0	0	0	0	1	
Kansas	3	0	0	1	0	0	0	0	0	0	1	1	
Las Vegas	6	0	0	0	0	0	0	0	0	0	0	5	
Texas	7	0	0	0	1	1	0	0	0	0	1	1	
Total	**81**	**0**	**0**	**4**	**6**	**3**	**4**	**3**	**4**	**4**	**4**	**20**	**2**
		0.0%	0.0%	4.9%	7.4%	3.7%	4.9%	3.7%	4.9%	4.9%	4.9%	24.7%	35

ack Performance

51 Mile–2.5 Mile

anta	52	1	1	2	2	1	2	2	6	3	2	7	23
lifornia	7	0	0	2	1	0	1	0	0	0	0	1	2
chigan	54	1	2	1	2	3	1	3	5	2	2	10	22
dianapolis	10	1	0	0	0	0	1	0	0	1	0	3	4
cono	49	1	3	2	2	1	4	5	0	1	2	11	17
tario	2	0	0	0	0	0	0	0	1	0	1	0	0
tal	**174**	**4**	**6**	**7**	**7**	**5**	**9**	**10**	**12**	**7**	**7**	**32**	**68**
		2.3%	3.4%	4.0%	4.0%	2.9%	5.2%	5.7%	6.9%	4.0%	4.0%	18.4%	39.1%

strictor Plate

ytona	54	0	0	2	3	2	1	4	2	6	1	15	18
ladega	54	0	0	4	4	2	0	1	1	1	0	13	28
tal	**108**	**0**	**0**	**6**	**7**	**4**	**1**	**5**	**3**	**7**	**1**	**28**	**46**
		0.0%	0.0%	5.6%	6.5%	3.7%	0.9%	4.6%	2.8%	6.5%	0.9%	25.9%	42.6%

ad Courses

erside	16	2	2	2	1	1	0	0	0	1	0	3	4
ars Point	15	2	1	2	3	1	0	1	0	0	0	2	3
tkins Glen	18	2	1	0	3	2	0	1	0	0	0	3	6
tal	**49**	**6**	**4**	**4**	**7**	**4**	**0**	**2**	**0**	**1**	**0**	**8**	**13**
		12.2%	8.2%	8.2%	14.3%	8.2%	0.0%	4.1%	0.0%	2.0%	0.0%	16.3%	26.5%

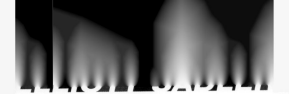

Elliott Sadler

Current Team: Robert Yates Racing
Residence: Charlotte, North Carolina
Hometown: Emporia, Virginia
Birthday: April 30, 1975
Height: 6 feet, 2 inches
Weight: 195

Races: 177
Running: 152 (85.9 percent)
Accidents: 18 (10.2 percent)
Mechanical Failures: 7 (4.0 percent)

2002–2003	Robert Yates Racing
1999–2002	Wood Brothers Racing
1998	Gary Bechtel

E lliott Sadler is another NASCAR driver who was driving a kart at a very early age. As he grew older, he followed the typical path of the stock car driver, running on short tracks in Virginia and surrounding states. Over the years he racked up hundreds of short track wins, and by the age of 20 was champion of South Boston Speedway, the same track that produced the Burton brothers.

In 1997 Elliott ran his first full season in the Busch Series. He was quite successful, winning three races and finishing fifth in the series championship. In 1998 Elliott ran the Busch Series again for Diamond Ridge Motorsports, chalking up two more wins and an 8th-place finish in the points. Elliott made his Winston Cup debut in 1998, qualifying 31st in a Chevrolet at Lowe's Motor Speedway. However, he finished 42nd after engine failure. Later in the year, he drove a race at Bristol and this time the results were better. He again qualified 31st, but finished a very respectable 24th.

In 1999 Elliott went Cup racing full-time for the legendary Wood Brothers. The team got off to a tough start, with Elliott involved in crashes in the first two races of the year, but as time went on things got better. In the sixth race, Elliott got his first top 10. It was his best finish of the year, and when the season ended, he finished second in the Rookie of the Year battle, behind Tony Stewart. Elliott won only one top 10 in 2000, but in 2001 he drove the Wood Brothers Ford to an exciting victory at Bristol, piloting the No. 21 car past its old nemesis, Petty's No. 43 car. In 2002, his last year in the Wood Brothers car, he had seven top 10s. He finished 2nd twice, once in the Daytona 500 and once at Darlington.

In 2002 it was announced that Elliott would leave the Wood Brothers to drive for Robert Yates Racing with a new car number and M&M's sponsorship. Neither Yates team was really outstanding in 2003, although Elliott had nine top 10s, a career best.

Elliott began driving for Robert Yates in 2003 in a car with a new number and sponsor for both Sadler and Yates.

After two hot years (1997 and 1998) on the Busch Series, Elliott landed one of the most-famed rides in NASCAR—the Wood Brothers Ford. His success with the team was limited but he did get an emotional win at Bristol in 2001.

Year-by-year Performance

	Races	Poles		Wins		Top 5		Top 10	
1998	2	0	0.0%	0	0.0%	0	0.0%	0	0.0%
1999	34	0	0.0%	0	0.0%	0	0.0%	1	2.9%
2000	33	0	0.0%	0	0.0%	0	0.0%	1	3.0%
2001	36	0	0.0%	1	2.8%	2	5.6%	2	5.6%
2002	36	0	0.0%	0	0.0%	2	5.6%	7	19.4%
2003	36	2	5.6%	0	0.0%	2	5.6%	9	25.0%
Total	**177**	**2**	**1.1%**	**1**	**0.6%**	**6**	**3.4%**	**20**	**11.3%**

rack Performance

ss than 1 Mile

	Starts	1st	2nd	3rd	4th	5th	6th	7th	8th	9th	10th	11–20	21–43
istol	11	1	0	0	0	0	0	1	0	0	0	1	8
artinsville	10	0	0	0	0	1	0	0	0	0	0	1	8
chmond	10	0	0	0	0	0	0	0	0	0	0	1	9
tal	**31**	**1**	**0**	**0**	**0**	**1**	**0**	**1**	**0**	**0**	**0**	**3**	**25**
		3.2%	0.0%	0.0%	0.0%	3.2%	0.0%	3.2%	0.0%	0.0%	0.0%	9.7%	80.6%

Mile–1.49 Mile

	Starts	1st	2nd	3rd	4th	5th	6th	7th	8th	9th	10th	11–20	21–43
ver	10	0	0	0	0	0	0	0	1	0	0	5	4
w Hamp.	10	0	0	0	0	0	0	0	1	0	1	5	3
Carolina	10	0	0	0	0	0	0	0	0	1	0	4	5
oenix	5	0	0	0	0	0	0	0	0	0	1	1	3
rlington	10	0	1	0	0	0	0	1	0	1	0	5	2
tal	**45**	**0**	**1**	**0**	**0**	**0**	**0**	**1**	**2**	**2**	**2**	**20**	**17**
		0.0%	2.2%	0.0%	0.0%	0.0%	0.0%	2.2%	4.4%	4.4%	4.4%	44.4%	37.8%

5 mile

	Starts	1st	2nd	3rd	4th	5th	6th	7th	8th	9th	10th	11–20	21–43
arlotte	11	0	0	0	0	0	0	0	0	0	0	4	7
icago	3	0	0	0	0	0	0	0	0	1	0	1	1
mestead	5	0	0	0	0	0	0	0	0	1	0	1	3
nsas	3	0	0	0	0	0	0	0	0	0	0	1	2
s Vegas	5	0	0	0	0	0	0	0	0	0	0	1	4
xas	5	0	0	0	0	0	0	0	0	0	1	2	2
tal	**32**	**0**	**0**	**0**	**0**	**0**	**0**	**0**	**0**	**2**	**1**	**10**	**19**
		0.0%	0.0%	0.0%	0.0%	0.0%	0.0%	0.0%	0.0%	6.3%	3.1%	31.3%	59.4%

Track Performance

1.51 Mile–2.5 Mile

	Starts	1st	2nd	3rd	4th	5th	6th	7th	8th	9th	10th	11–20	21–43
Atlanta	11	0	0	0	0	0	1	0	0	0	0	6	4
California	5	0	0	0	0	0	0	0	0	0	0	0	5
Michigan	10	0	0	0	0	0	0	0	0	0	0	4	6
Indianapolis	5	0	0	0	0	0	0	0	0	0	0	0	5
Pocono	10	0	0	0	0	0	0	0	0	1	0	5	4
Total	**41**	**0**	**0**	**0**	**0**	**0**	**1**	**0**	**0**	**1**	**0**	**15**	**24**
		0.0%	0.0%	0.0%	0.0%	0.0%	2.4%	0.0%	0.0%	2.4%	0.0%	36.6%	58.5%

Restrictor Plate

	Starts	1st	2nd	3rd	4th	5th	6th	7th	8th	9th	10th	11–20	21–43
Daytona	10	0	1	1	0	0	0	0	0	0	0	3	5
Talladega	9	0	0	1	0	0	0	0	0	0	0	1	7
Total	**19**	**0**	**1**	**2**	**0**	**0**	**0**	**0**	**0**	**0**	**0**	**4**	**12**
		0.0%	5.3%	10.5%	0.0%	0.0%	0.0%	0.0%	0.0%	0.0%	0.0%	21.1%	63.2%

Road Courses

	Starts	1st	2nd	3rd	4th	5th	6th	7th	8th	9th	10th	11–20	21–43
Sears Point	5	0	0	0	0	0	1	0	0	0	0	2	2
Watkins Glen	5	0	0	0	0	0	0	0	0	0	0	2	3
Total	**10**	**0**	**0**	**0**	**0**	**0**	**1**	**0**	**0**	**0**	**0**	**4**	**5**
		0.0%	0.0%	0.0%	0.0%	0.0%	10.0%	0.0%	0.0%	0.0%	0.0%	40.0%	50.0%

Ken Schrader

Current Team: BAM Racing
Residence: Concord, North Carolina
Hometown: Fenton, Missouri
Birthday: May 25, 1955
Height: 5 feet, 10 inches
Weight: 190

Races: 596
Running: 500 (83.9 percent)
Accidents: 42 (7.0 percent)
Mechanical Failures: 54 (9.1 percent)

2003	BAM Racing
2000–2002	Nelson Bowers
1997–1999	Andy Petree Racing
1989–1996	Hendrick Motorsports
1988	Hendrick Motorsports
	Buddy Arrington
1985–1987	Junie Donlavey
1984	Elmo Langley

Many in the motoring sports can be called drivers, but Ken Schrader is a pure racer. While many Nextel Cup drivers are content to drive once a week, Schrader is not. He can be found in Craftsman Trucks, ARCA races, the Winston West Series, and at dirt tracks across the country. It is not out of the ordinary for Ken to run 100 races in a year. He was only three years old when he got his first kart, which his father attached to a pole in the backyard with a cable. Thus began Ken's long career of driving in circles.

By the early 1980s Ken was driving open-wheel cars throughout the Midwest. He won the USAC Silver Crown Championship in 1982 and the USAC Sprint Car Championship in 1983. In 1984 he wanted to go stock car racing, but it was well before the time when promising young rookies were given multimillion dollar rides. Instead, Ken made an agreement to rent a Ford race car from NASCAR legend Elmo Langley for three races in 1984. His best finish was 19th, but Langley was so impressed that the new racer managed not to tear up his race car that he let him race two more times. His short appearance impressed another NASCAR legend, owner Junie Donlavey, who hired Ken to drive his race car

Ken took advantage of the opportunity and won the 1985 Rookie of the Year award. Schrader stayed with Donlavey until 1988, when Hendrick

Motorsports hired him. His first win came in 1988 at Talladega, and he had 17 top-10 finishes in 29 races. He won again the next year, this time at Charlotte. The team went winless in 1990, but in 1991 he won at Atlanta and Darlington. Ken stayed with Hendrick Motorsports until the end of the 1996 season, but did not win another race with the team. His next stop was with Andy Petree Racing, where he stayed until he moved to MB2 Motorsports in 2000.

At the end of the 2002 season, Schrader left MB2 to go to the new BAM Racing team. For the 2003 campaign, the team ran without sponsorship but still managed to put together some respectable runs, including a 3rd at Bristol and a 4th at Martinsville. While many things in NASCAR racing have changed over the last 20 years, Ken has not. Even though he is approaching his 50th birthday, he has not slowed down. He again has plans to race in not only the Nextel Cup Series in 2004, but also in the Craftsman Truck Series, the Winston West Series, and ARCA. And, of course, Ken Schrader will still show up at the local dirt tracks.

Ken Schrader began driving for BAM Racing in 2003. The young team ran many races without a sponsor before landing Schwan's for the 2004 campaign.

From 1988 to 1996, Ken raced for Rick Hendrick, and it was with this team that he scored his four Winston Cup wins.

Year-by-year Performance

	Races	Poles		Wins		Top 5		Top 10	
1984	5	0	0.0%	0	0.0%	0	0.0%	0	0.0%
1985	28	0	0.0%	0	0.0%	0	0.0%	3	10.7%
1986	29	0	0.0%	0	0.0%	0	0.0%	4	13.8%
1987	29	1	3.4%	0	0.0%	1	3.4%	10	34.5%
1988	29	2	6.9%	1	3.4%	4	13.8%	17	58.6%
1989	29	4	13.8%	1	3.4%	10	34.5%	14	48.3%
1990	29	3	10.3%	0	0.0%	7	24.1%	14	48.3%
1991	29	0	0.0%	2	6.9%	10	34.5%	18	62.1%
1992	29	1	3.4%	0	0.0%	4	13.8%	11	37.9%
1993	30	6	20.0%	0	0.0%	9	30.0%	15	50.0%
1994	31	0	0.0%	0	0.0%	9	29.0%	18	58.1%
1995	31	1	3.2%	0	0.0%	2	6.5%	10	32.3%
1996	31	0	0.0%	0	0.0%	3	9.7%	10	32.3%
1997	32	2	6.3%	0	0.0%	2	6.3%	8	25.0%
1998	33	2	6.1%	0	0.0%	3	9.1%	11	33.3%
1999	34	1	2.9%	0	0.0%	0	0.0%	6	17.6%
2000	34	0	0.0%	0	0.0%	0	0.0%	2	5.9%
2001	36	0	0.0%	0	0.0%	0	0.0%	5	13.9%
2002	36	0	0.0%	0	0.0%	0	0.0%	0	0.0%
2003	32	0	0.0%	0	0.0%	0	0.0%	2	6.3%
Total	**596**	**23**	**3.9%**	**4**	**0.7%**	**64**	**10.7%**	**178**	**29.9%**

Track Performance

Less than 1 Mile

	Starts	1st	2nd	3rd	4th	5th	6th	7th	8th	9th	10th	11–20	21–43
Bristol	37	0	1	3	0	0	3	0	0	0	3	12	15
Martinsville	38	0	0	0	2	0	3	6	0	3	4	10	10
Richmond	37	0	0	0	3	0	0	0	1	4	3	16	10
N. Wilkes	25	0	0	1	0	2	0	0	3	2	1	14	2
Nashville	1	0	0	0	0	0	0	0	0	0	0	1	0
Total	**138**	**0**	**1**	**4**	**5**	**2**	**6**	**6**	**4**	**9**	**11**	**53**	**37**
		0.0%	0.7%	2.9%	3.6%	1.4%	4.3%	4.3%	2.9%	6.5%	8.0%	38.4%	26.8%

1 Mile–1.49 Mile

	Starts	1st	2nd	3rd	4th	5th	6th	7th	8th	9th	10th	11–20	21–43
Dover	38	1	2	3	1	1	2	0	0	0	4	7	17
New Hamp.	18	0	0	0	0	0	0	0	1	1	2	4	10
N. Carolina	38	0	1	1	1	3	0	0	1	1	2	10	18
Phoenix	16	0	1	0	1	0	1	0	0	0	1	6	6
Darlington	38	0	0	1	2	2	0	1	1	2	4	13	12
Total	**148**	**1**	**4**	**5**	**5**	**6**	**3**	**1**	**3**	**4**	**13**	**40**	**63**
		0.7%	2.7%	3.4%	3.4%	4.1%	2.0%	0.7%	2.0%	2.7%	8.8%	27.0%	42.6%

1.5 mile

	Starts	1st	2nd	3rd	4th	5th	6th	7th	8th	9th	10th	11–20	21–43
Charlotte	38	1	1	1	2	1	1	3	0	1	1	5	21
Chicago	3	0	0	0	0	0	0	0	0	0	0	0	3
Homestead	4	0	0	0	0	0	0	0	0	0	0	0	4
Kansas	3	0	0	0	0	0	0	0	0	0	0	0	3
Las Vegas	6	0	0	0	0	0	0	0	0	0	0	2	4
Texas	7	0	0	0	0	0	0	0	0	0	1	3	3
Total	**61**	**1**	**1**	**1**	**2**	**1**	**1**	**3**	**0**	**1**	**2**	**10**	**38**
		1.6%	1.6%	1.6%	3.3%	1.6%	1.6%	4.9%	0.0%	1.6%	3.3%	16.4%	62.3%

Track Performance

1.51 Mile–2.5 Mile

Atlanta	39	1	0	0	2	0	2	1	2	0	0	10	21
California	7	0	0	0	0	0	0	0	0	0	0	2	5
Michigan	39	0	0	0	0	0	3	0	1	0	1	20	14
Indianapolis	9	0	0	0	0	0	0	1	0	0	1	5	2
Pocono	38	0	2	2	2	0	1	2	1	2	1	14	11
Total	**132**	**1**	**2**	**2**	**4**	**0**	**6**	**4**	**4**	**2**	**3**	**51**	**53**
		0.8%	1.5%	1.5%	3.0%	0.0%	4.5%	3.0%	3.0%	1.5%	2.3%	38.6%	40.2%

Restrictor Plate

Daytona	38	0	1	3	2	1	4	3	3	3	1	6	11
Talladega	38	1	0	0	3	2	2	2	1	1	0	6	20
Total	**76**	**1**	**1**	**3**	**5**	**3**	**6**	**5**	**4**	**4**	**1**	**12**	**31**
		1.3%	1.3%	3.9%	6.6%	3.9%	7.9%	6.6%	5.3%	5.3%	1.3%	15.8%	40.8%

Road Courses

Riverside	7	0	0	0	0	0	0	0	0	0	2	3	2
Sears Point	15	0	0	0	1	1	0	0	1	3	0	3	6
Watkins Glen	17	0	0	0	1	1	0	0	0	1	1	6	7
Total	**39**	**0**	**0**	**0**	**2**	**2**	**0**	**0**	**1**	**4**	**3**	**12**	**15**
		0.0%	0.0%	0.0%	5.1%	5.1%	0.0%	0.0%	2.6%	10.3%	7.7%	30.8%	38.5%

Jimmy Spencer

Current Team: Ultra Motorsports
Residence: Cornelius, North Carolina
Hometown: Berwick, Pennsylvania
Birthday: February 15, 1957
Height: 6 feet, 0 inches
Weight: 230

Races: 439
Running: 345 (78.6 percent)
Accidents: 48 (10.9 percent)
Mechanical Failures: 46 (10.5 percent)

2003	Ultra Motorsports
2002	Chip Ganassi Racing
1995–2001	Travis Carter
1994	Junior Johnson
1993	Bobby Allison Motorsports
1992	Bobby Allison Motorsports
	Dick Moroso
	Travis Carter
1991	Travis Carter
1990	Rod Osterlund
1989	Baker-Schiff

Jimmy Spencer is another driver who was captivated by racing as he watched his father compete on the track. Jimmy began his pro career when he was 19 years old, running in late models. He won his first late-model race in 1976 and by 1979 had won the Rookie of the Year title at the Shangri-La Speedway in the asphalt modified division. The track was a good place for Jimmy, as he won the modified track championships in 1982 and 1983.

Early in his career he was tagged "Mr. Excitement," and this appropriate title has followed Jimmy throughout his career. By the mid-1980s Spencer was driving in the Winston Modified Series, and he won the series title in both 1986 and 1987. In 1988 Jimmy graduated to the Busch Series, running the entire season. The next year he got his first Busch Series win at Hickory Motor Speedway. It was in the same year that Jimmy started his Winston Cup career, in a Baker-Schiff Pontiac. He ran in 17 races for the team and managed three top-10 finishes.

In 1991 Jimmy drove his first full year on the Winston Cup circuit, this time for Travis Carter, with his best finish being a 3rd at the half-mile North Wilkesboro track. He only ran 12 races the next year (for three different owners) but finished in the top five in 25 percent of the races that he ran. Team owners were taking notice of Jimmy, and beginning in 1993 he became a full-time Cup driver. He finished the 1993 campaign with 10 top-10 finishes and eagerly started the 1994 season, which was his best year. He drove the entire year for Junior Johnson and won twice, taking a race at both Daytona and Talladega. At North Wilkesboro, he also won his first Winston Cup pole.

The next year, Spencer left Johnson to begin driving for Travis Carter; while Jimmy did not win a points race, he did win the Winston Select Open race. Since 1994 Jimmy has driven for Travis Carter, Chip Ganassi Racing, and Ultra Motorsports, and while he has had many good runs, he has not been able to put together a win on the Winston Cup circuit. However, he has certainly been a factor on the Busch Series. In the mid-1990s, he started his own Busch Series team and won two races that year. Since then, Jimmy has been a threat whenever he runs a Busch Series event.

Jimmy started the 2004 season without a ride, but early in the year he got the call to drive the Morgan-McClure Chevrolet.

Jimmy's longest driving tenure was with owner Travis Carter. Jimmy drove for the team from 1995 to 2001.

Year-by-year Performance

	Races	Poles		Wins		Top 5		Top 10	
1989	17	0	0.0%	0	0.0%	0	0.0%	3	17.6%
1990	26	0	0.0%	0	0.0%	0	0.0%	2	7.7%
1991	29	0	0.0%	0	0.0%	1	3.4%	6	20.7%
1992	12	0	0.0%	0	0.0%	3	25.0%	3	25.0%
1993	30	0	0.0%	0	0.0%	5	16.7%	10	33.3%
1994	29	1	3.4%	2	6.9%	3	10.3%	4	13.8%
1995	29	0	0.0%	0	0.0%	0	0.0%	4	13.8%
1996	31	0	0.0%	0	0.0%	2	6.5%	9	29.0%
1997	32	1	3.1%	0	0.0%	1	3.1%	4	12.5%
1998	31	0	0.0%	0	0.0%	3	9.7%	8	25.8%
1999	34	0	0.0%	0	0.0%	2	5.9%	4	11.8%
2000	34	0	0.0%	0	0.0%	2	5.9%	5	14.7%
2001	36	2	5.6%	0	0.0%	3	8.3%	8	22.2%
2002	34	0	0.0%	0	0.0%	2	5.9%	6	17.6%
2003	35	0	0.0%	0	0.0%	1	2.9%	4	11.4%
Total	**439**	**4**	**0.9%**	**2**	**0.5%**	**28**	**6.4%**	**80**	**18.2%**

ack Performance

ss than 1 Mile

	Starts	1st	2nd	3rd	4th	5th	6th	7th	8th	9th	10th	11–20	21–43
istol	25	0	2	0	1	0	0	1	3	0	0	13	5
artinsville	25	0	0	1	0	0	1	1	0	1	0	13	8
chmond	28	0	0	0	0	0	0	0	1	2	1	7	17
Wilkes	14	0	0	1	0	0	0	0	0	0	0	5	8
tal	92	0	2	2	1	0	1	2	4	3	1	38	38
		0.0%	2.2%	2.2%	1.1%	0.0%	1.1%	2.2%	4.3%	3.3%	1.1%	41.3%	41.3%

Mile–1.49 Mile

	Starts	1st	2nd	3rd	4th	5th	6th	7th	8th	9th	10th	11–20	21–43
over	28	0	0	0	0	0	2	0	1	0	1	6	18
ew Hamp.	18	0	0	0	1	0	0	1	0	1	0	10	5
Carolina	28	0	0	0	1	0	0	0	1	0	1	8	17
oenix	14	0	0	0	0	1	0	1	0	0	1	4	7
arlington	28	0	0	0	1	0	0	0	0	0	0	5	22
tal	116	0	0	0	3	1	2	2	2	1	3	33	69
		0.0%	0.0%	0.0%	2.6%	0.9%	1.7%	1.7%	1.7%	0.9%	2.6%	28.4%	59.5%

5 mile

	Starts	1st	2nd	3rd	4th	5th	6th	7th	8th	9th	10th	11–20	21–43
arlotte	29	0	0	0	2	0	2	1	0	0	1	10	13
icago	3	0	0	0	0	1	0	0	0	0	0	0	2
omestead	5	0	0	0	0	1	0	0	0	0	0	2	2
ansas	3	0	0	0	0	0	0	0	0	0	0	1	2
s Vegas	6	0	0	0	0	0	0	1	0	0	2	1	2
xas	7	0	0	0	0	0	0	1	1	0	0	1	4
tal	53	0	0	0	2	2	2	3	1	0	3	15	25
		0.0%	0.0%	0.0%	3.8%	3.8%	3.8%	5.7%	1.9%	0.0%	5.7%	28.3%	47.2%

Track Performance

1.51 Mile–2.5 Mile

	Starts	1st	2nd	3rd	4th	5th	6th	7th	8th	9th	10th	11-20	21-43
Atlanta	28	0	0	0	1	0	1	2	0	1	2	7	14
California	7	0	0	0	0	1	0	1	0	0	0	0	5
Michigan	27	0	0	0	1	0	0	1	1	0	1	13	10
Indianapolis	10	0	0	0	0	0	0	0	1	0	0	3	6
Pocono	28	0	0	0	1	0	0	1	1	1	1	10	13
Total	**100**	**0**	**0**	**0**	**3**	**1**	**1**	**5**	**3**	**2**	**4**	**33**	**48**
		0.0%	0.0%	0.0%	3.0%	1.0%	1.0%	5.0%	3.0%	2.0%	4.0%	33.0%	48.0%

Restrictor Plate

	Starts	1st	2nd	3rd	4th	5th	6th	7th	8th	9th	10th	11-20	21-43
Daytona	25	1	0	0	1	0	0	0	0	1	2	8	12
Talladega	28	1	2	0	2	2	0	1	0	2	1	2	15
Total	**53**	**2**	**2**	**0**	**3**	**2**	**0**	**1**	**0**	**3**	**3**	**10**	**27**
		3.8%	3.8%	0.0%	5.7%	3.8%	0.0%	1.9%	0.0%	5.7%	5.7%	18.9%	50.9%

Road Courses

	Starts	1st	2nd	3rd	4th	5th	6th	7th	8th	9th	10th	11-20	21-43
Sears Point	13	0	0	0	0	1	0	0	0	0	0	2	10
Watkins Glen	12	0	0	1	0	0	0	0	0	0	0	4	7
Total	**25**	**0**	**0**	**1**	**0**	**1**	**0**	**0**	**0**	**0**	**0**	**6**	**17**
		0.0%	0.0%	4.0%	0.0%	4.0%	0.0%	0.0%	0.0%	0.0%	0.0%	24.0%	68.0%

Tony Stewart

Current Team: Joe Gibbs Racing
Residence: Cornelius, North Carolina,
and Columbus, Indiana
Hometown: Rushville, Indiana
Birthday: May 20, 1971
Height: 5 feet, 9 inches
Weight: 165

Races: 176
Running: 155 (88.1 percent)
Accidents: 12 (6.8 percent)
Mechanical Failures: 9 (5.1 percent)

1999–2003   Joe Gibbs Racing

Tony Stewart, at 31, has proven he can drive just about anything with wheels, and he has put together one of the most impressive trophy cases the world of auto racing has ever seen. He started driving in karts, with his father acting as crew chief, and at the age of eight won his first local championship. He later added an International Karting Federation National Championship and a World Karting Association National Championship.

In the late 1980s Tony moved up to the open-wheel ranks running quarter midgets. After gaining a couple of years of experience, he entered into USAC competition where he won Rookie of the Year in 1991 and a National USAC Midget Championship in 1994. In 1995 Tony turned heads by becoming the first driver ever to win the Midget, Sprint, and Silver Crown Championships in the same year. Tony's next stop was the Indy Racing League, formed after a split from the CART Series. He won Rookie of the Year in the series in 1996 and in 1997 won the IRL Championship.

In 1998 he shocked the open-wheel community when, as the hottest commodity in the sport, he opted to enter stock car racing. It was announced that Tony, driving for Joe Gibbs Racing, would run a limited schedule in the Busch Series in 1998 to gain experience. While he was hardly new to racing, he was named Rookie of the Year, claiming three victories in 22 races. After his brief one-year stint in the Busch Series, Tony started his Winston Cup career in 1999 and had an impressive first year. Needless to say, he won Rookie of the Year honors, but he also finished fourth in the Winston Cup Championship. In 34 races Tony finished outside the top 20 only three times. He won three races and had 12 top 5s and 21 top 10s. The next year he upped the ante with six wins and a 6th-place finish in the points.

In 2001 he finished 2nd in the points race, losing the championship to Jeff Gordon. However, in 2002 Tony added another national title to his resume, and this time it was a Winston Cup Championship. He finished in the top five in one-third of the year's races and in the top 10 in half of them. In his first five years of stock car racing, Tony has won multiple races in each year.

While he has become a NASCAR legend in a half-decade, fans can still see him drive in other racing series, from dirt track features to the Indianapolis 500. In 1999 he became the first person to complete the Indianapolis 500 and Coca-Cola 600 on the same day, finishing 9th and 4th, respectively. He did it again in 2001, finishing 6th at Indianapolis and 3rd at Charlotte.

In 2004 Tony will begin his sixth year with Joe Gibbs Racing. Their first five years together produced 17 wins and over 100 top-10 finishes.

Despite some occasional trouble after the 2002 campaign, Tony was able to put a Winston Cup Championship trophy in his trophy case, which also contains an IRL Championship trophy.

Year-by-year Performance

	Races	Poles		Wins		Top 5		Top 10	
1999	34	2	5.9%	3	8.8%	12	35.3%	21	61.8%
2000	34	2	5.9%	6	17.6%	12	35.3%	23	67.6%
2001	36	0	0.0%	3	8.3%	15	41.7%	22	61.1%
2002	36	2	5.6%	3	8.3%	15	41.7%	21	58.3%
2003	36	1	2.8%	2	5.6%	12	33.3%	18	50.0%
Total	**176**	**7**	**4.0%**	**17**	**9.7%**	**66**	**37.5%**	**105**	**59.7%**

Track Performance

Less than 1 Mile

Bristol	10	1	1	0	0	1	0	0	0	0	0	2	5
Martinsville	10	1	0	2	0	0	2	1	0	0	0	2	2
Richmond	10	3	0	0	0	0	1	1	1	0	0	1	3
Total	**30**	**5**	**1**	**2**	**0**	**1**	**3**	**2**	**1**	**0**	**0**	**5**	**10**
		16.7%	3.3%	6.7%	0.0%	3.3%	10.0%	6.7%	3.3%	0.0%	0.0%	16.7%	33.3%

1 Mile–1.49 Mile

Dover	10	2	1	1	2	2	0	1	0	0	0	1	0
New Hamp.	10	1	1	1	0	2	0	0	0	0	1	1	3
N. Carolina	10	0	0	0	3	0	0	2	0	1	0	4	0
Phoenix	5	1	0	0	0	1	0	0	1	0	0	2	0
Darlington	10	0	0	0	2	0	1	0	1	1	1	3	1
Total	**45**	**4**	**2**	**2**	**7**	**5**	**1**	**3**	**2**	**2**	**2**	**11**	
		8.9%	4.4%	4.4%	15.6%	11.1%	2.2%	6.7%	4.4%	4.4%	4.4%	24.4%	8.9%

1.5 mile

Charlotte	10	1	1	2	2	0	1	0	0	0	0	2	
Chicago	3	0	1	1	0	0	0	0	0	0	0	0	
Homestead	5	2	0	0	0	0	0	1	0	0	0	2	
Kansas	3	0	0	0	1	0	0	0	2	0	0	0	
Las Vegas	5	0	1	0	0	2	0	0	0	0	0	1	
Texas	5	0	0	0	0	1	1	0	0	1	0	0	
Total	**31**	**3**	**3**	**3**	**3**	**3**	**2**	**1**	**2**	**1**	**0**	**5**	
		9.7%	9.7%	9.7%	9.7%	9.7%	6.5%	3.2%	6.5%	3.2%	0.0%	16.1%	16.1%

Track Performance

1.51 Mile–2.5 Mile

Atlanta	10	1	1	0	1	1	0	0	0	1	0	2	3
California	5	0	0	0	2	0	0	0	0	0	1	0	2
Michigan	10	1	1	2	0	0	0	0	1	1	0	1	3
Indianapolis	5	0	0	0	0	1	0	1	0	0	0	3	0
Pocono	10	1	0	1	1	0	2	3	0	0	0	0	2
Total	**40**	**3**	**2**	**3**	**4**	**2**	**2**	**4**	**1**	**2**	**1**	**6**	**10**
		7.5%	5.0%	7.5%	10.0%	5.0%	5.0%	10.0%	2.5%	5.0%	2.5%	15.0%	25.0%

Restrictor Plate

Daytona	10	0	0	0	0	0	2	1	0	0	0	1	6
Talladega	10	0	3	1	0	1	1	0	0	0	0	0	4
Total	**20**	**0**	**3**	**1**	**0**	**1**	**3**	**1**	**0**	**0**	**0**	**1**	**10**
		0.0%	15.0%	5.0%	0.0%	5.0%	15.0%	5.0%	0.0%	0.0%	0.0%	5.0%	50.0%

Road Courses

Sears Point	5	1	1	0	0	0	0	0	0	0	1	2	0
Watkins Glen	5	1	0	0	0	0	2	0	0	0	0	1	1
Total	**10**	**2**	**1**	**0**	**0**	**0**	**2**	**0**	**0**	**0**	**1**	**3**	**1**
		20.0%	10.0%	0.0%	0.0%	0.0%	20.0%	0.0%	0.0%	0.0%	10.0%	30.0%	10.0%

Rusty Wallace

Current Team: Penske Racing
Residence: Lake Norman, North Carolina
Hometown: Fenton, Missouri
Birthday: August 14, 1956
Height: 6 feet, 0 inches
Weight: 180

Races: 634
Running: 520 (82.0 percent)
Accidents: 38 (6.0 percent)
Mechanical Failures: 76 (12.0 percent)

1991–2003	Roger Penske
1986–1990	Ray Beadle
1984–1985	Cliff Stewart
1983	Ron Childs
1982	Rusty Wallace
1981	Rusty Wallace
	Ron Benefield
1980	Roger Penske

Rusty Wallace's 54 victories give him a career ranking of 9th in all-time wins and 7th in the Modern Era, and certify him as one of the greatest of all NASCAR drivers. He wins poles (his 36 poles rank him 8th in the Modern Era), and he wins races. He can run fast on every type of track, from superspeedways to road courses, but when you hear his name, you typically think of a down-home, hard-nosed short track racer. He'll move you out of the way if he has to, and will complain if he gets hit (and that's the way it ought to be).

He started racing in the early 1970s in his home state of Missouri. He ran the local tracks for about six years, racking up win after win, and in 1979 moved onto the USAC Stock Car circuit. He won Rookie of the Year, winning five times and finishing second in points. The next year, Rusty made his Winston Cup debut at Atlanta. It was quite a debut, as he qualified 7th and finished 2nd, behind Dale Earnhardt. Late in the season he ran at Charlotte and finished 14th. But it was before the days of rookies getting a top-line ride, and Rusty ran in only seven more races over the next two years. While he was waiting for a full-time Cup ride, he went into the ASA ranks and in 1983 won the series championship.

The next year, 1984, he ran his first full Cup season, driving for Cliff Stewart in a Pontiac. He ran well, but had only four top 10s—still good enough to win the Rookie of the Year. In 1985 he moved to a Blue Max Racing Pontiac. In the first year, Rusty again ran well, with eight top 10s, but in 1986 the team really took off. Rusty got his first win at Bristol, won again at Martinsville, and cruised to a 6th-place finish in the points. Rusty and the Blue Max team won two races in 1987, six in 1988, and six in 1989. The 1989 performance earned Rusty a Winston Cup Championship. To add to the year, he also won the Winston All Star race.

The team won two more races the next year, before Rusty changed rides and resumed his relationship with Roger Penske. In their first year together, they won twice and finished 10th in points. In 1991 Rusty also added an IROC Championship to his long list of accomplishments. Through his first 10 years with his Penske team, Rusty won at least one race each year and often more. In 1993 the team won 10 races, but some bad breaks cost Rusty a second championship.

For 10 straight years, Rusty and Penske finished in the top 10 in championship points, and in four years they were in the top 5. In 2002 Rusty's winning streak came to an end after 16 years, and he went winless again in 2003. But Rusty was still competitive, as in those two years he drove to 29 top-10 finishes, including four 2nd-place finishes.

2004 will be Rusty Wallace's 24th year in NASCAR's top ranks, and his enthusiasm does not seem to have dimmed one bit. Rusty joined Roger Penske full time in 1991, where he remains to this day.

RUSTY WALLACE

Rusty drove Pontiacs for Raymond Beadle from 1986 to 1990. While together they won 18 races and the Winston Cup Championship in 1989.

Year-by-year Performance

	Races	Poles		Wins		Top 5		Top 10	
1980	2	0	0.0%	0	0.0%	1	50.0%	1	50.0%
1981	4	0	0.0%	0	0.0%	0	0.0%	1	25.0%
1982	3	0	0.0%	0	0.0%	0	0.0%	0	0.0%
1984	30	0	0.0%	0	0.0%	2	6.7%	4	13.3%
1985	28	0	0.0%	0	0.0%	2	7.1%	8	28.6%
1986	29	0	0.0%	2	6.9%	4	13.8%	16	55.2%
1987	29	1	3.4%	2	6.9%	9	31.0%	16	55.2%
1988	29	2	6.9%	6	20.7%	19	65.5%	23	79.3%
1989	29	4	13.8%	6	20.7%	13	44.8%	20	69.0%
1990	29	2	6.9%	2	6.9%	9	31.0%	16	55.2%
1991	29	2	6.9%	2	6.9%	9	31.0%	14	48.3%
1992	29	1	3.3%	1	3.3%	5	16.7%	12	40.0%
1993	30	3	9.7%	10	32.3%	19	61.3%	21	67.7%
1994	31	2	6.5%	8	25.8%	17	54.8%	20	64.5%
1995	31	0	0.0%	2	6.5%	15	48.4%	19	61.3%
1996	31	1	3.1%	5	15.6%	8	25.0%	18	56.3%
1997	32	1	3.0%	1	3.0%	8	24.2%	12	36.4%
1998	33	4	11.8%	1	2.9%	15	44.1%	21	61.8%
1999	34	4	11.8%	1	2.9%	7	20.6%	16	47.1%
2000	34	9	25.0%	4	11.1%	12	33.3%	20	55.6%
2001	36	0	0.0%	1	2.8%	8	22.2%	14	38.9%
2002	36	1	2.8%	0	0.0%	7	19.4%	17	47.2%
2003	36	0	0.0%	0	0.0%	2	5.6%	12	33.3%
Total	**634**	**37**	**5.8%**	**54**	**8.5%**	**191**	**30.1%**	**321**	**50.6%**

ack Performance

ss than 1 Mile

	Starts	1st	2nd	3rd	4th	5th	6th	7th	8th	9th	10th	11–20	21–43
istol	40	9	6	1	1	3	1	2	0	3	1	8	5
artinsville	40	6	4	2	2	1	1	2	1	1	2	8	10
chmond	40	6	2	5	2	6	2	3	0	0	2	8	4
. Wilkes	26	3	3	0	5	1	1	2	1	2	3	0	5
ashville	2	0	0	0	0	0	1	0	0	0	0	1	0
tal	148	24	15	8	10	11	6	9	2	6	8	25	24
		16.2%	10.1%	5.4%	6.8%	7.4%	4.1%	6.1%	1.4%	4.1%	5.4%	16.9%	16.2%

Mile–1.49 Mile

	Starts	1st	2nd	3rd	4th	5th	6th	7th	8th	9th	10th	11–20	21–43
over	40	3	1	4	0	2	2	3	1	2	2	12	8
ew Hamp.	18	1	0	2	2	1	3	1	1	0	0	4	3
. Carolina	40	5	3	1	0	3	3	1	2	2	1	7	12
oenix	16	1	2	0	2	2	0	0	0	0	0	4	5
arlington	40	0	2	3	3	3	2	3	2	1	1	5	15
tal	154	10	8	10	7	11	10	8	6	5	4	32	43
		6.5%	5.2%	6.5%	4.5%	7.1%	6.5%	5.2%	3.9%	3.2%	2.6%	20.8%	27.9%

5 mile

	Starts	1st	2nd	3rd	4th	5th	6th	7th	8th	9th	10th	11–20	21–43
arlotte	44	2	4	0	1	1	1	1	6	1	3	8	16
icago	3	0	0	0	0	0	0	0	0	0	0	1	2
mestead	5	0	0	0	0	0	0	0	0	0	0	4	1
ansas	3	0	0	1	1	0	0	0	0	1	0	0	0
s Vegas	6	0	0	1	0	0	0	0	0	1	0	2	2
xas	7	0	0	0	2	0	0	0	0	0	0	4	1
tal	68	2	4	2	4	1	1	1	6	3	3	19	22
		2.9%	5.9%	2.9%	5.9%	1.5%	1.5%	1.5%	8.8%	4.4%	4.4%	27.9%	32.4%

Track Performance

1.51 Mile–2.5 Mile

	Starts	1st	2nd	3rd	4th	5th	6th	7th	8th	9th	10th	11–20	21–43
Atlanta	42	2	2	3	1	0	2	1	1	1	3	13	13
California	7	1	0	1	0	0	0	0	2	0	0	2	1
Michigan	40	5	2	3	2	3	2	3	0	0	0	10	10
Indianapolis	10	0	3	0	2	0	0	1	2	0	1	0	1
Pocono	40	4	3	2	0	0	4	0	0	2	1	10	14
Total	**139**	**12**	**10**	**9**	**5**	**3**	**8**	**5**	**5**	**3**	**5**	**35**	**39**
		8.6%	7.2%	6.5%	3.6%	2.2%	5.8%	3.6%	3.6%	2.2%	3.6%	25.2%	28.1%

Restrictor Plate

	Starts	1st	2nd	3rd	4th	5th	6th	7th	8th	9th	10th	11–20	21–43
Daytona	41	0	1	2	1	2	1	3	5	1	0	10	15
Talladega	41	0	0	0	0	1	3	0	3	1	4	13	16
Total	**82**	**0**	**1**	**2**	**1**	**3**	**4**	**3**	**8**	**2**	**4**	**23**	**31**
		0.0%	1.2%	2.4%	1.2%	3.7%	4.9%	3.7%	9.8%	2.4%	4.9%	28.0%	37.8%

Road Courses

	Starts	1st	2nd	3rd	4th	5th	6th	7th	8th	9th	10th	11–20	21–43
Riverside	10	2	0	0	1	0	0	0	1	0	0	1	5
Sears Point	15	2	1	1	1	3	0	1	1	0	0	1	4
Watkins Glen	18	2	1	2	2	0	2	0	0	0	0	3	6
Total	**43**	**6**	**2**	**3**	**4**	**3**	**2**	**1**	**2**	**0**	**0**	**5**	**15**
		14.0%	4.7%	7.0%	9.3%	7.0%	4.7%	2.3%	4.7%	0.0%	0.0%	11.6%	34.9%

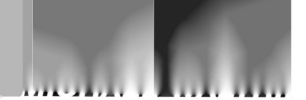

Current Team: Dale Earnhardt Incorporated
Residence: Sherrills Ford, North Carolina
Hometown: Owensboro, Kentucky
Birthday: April 30, 1963
Height: 6 feet, 5 inches
Weight: 210

Races: 570
Running: 456 (80.0 percent)
Accidents: 44 (7.7 percent)
Mechanical Failures: 70 (12.3 percent)

2001–2003	Dale Earnhardt Incorporated
2000	Jim Smith
	Jim Mattei
1999	Jim Mattei
1996–1998	Wood Brothers Racing
1988–1995	Chuck Rider
1985–1987	Dick Bahre

Michael Waltrip

Michael Waltrip has emerged as one of NASCAR's most entertaining figures, both on and off the track. The younger brother of three-time Winston Cup Champion Darrell Waltrip, Michael began his driving career racing karts. By the early 1980s, he was driving modifieds, and in 1982 moved to the Goody's Dash Series, where he won the championship in 1983.

In 1985 he raced in his first Winston Cup event, the prestigious Coca-Cola 600 at Charlotte. Michael held his own (considering he had mechanical problems), starting 24th and finishing 28th in the grueling event. He ran a total of five races that year, and his only trouble-free race was at Michigan, where he finished 18th. The next year Michael ran 28 of the seasons 29 races for Dick Bahre, and while he still did not crack the top 10, he finished in 11th place twice. The next year (1987) Michael scored his first top 10, with a good run at Martinsville. At the end of the year he changed teams and began driving for Chuck Rider.

Every year Michael scored more and more top finishes. In 1995 he finished 12th in the points race, and again switched teams, leaving Chuck Rider for the Wood Brothers Ford. In 1996 Michael finally won an event, the Winston All Star Race and he did it in dramatic fashion. With a hot car, he out-drove the sport's best in the all-out non-points race. Even without a points win, it was a good year for Michael, as he finished the year in 14th place in the points. Michael was out of the Wood Brothers car in 1999 and with a new team, Mattei Motorsports. The results were not good, with Michael scoring only one top five, but he led at a couple of superspeedway races, showing he could run up front.

In 2000 Michael drove for both Mattei and Jim Smith. It was another difficult year for Michael, as he scored only one top five and finished 27th in the points. But things were about to take a swing for the better. One guy thought Michael could win races, and in 2000, friend and fellow driver Dale Earnhardt hired Michael to drive the No. 15 DEI NAPA Chevrolet for the 2001 season. Michael moved into a car fielded by an organization that was becoming one of the best in the business. He started his career with his new team in style—by winning the Daytona 500. While the events of the day made it a somber win, Michael had still won the big one.

In 2002 he started the year winning one of the Gatorade Twin-125 qualifying races, following with a win in Daytona's second race, the Pepsi 400. He finished the year with 10 top 10s and a 14th-place finish in points. Michael's first multiple-win season was 2003, when he again took home the Daytona 500 trophy, with a win at Talladega later in the year.

Michael Waltrip has gone to victory lane four times behind the wheel of his Dale Earnhardt Incorporated NAPA Monte Carlo. He ended his long winless streak with a victory in the 2001 Daytona 500.

From 1986 to 1995, Michael drove General Motors brands (usually Pontiacs) for Chuck Rider's team.

Year-by-year Performance

	Races	Poles		Wins		Top 5		Top 10	
1985	5	0	0.0%	0	0.0%	0	0.0%	0	0.0%
1986	28	0	0.0%	0	0.0%	0	0.0%	0	0.0%
1987	29	0	0.0%	0	0.0%	0	0.0%	1	3.4%
1988	29	0	0.0%	0	0.0%	2	6.9%	3	10.3%
1989	29	0	0.0%	0	0.0%	0	0.0%	5	17.2%
1990	29	0	0.0%	0	0.0%	5	17.2%	10	34.5%
1991	29	2	6.9%	0	0.0%	4	13.8%	12	41.4%
1992	29	0	0.0%	0	0.0%	1	3.4%	2	6.9%
1993	30	0	0.0%	0	0.0%	0	0.0%	5	16.7%
1994	31	0	0.0%	0	0.0%	2	6.5%	10	32.3%
1995	31	0	0.0%	0	0.0%	2	6.5%	8	25.8%
1996	31	0	0.0%	0	0.0%	1	3.2%	11	35.5%
1997	32	0	0.0%	0	0.0%	0	0.0%	6	18.8%
1998	32	0	0.0%	0	0.0%	0	0.0%	5	15.6%
1999	35	0	0.0%	0	0.0%	1	2.9%	3	8.6%
2000	35	0	0.0%	0	0.0%	1	2.9%	1	2.9%
2001	36	0	0.0%	1	2.8%	3	8.3%	3	8.3%
2002	36	0	0.0%	1	2.8%	4	11.1%	10	27.8%
2003	36	0	0.0%	2	5.6%	8	22.2%	11	30.6%
Total	**572**	**2**	**0.3%**	**4**	**0.7%**	**34**	**5.9%**	**106**	**18.5%**

Track Performance

Less than 1 Mile

	Starts	1st	2nd	3rd	4th	5th	6th	7th	8th	9th	10th	11–20	21–4
Bristol	36	0	0	0	0	1	1	1	0	2	1	14	16
Martinsville	36	0	0	1	0	0	0	1	2	0	1	14	17
Richmond	36	0	0	0	0	0	0	0	0	0	0	12	24
N. Wilkes	22	0	0	0	0	0	0	1	0	0	0	9	12
Total	**130**	**0**	**0**	**1**	**0**	**1**	**1**	**3**	**2**	**2**	**2**	**49**	**69**
		0.0%	0.0%	0.8%	0.0%	0.8%	0.8%	2.3%	1.5%	1.5%	1.5%	37.7%	53.1%

1 Mile–1.49 Mile

	Starts	1st	2nd	3rd	4th	5th	6th	7th	8th	9th	10th	11–20	21–4
Dover	36	0	0	0	0	2	1	2	1	1	0	12	1?
New Hamp.	18	0	0	0	0	0	0	1	0	0	1	4	1?
N. Carolina	36	0	0	0	1	0	0	1	0	0	1	18	1?
Phoenix	15	0	0	0	0	1	0	0	0	2	0	3	?
Darlington	37	0	0	1	0	2	0	2	0	3	0	11	1?
Total	**142**	**0**	**0**	**1**	**1**	**5**	**1**	**6**	**1**	**6**	**2**	**48**	**7**
		0.0%	0.0%	0.7%	0.7%	3.5%	0.7%	4.2%	0.7%	4.2%	1.4%	33.8%	50.0

1.5 mile

	Starts	1st	2nd	3rd	4th	5th	6th	7th	8th	9th	10th	11–20	21–4
Charlotte	38	0	0	2	1	0	1	1	2	1	2	14	1
Chicago	3	0	0	0	0	1	0	0	0	0	0	0	
Homestead	5	0	1	0	0	0	0	0	0	0	0	0	
Kansas	3	0	0	0	0	0	0	0	0	0	0	0	
Las Vegas	6	0	0	1	0	0	0	0	0	0	0	2	
Texas	7	0	0	0	0	0	0	0	0	2	0	2	
Total	**62**	**0**	**1**	**3**	**1**	**1**	**1**	**1**	**2**	**3**	**2**	**18**	**2**
		0.0%	1.6%	4.8%	1.6%	1.6%	1.6%	1.6%	3.2%	4.8%	3.2%	29.0%	46.8

188

rack Performance

51 Mile–2.5 Mile

lanta	37	0	0	0	0	1	1	2	0	1	2	12	18
alifornia	7	0	0	0	0	0	0	1	0	0	1	2	3
ichigan	37	0	0	0	1	1	0	2	1	1	0	11	20
dianapolis	10	0	0	0	0	0	0	0	1	0	0	4	5
cono	36	0	1	0	1	0	0	0	1	1	1	19	12
tal	**127**	**0**	**1**	**0**	**2**	**2**	**1**	**5**	**3**	**3**	**4**	**48**	**58**
		0.0%	0.8%	0.0%	1.6%	1.6%	0.8%	3.9%	2.4%	2.4%	3.1%	37.8%	45.7%

strictor Plate

aytona	35	3	1	0	0	2	2	0	1	1	1	8	16
lladega	36	1	1	1	0	3	0	2	1	2	1	8	16
tal	**71**	**4**	**2**	**1**	**0**	**5**	**2**	**2**	**2**	**3**	**2**	**16**	**32**
		5.6%	2.8%	1.4%	0.0%	7.0%	2.8%	2.8%	2.8%	4.2%	2.8%	22.5%	45.1%

ad Courses

verside	5	0	0	0	0	0	0	0	0	0	0	1	4
ears Point	15	0	0	0	0	0	0	1	0	1	4	5	4
atkins Glen	18	0	0	0	1	0	0	1	0	1	1	8	6
tal	**38**	**0**	**0**	**0**	**1**	**0**	**0**	**2**	**0**	**2**	**5**	**14**	**14**
		0.0%	0.0%	0.0%	2.6%	0.0%	0.0%	5.3%	0.0%	5.3%	13.2%	36.8%	36.8%

Rookies

BRENDAN GAUGHAN

KASEY KAHNE

SCOTT RIGGS

BRIAN VICKERS

SCOTT WIMMER

Current Team: Penske/Jasper Racing
Residence: Cornelius, North Carolina
Hometown: Las Vegas, Nevada
Birthday: July 10, 1975
Height: 5 feet, 9 inches
Weight: 190

Brendan Gaughan

Brendan Gaughan's road to NASCAR was a bit different from most other drivers. While most cut their teeth in late models on short tracks, Gaughan learned to race in the wide-open deserts of Nevada. He was born in Las Vegas, where his father took him to the off-road races when he was young. When Brendan saw them, he was hooked. Before he was licensed to drive on the road, he was flying across desert trails.

Throughout most of the 1990s while he was in off-road racing, Brendan worked with Walker Evans Racing, one of the best firms in the business. Before he was done, Gaughan had collected the 1996, 1997, and 1998 SODA World Championships. One of Gaughan's competitors in the desert was future NASCAR winner Jimmie Johnson. But Brendan was more than a good driver. During his tenure at Georgetown University, he was a member of the men's basketball team when they won two Big East regular season championships, and he played in four NCAA tournaments. He was also on Georgetown's football team, earning all-conference honors. Brendan graduated from Georgetown University with a degree in business management, but he wanted to be a racer, so after graduation he was back to the track.

He drove his first Craftsman Truck Series race in 1997. Over the next five years, he drove in 17 truck events. Before going to the trucks full-time, Brendan ran in the Winston West Series, where he won championships in 2000 and 2001. In 2002 he ran 22 Craftsman Truck races and began to show much promise. He finished the year with two wins, both at Texas, and took the Rookie of the Year award. In 2003 it got better. In 25 races, Brendan won six times, and despite an accident not of his making, he very well might have won the Truck Series Championship. In 2003 Brendan was named to drive the No. 77 Jasper car at a time when the Jasper team was merging with Penske Racing. Brendan joined Rusty Wallace and Ryan Newman in a premier Dodge organization.

Brendan Gaughan began his career behind the wheel of a newly reorganized team. The Jasper Motorsports team joined forces with Penske Racing for the 2004 season with Kodak as the new primary sponsor.

Current Team: Evernham Motorsports
Residence: Mooresville, North Carolina
Hometown: Enumclaw, Washington
Birthday: August 10, 1980
Height: 5 feet, 9 inches
Weight: 145

Kasey Kahne

Kasey Kahne's rise to a Nextel Cup driver has been fast both on and off the track. He began racing in micro midgets and mini sprint cars, winning more often than not, and after two seasons of racing had won two championships. By the late 1990s, he had graduated to full-size sprint cars and again proved himself to be a winner.

In 2000 Steve Lewis, the same car owner who had employed Jeff Gordon and Tony Stewart, gave Kasey a ride. Kasey made the most of the opportunity, running the entire USAC schedule, racing a sprint car, a midget, and a Silver Crown car. He won the USAC Midget Series Championship, the USAC Silver Crown Rookie of the Year trophy, and the Driver of the Year award. In 2000 he also drove a few races in the Toyota Atlantic Series, and in 2001 he did the same in the Formula Ford 2000 Series.

Kasey's next major career move was in 2002, when he joined Robert Yates to run a limited Busch schedule. It was a new challenge for Kasey, learning to drive cars that were much heavier than the open-wheel cars he had grown up driving. He gained valuable experience in 2002, running in 20 races, with his best finish a 10th at Michigan. His efforts in 2002 were good enough to land him a full-time Busch Series ride in 2003, this time with Akins Motorsports. Over the season's 34 races, Kasey had 15 top-10 finishes, four top 5s, and his first Busch win, at Homestead. His effort was good enough for a 7th-place finish in the Busch Series Championship.

Late in 2003 it was announced that Kasey would move from the Ford camp to the Dodge camp, and would be in the No. 9 Evernham Dodge for the 2004 Nextel Cup season, taking over for a semi-retired Bill Elliott.

After two tears in the Busch Series, Kasey Kahne took over the driving duties of the No. 9 Evernham Dodge in 2004. He climbed into the seat vacated by the legendary Bill Elliott.

Current Team: MBV Motorsports
Residence: Bahama, North Carolina
Hometown: Bahama, North Carolina
Birthday: January 1, 1971
Height: 5 feet, 6 inches
Weight: 165

Scott Riggs

Scott Riggs will enter the 2004 season as another one of the Nextel Cup's many new talents. But Scott is not new to racing. Over the last 20 years he has evolved from a teen racing motorcycles to a 33-year-old rookie in NASCAR's most elite division. Scott raced motocross in the mid-1980s, wining races and finishing 3rd in an AMA National competition in 1987.

He changed from two wheels to four, and beginning in 1988 he raced in a NASCAR-sanctioned mini-stock division. Through the 1990s he competed primarily in NASCAR late models, continuing to win and gaining experience. In 1999 he got a couple of starts in the Craftsman Truck Series, and the following year Scott was at last going big-time racing. In 2000 he ran 17 of the season's truck races, finishing in the top 10 in eight of the races, with one top 5.

When racing the truck wasn't keeping him busy, he occasionally raced his late-model car, starting four races in 2000 and winning once. In 2001 Scott ran the entire Truck Series, racing in all 24 events. He put all his experience to work, winning five races and four poles and finishing 14 times in the top five. He finished the season in 5th place in points. After 15 years of racing, Scott Riggs was an overnight success. In 2002 he moved to the Busch Series, winning the Rookie of the Year award with two wins and eight top fives in 34 races, and finishing a respectable 10th place in the championship points race. In 2003 he was again in a Busch Series car and added another pair of wins to his resume.

After Scott's 6th-place finish in the points, it was announced that he would be the new driver at MBV Motorsports for the 2004 season. At the age of 33, Scott begins his rookie year in the Nextel Cup Series.

Scott Riggs won five times in the Craftsman Truck Series, four times in the Busch Series, and now tests his skill in the Nextel Cup Series. He is behind the wheel of owner James Rocco's Valvoline Chevrolet.

BRIAN VICKERS

Brian Vickers

Current Team: Hendrick Motorsports
Residence: Thomasville, North Carolina
Hometown: Thomasville, North Carolina
Birthday: October 24, 1983
Height: 5 feet, 11 inches
Weight: 160

Brian was born in North Carolina, in the heart of the professional stock car community. He began racing karts at age nine and quickly proved his ability to drive. By the mid-1990s he was a three-time World Karting Association national champion and a four-time state champion. Brian was equally good at racing on dirt or paved tracks.

Brian then graduated to the Allison Legacy Car Series, and won five races in 1998. The next year he competed in NASCAR late models and won six times. In 2000 he ran in the USAR Hooter's Pro Cup Series and became their youngest-ever Rookie of the Year. He ran the series again in 2001, finishing second in points. In 2001 he also began his Busch Series career, starting four races in a family-owned car. His schedule expanded to 21 Busch races in 2002, finishing the year with a single top 10. In 2002 Brian graduated from high school and it wasn't long before he landed a top job. In

December of that year, he joined forces with Hendrick Motorsports, and 2003 was a break-out year for Brian. He ran the entire Busch Series schedule for the first time and became the youngest champion in the series history. In 34 races, he won three times, finished in the top five 13 times, and in the top ten 21 times. It was Hendrick Motorsports' first Busch Series Championship. Brian's great year did not go unrewarded. In 2003 he started five Winston Cup races, and it was announced that he would drive the entire schedule in 2004 in a Hendrick Motorsports Chevrolet.

Brian graduated to NASCAR's highest division late in 2003, driving in five of the last six races of the season. He is set to run the entire 2004 season for Rick Hendrick.

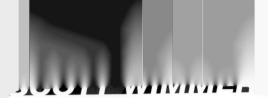

Scott Wimmer

Current Team: Bill Davis Racing
Residence: High Point, North Carolina
Hometown: Wausau, Wisconsin
Birthday: January 26, 1976
Height: 6 feet
Weight: 180

Scott Wimmer began off-road racing on three-wheelers, and at the age of nine finished 2nd in the National Amateur Off-Road Championship. He began racing cars at the Wausau Speedway in 1991 when he was 15 years old. By 1994 he was traveling to tracks all over Wisconsin. Scott raced whenever he could, and it kept him busy. In 1996 he ran 97 races, winning nine of them and finishing 68 times in the top 10.

By 1997 he was racing in the Hooter's Late Model Series, where he won Rookie of the Year. In 1998 he ran in the Hooter's Pro Cup Series and took home another Rookie of the Year award. He ran the series again in 1999 before graduating to the ASA Series in 2000. He won the first two ASA races that he entered and at season's end finished 2nd in the Rookie of the Year. By 2001 he was ready to take the next step and run the Busch Series. He had run three Busch Series races in 2000 for Bill Davis Racing, and in 2001 ran the entire schedule. Together, Davis and Wimmer ended the year with two top 5s, eight top 10s, an 11th-place finish in the Busch Series point race, and a 2nd place in the Rookie of the Year honors.

In 2002 Scott returned to the Busch Series, and this time broke into victory lane, winning four times with 11 top fives. He finished in the top ten in half of the seasons races, and finished 3rd in points. The year 2003 yielded one more win in the Busch Series, but also presented Scott with his next opportunity. It was announced late in the season that Scott would be driving for a winning team, as he was slated to drive for Davis' Winston Cup team. Scott had driven in a handful of Cup events in 2002, and he drove in the last six races of 2003, scoring one top 10 at Phoenix International Raceway. He also finished 12th in the season-ending race at Homestead.

Beginning in 2000, Scott Wimmer began driving the occasional Winston Cup race for Bill Davis Racing. Late in 2003 he was awarded a full-time ride and will run his first complete Cup schedule in 2004.

Modern Era

Greats

ERNIE IRVAN
BOBBY ISAAC
ALAN KULWICKI
FRED LORENZEN
BENNY PARSONS
DAVID PEARSON
RICHARD PETTY
TIM RICHMOND
DARRELL WALTRIP
CALE YARBOROUGH

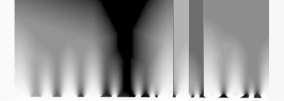

Only a few drivers have more wins than Bobby Allison, and probably no other driver has had the combination of driving talent and mechanical and engineering ability that he did. Throughout his career, he was one of the sports greatest in the building and setting up of race cars.

Bobby Allison was born on December 3, 1937, in Miami, Florida, although he now calls Hueytown, Alabama, his hometown. Bobby came from a large family and was the fourth of 10 children. He started racing a car he prepared himself while he was still going to high school, and in his first race, with the track packed with over 50 cars, Bobby drove to a 10th-place finish. However, it appeared that his career might end as quickly as it began. Bobby had to stop racing on his father's orders after flipping his car twice in a race.

When he wasn't racing, Bobby was involved in anything mechanical, even making money behind the wheel as a test driver for Mercury Marine. It was here that he met many of the people who would help him get back into racing. After leaving Mercury, Bobby worked as a mechanic and garage owner before returning to driving. While a mechanic, Bobby was still around race cars and he could not resist the urge to get back behind the wheel. When he resumed his driving career, he drove under the alias Bob Sunderman, so his parents wouldn't know. His first big win came at a track in Montgomery, Alabama, in 1959.

Bobby was running modifieds, and in 1961 he tried a couple of Grand National races. Still, before he made the move to the top ranks full-time, he stayed in modifieds, honing his driving skills in the tough Alabama Modified and Sportsman circuits. He won his first national NASCAR Modified Special Crown in 1962, won it again in 1963, and in 1964 won NASCAR's Modified

Crown. In 1966 he built his own car and went Grand National racing full-time. During the 1966 season, he came into the spotlight as an aggressive competitor, ensuring much better rides from 1967 on. His first win in NASCAR's highest level came in 1966 at Oxford Plains Speedway, driving a Chevrolet he prepared himself. He added two more wins that year and six more in 1967.

For the next two decades, he was one of the winningest drivers in the sport. Throughout his career, Bobby was either driving for a top team or in a car he built himself. He drove for Holman-Moody, Junior Johnson, Roger Penske, Bud Moore, DiGard Racing, and the Stavola Brothers. While Bobby was primarily a stock car racer, he also raced on the SCCA's Trans-Am Series, and in 1973 he raced in the Indianapolis 500. His driving was not his only contribution to the sport, as he engineered many of the systems still used on the race car, and he was one of the first to campaign an independent Chevrolet Chevelle against the factory teams.

His career achievements include 84 official Winston Cup victories, being voted the Most Popular Driver for NASCAR's Winston Cup division six times, winning the 1983 Winston Cup Championship, three Daytona 500s, the 1980 IROC Championship, and he was the only Ford Winner from 1978 to 1980.

Like many other drivers, Allison drove a winged Dodge during the 1970 season. In some of the year's races, he drove a car owned by Mario Rossi and in some he competed in a car he owned.

In 1982, Allison began driving for DiGard
Racing and the results were impressive.
From 1982 to 1984, the DiGard team
racked up 16 wins.

Year-by-year Performance

	Races	Wins		Top 5		Top 10	
1961	4	0	0.0%	0	0.0%	0	0.0%
1965	8	0	0.0%	0	0.0%	3	37.5%
1966	34	3	8.8%	10	29.4%	15	44.1%
1967	45	6	13.3%	21	46.7%	27	60.0%
1968	37	2	5.4%	16	43.2%	20	54.1%
1969	27	5	18.5%	13	48.1%	15	55.6%
1970	46	3	6.5%	30	65.2%	35	76.1%
1971	40	10	25.0%	27	67.5%	29	72.5%
1972	31	10	32.3%	25	80.6%	27	87.1%
1973	27	2	7.4%	15	55.6%	16	59.3%
1974	27	2	7.4%	17	63.0%	17	63.0%
1975	19	3	15.8%	10	52.6%	10	52.6%
1976	30	0	0.0%	10	33.3%	15	50.0%
1977	30	0	0.0%	10	33.3%	15	50.0%
1978	30	5	16.7%	14	46.7%	22	73.3%
1979	31	5	16.1%	18	58.1%	22	71.0%
1980	31	4	12.9%	12	38.7%	18	58.1%
1981	31	5	16.1%	21	67.7%	26	83.9%
1982	30	8	26.7%	14	46.7%	20	66.7%
1983	30	6	20.0%	18	60.0%	25	83.3%
1984	30	2	6.7%	13	43.3%	19	63.3%
1985	28	0	0.0%	7	25.0%	11	39.3%
1986	29	1	3.4%	6	20.7%	15	51.7%
1987	29	1	3.4%	4	13.8%	13	44.8%
1988	13	1	7.7%	3	23.1%	6	46.2%
Total	**717**	**84**	**11.7%**	**334**	**46.6%**	**441**	**61.5%**

Davey Allison was perhaps the first of the modern-style rookies. After running a handful of races in 1985 and 1986, he burst onto the scene in 1987 driving 22 races for Harry Ranier, capturing two victories and taking home five poles and ten top 10s.

Davey Allison was one of the fastest risers in the history of the sport. Davey was born on February 25, 1961, the son of racing legend Bobby Allison, and naturally he grew up around racing. His first experience came from working at his dad's shop after school and at night. His behind-the-wheel career began in 1979 at Birmingham International Raceway, where he finished 5th in his first feature race. He won later that year in his 6th start.

On his way to the Winston Cup, he won over 40 races in ARCA, All-Pro, DIRT, ASA, NASCAR Winston West, Busch Grand National, Grand American, and the Dash Series. In 1984 he won two ARCA races, finished second in the ARCA points, and won Rookie of the Year honors. Davey ran his first Winston Cup race at Talladega in 1985, finishing 10th in Hoss Ellington's Chevrolet (he also ran in two more Winston Cup events that season). In 1986 he ran five races and added another top-10 finish. In 1987 Davey teamed up with crew chief Joey Knuckles in the Ranier/Lundy Ford, driving in 22 of the season's races.

In 1987 at Talladega, he drove to his first win, following with another win later that year in Dover. His efforts resulted in his winning the 1987 Rookie of the Year honors. Davey won two races in 1988, 1989, and 1990, but during this period his most memorable moment was a father-son duel in the 1988 Daytona 500. Bobby won the race, and Davey finished a close second.

The team for which Davey was driving was bought out, and suddenly Davey was racing for Robert Yates. It turned out to be a good match. In 1991 Davey won five races, and he repeated the feat in 1992. Davey was fast on the big tracks—two of his 1992 wins came in the Daytona 500 and the Winston 500. He won three other races, but spent much of the year banged up with injuries he suffered in crashes at Bristol and Pocono. A wreck in the final race at Atlanta, caused by another driver, cost Davey a shot at the 1992 Winston Cup Championship.

Davey Allison was killed in a helicopter crash at the Talladega Superspeedway halfway through the 1993 season. In his short career, he won 19 NASCAR Winston Cup races and drove to 14 poles.

In 1989, the No. 28 car became owned by Robert Yates, but the ownership change did not faze Davey as he continued to win multiple races every year. Here, he prepares to run the high banks of Bristol.

Year-by-year Performance

	Races	Wins		Top 5		Top 10	
1985	3	0	0.0%	0	0.0%	1	33.3%
1986	5	0	0.0%	0	0.0%	1	20.0%
1987	22	2	9.1%	9	40.9%	10	45.5%
1988	29	2	6.9%	12	41.4%	16	55.2%
1989	29	2	6.9%	7	24.1%	13	44.8%
1990	29	2	6.9%	5	17.2%	10	34.5%
1991	29	5	17.2%	12	41.4%	16	55.2%
1992	29	5	17.2%	15	51.7%	17	58.6%
1993	16	1	6.3%	6	37.5%	8	50.0%
Total	**191**	**19**	**9.9%**	**66**	**34.6%**	**92**	**48.2%**

Donnie Allison, younger brother to Bobby, had a career that spanned 20 years and resulted in 10 wins and 115 top-10 finishes in 242 starts.

When he was a youngster, Donnie Allison wanted to race—not in cars, but on horses. He was born September 7, 1939, in Miami, and grew up wanting to be a jockey until he finally outgrew it, size-wise. An all-around good athlete, by the age of 15, Donnie had won both swimming and diving championships.

Ironically, the younger brother of racing legend Bobby Allison was not interested in racing— that is, until Bobby began his career. One night while accompanying his brother to the track, Donnie convinced a local car owner to let him drive his race car for the night. He ran the car faster than the regular driver, and in that moment his racing career began. Throughout his career, Donnie drove just about everything with wheels. He raced in modifieds, late models, Busch cars, Winston Cup cars, IROC, Indy cars, and winged super modifieds.

In 1966 Donnie began his Grand National career with a 9th-place finish at Rockingham. Donnie also won the 1967 Rookie of the Year trophy. In 1970 Donnie entered the racing history books by finishing 4th in the

Indianapolis 500, earning the Indy Rookie of the Year award. He then won the World 600 at Charlotte Motor Speedway, all in the same weekend. Donnie raced in Winston Cup from 1966 to 1988, driving for many of the best teams in racing, including Hoss Ellington, Banjo Mathews, Herb Nab, and the Wood Brothers.

In 242 starts, he has 10 wins, 78 top 5s, and 115 top 10s. He won 17 poles (15 of them on superspeedways). He was always a threat on the fast tracks in his mostly part-time career. He won the World 600 and the National 500 at Charlotte Motor Speedway, the Firecracker 400 at Daytona, a 125-mile qualifying race at Daytona, the Atlanta Journal 500 at Atlanta, and both the Winston Select 500 and the Die Hard 500 at Talladega.

Donnie has held many jobs other than driver in his racing career. He has been a crew chief for his son-in-law, Hut Stricklin, and also for Joe Nemechek. He has been employed as a team manager for Winston Cup, Busch Grand National, and Craftsman Truck teams; a crew chief for Winston Cup and Busch Grand National teams; and a driver consultant. He has also been an announcer for ABC, CBS, and various radio stations.

Much of Donnie's early success came behind the wheel of a big-block Mercury prepared by Banjo Mathews. Here, he battles for position with his brother Bobby, who is driving a self-owned Dodge. From 1968 to 1970, Donnie won five times behind the wheel of his Mercury.

Year-by-year Performance

	Races	Wins		Top 5		Top 10	
1966	1	0	0.0%	0	0.0%	1	100.0%
1967	20	0	0.0%	4	20.0%	7	35.0%
1968	13	1	7.7%	5	38.5%	8	61.5%
1969	16	1	6.3%	10	62.5%	11	68.8%
1970	19	3	15.8%	10	52.6%	12	63.2%
1971	13	1	7.7%	7	53.8%	9	69.2%
1972	10	0	0.0%	2	20.0%	3	30.0%
1973	14	0	0.0%	2	14.3%	5	35.7%
1974	21	0	0.0%	6	28.6%	10	47.6%
1975	14	0	0.0%	3	21.4%	6	42.9%
1976	9	1	11.1%	2	22.2%	5	55.6%
1977	17	2	11.8%	9	52.9%	10	58.8%
1978	17	1	5.9%	7	41.2%	8	47.1%
1979	20	0	0.0%	7	35.0%	10	50.0%
1980	18	0	0.0%	3	16.7%	6	33.3%
1981	6	0	0.0%	1	16.7%	1	16.7%
1982	9	0	0.0%	0	0.0%	3	33.3%
1983	3	0	0.0%	0	0.0%	0	0.0%
1986	1	0	0.0%	0	0.0%	0	0.0%
1988	1	0	0.0%	0	0.0%	0	0.0%
Total	**242**	**10**	**4.1%**	**78**	**32.2%**	**115**	**47.5%**

Buck Baker was a fixture in the NASCAR circuit from its first year until well into the Winston Cup era. He had 46 wins and finished in the top 10 in well over half of the 600-plus races that he drove in.

Buck Baker was born in Hartville, South Carolina, in 1919. In 1939 he began a racing career that ran from the first year of NASCAR all the way to the Modern Era. Buck drove modifieds, but also had a great interest in Indy cars. Before making a career of racing, Buck was a sailor during World War II, and he had another driving career: piloting Greyhound buses.

In the early years of NASCAR, Buck was one of the most dominant racers on the circuit. Buck worked to stay in shape by squeezing rubber balls while watching TV—sitting in a bucket seat with a steering wheel attached. While he was a bus driver in Charlotte, North Carolina, Buck attended his first stock car race. Buck figured he could be a driver because he had driven most of his life, and on the track it was all one-way traffic. In his first race a tire came off, and he was lucky to get off the track. Although it was a rough start, Baker went on to become one of the greatest drivers in NASCAR history.

He won the Grand National (now Nextel Cup) Championship in 1956 and 1957. He was second in the final point standings twice, in 1955 and 1958, and in four other years placed among the top five. Baker had 682 NASCAR starts, and his 46 wins place him 13th on the all-time victory list. He won the coveted Southern 500 at Darlington Raceway three times, in 1953, 1960, and 1964. By 1967 Buck had changed series and was driving in NASCAR's Grand American division, where he was also very successful. In 1972, for example, he made an astounding 109 starts and won eight times. Buck continued to drive occasionally well into the late 1970s.

Buck began his career when the sport was barely organized and the action on the track was often chaotic. In this photo, he is holding hard on the brakes in the No. 7 car on the far right.

In 1956, Baker won 14 races driving Dodges and Chryslers for Carl Kiekhaefer. Here, he makes an outside move in the No. 300 car at the Ashville-Weaverville Speedway; however, a broken spindle would cost him a chance at victory on this day.

Year-by-year Performance

	Races	Wins		Top 5		Top 10	
1949	2	0	0.0%	0	0.0%	0	0.0%
1950	9	0	0.0%	2	22.2%	5	55.6%
1951	11	0	0.0%	4	36.4%	5	45.5%
1952	14	1	7.1%	3	21.4%	6	42.9%
1953	33	4	12.1%	16	48.5%	26	78.8%
1954	34	4	11.8%	23	67.6%	28	82.4%
1955	42	3	7.1%	25	59.5%	34	81.0%
1956	48	14	29.2%	31	64.6%	39	81.3%
1957	40	10	25.0%	30	75.0%	39	97.5%
1958	44	3	6.8%	23	52.3%	35	79.5%
1959	35	1	2.9%	14	40.0%	19	54.3%
1960	37	2	5.4%	15	40.5%	24	64.9%
1961	42	1	2.4%	11	26.2%	15	35.7%
1962	37	0	0.0%	6	16.2%	14	37.8%
1963	46	1	2.2%	17	37.0%	30	65.2%
1964	34	2	5.9%	15	44.1%	18	52.9%
1965	31	0	0.0%	2	6.5%	12	38.7%
1966	34	0	0.0%	7	20.6%	14	41.2%
1967	20	0	0.0%	0	0.0%	5	25.0%
1968	17	0	0.0%	1	5.9%	3	17.6%
Total	**610**	**46**	**7.5%**	**245**	**40.2%**	**371**	**60.8%**

Like his father Buck, Buddy Baker saw great changes in the sport of auto racing over the course of his career. He began racing in 1959 when the cars were mainly stock and ended his career in 1992, when the cars were hand-crafted racing machines. In more than 33 years behind the wheel, Buddy won 19 events in NASCAR's highest division.

Buddy Baker was born January 25, 1941, in Florence, South Carolina, son of racing great Buck Baker. Not surprisingly, Buddy also decided to be a race car driver. He pretty much grew up in the garages and pits and entered his first race in 1958 at the age of 17. At 6 foot, 5 inches tall, and weighing 215 pounds, Buddy was not hard to notice at the track.

When he wasn't racing, he concentrated on tire testing, learning about setups, and running fast in the turns like his father. He carefully studied the moves of great racers like his dad and "Fireball" Roberts, and he

In the late 1960s, Buddy was behind the wheel of Ray Fox's Dodge. He won twice for that team before leaving in 1969.

worked hard to be precise and to drive as well as they did. He would set his car up like his father's, and then follow his father's line around the track. But Buck always worked to make the car last and finish the race, while Buddy was mostly a hard charger, always running the car to the edge of its limits. As a result, he was one of the most popular drivers with the fans. In the long run, studying and charging paid off for Buddy.

His first racing ride was in the now-defunct convertible division at Columbia, South Carolina. He got his first win in NASCAR Winston Cup and moved into the top echelon of drivers in 1967, when he took the checkered flag at the National 500 at Charlotte Motor Speedway. On March 24, 1970, while testing his famous blue Dodge Daytona for the first running of the Alabama 500 at the Talladega Superspeedway, Buddy set a world closed-course record by running a 200.447-mile-per-hour lap around the 2.66-mile track. He was the first driver to exceed 200 miles per hour on a closed course. Buddy became one of the best on the highest-speed tracks, Daytona and Talladega, winning on them with regularity. He won the Winston 500 in 1975, 1976, and 1980; the Talladega 500 in 1975; the Daytona 500 in 1980; and the Firecracker 400 in 1983.

NASCAR credits Buddy with 688 Winston Cup career starts, resulting in 40 poles, 19 wins, 198 top 5s, and 299 top 10s. The popularity Buddy generated with fans followed him when he left racing, and after retiring from the Winston Cup circuit, he became one of motorsport's most prominent stock car commentators.

In 1971, he drove 18 races for Petty Enterprises, winning one of those events.

Year-by-year Performance

	Races	Wins		Top 5		Top 10	
1959	12	0	0.0%	1	8.3%	5	41.7%
1960	15	0	0.0%	0	0.0%	1	6.7%
1961	14	0	0.0%	1	7.1%	3	21.4%
1962	31	0	0.0%	5	16.1%	10	32.3%
1963	8	0	0.0%	1	12.5%	2	25.0%
1964	32	0	0.0%	3	9.4%	7	21.9%
1965	42	0	0.0%	12	28.6%	17	40.5%
1966	41	0	0.0%	1	2.4%	7	17.1%
1967	21	1	4.8%	6	28.6%	7	33.3%
1968	38	1	2.6%	16	42.1%	18	47.4%
1969	18	0	0.0%	9	50.0%	11	61.1%
1970	18	1	5.6%	6	33.3%	8	44.4%
1971	19	1	5.3%	13	68.4%	16	84.2%
1972	17	2	11.8%	8	47.1%	9	52.9%
1973	27	2	7.4%	16	59.3%	20	74.1%
1974	19	0	0.0%	11	57.9%	12	63.2%
1975	23	4	17.4%	12	52.2%	13	56.5%
1976	30	1	3.3%	16	53.3%	16	53.3%
1977	19	0	0.0%	4	21.1%	8	42.1%
1978	19	0	0.0%	4	21.1%	8	42.1%
1979	26	3	11.5%	12	46.2%	15	57.7%
1980	19	2	10.5%	10	52.6%	12	63.2%
1981	16	0	0.0%	6	37.5%	9	56.3%
1982	23	0	0.0%	4	17.4%	11	47.8%
1983	21	1	4.8%	6	28.6%	12	57.1%
1984	21	0	0.0%	4	19.0%	12	57.1%
1985	28	0	0.0%	2	7.1%	7	25.0%
1986	17	0	0.0%	6	35.3%	6	35.3%
1987	20	0	0.0%	3	15.0%	10	50.0%
1988	17	0	0.0%	0	0.0%	7	41.2%
1990	8	0	0.0%	0	0.0%	0	0.0%
1991	6	0	0.0%	0	0.0%	0	0.0%
1992	3	0	0.0%	0	0.0%	0	0.0%
Total	**688**	**19**	**2.8%**	**198**	**28.8%**	**299**	**43.5%**

Geoffrey Bodine has enjoyed the stress-filled life of the modern stock car driver. Bodine began his career in 1979 and will still occasionally climb into a Nextel Cup car. Through the years, he has racked up 18 wins and 100 top-five finishes.

Geoffrey Bodine hails from Chemung, New York, where he was born on April 18, 1949. A year after he was born, his father and grandfather built Chemung Speedrome when local drivers persuaded the Bodines to convert a cornfield into a racetrack. Geoff pretty much grew up at the track, and it served as the roots of his racing career. When Geoffrey wasn't working on the family farm, he was working at the track.

His racing career began in the mid-1950s driving micro midgets at—where else—Chemung Speedrome. Geoffrey moved from the midgets to modifieds, where he enjoyed great success. He won on both dirt and asphalt, and in one year won an amazing 55 races. In 1977 he finished second in the national modified standings. Geoffrey got his first Winston Cup start in 1979, driving in three races for Jack Beebe. In 1981 he ran five races, two for Dick Bahre and three for Emanuel Zervakis. His first true Winston Cup effort was in 1982, when he ran 25 races (24 of them for Cliff Stewart) in his rookie year. He ended the season with four top 5s and 10 top 10s and won the pole for the Firecracker 400 at Daytona in only his 19th start. His efforts were rewarded when he took home the Rookie of the Year award. It was also in 1982 that Geoffrey began his Busch Series career.

Throughout his career, he ran in both the Winston Cup Series and the Busch Series, where he accumulated six wins. His first Winston Cup win came in 1984 at Martinsville, in his 69th start, driving for Rick Hendrick. He added wins at Nashville and Riverside later in the year. Geoffrey began 1986 in style, winning the Daytona 500 in one of Rick Hendricks' Chevrolets. Throughout the rest of the 1980s and well into the 1990s, Geoffrey was a consistent winner on the Cup circuit. In 1990 he began driving for Junior Johnson and finished third, his personal best, in the Winston Cup Championship. In 1992 he left Junior to drive for Bud Moore.

After two years with Moore, Geoffrey became an owner-driver when he bought the late Alan Kulwicki's team, and he won three races and five poles. He owned his own team until he began driving for Jim Mattei in 1998 and Joe Bessy in 1999. During the next few years, he made a handful of starts each for different owners. When he had a good car, he was still competitive—which he proved by finishing 3rd in the 2002 Daytona 500. Throughout his career, Geoffrey proved himself to be a versatile racer, winning on short tracks, superspeedways, and road courses.

In 1994, Geoffrey decided to control his own destiny when he became an owner-driver. Over a three-year period, he won four races, but by 1998 he was back driving for another owner—Jim Mattei.

Year-by-year Performance

	Races	Wins		Top 5		Top 10	
1979	3	0	0.0%	0	0.0%	0	0.0%
1981	5	0	0.0%	0	0.0%	1	20.0%
1982	25	0	0.0%	4	16.0%	10	40.0%
1983	28	0	0.0%	5	17.9%	9	32.1%
1984	30	3	10.0%	7	23.3%	14	46.7%
1985	28	0	0.0%	10	35.7%	14	50.0%
1986	29	2	6.9%	10	34.5%	15	51.7%
1987	29	0	0.0%	3	10.3%	10	34.5%
1988	29	1	3.4%	10	34.5%	16	55.2%
1989	29	1	3.4%	9	31.0%	11	37.9%
1990	29	3	10.3%	11	37.9%	19	65.5%
1991	27	1	3.7%	6	22.2%	12	44.4%
1992	29	2	6.9%	7	24.1%	11	37.9%
1993	30	1	3.3%	2	6.7%	9	30.0%
1994	31	3	9.7%	7	22.6%	10	32.3%
1995	31	0	0.0%	1	3.2%	4	12.9%
1996	31	1	3.2%	2	6.5%	6	19.4%
1997	29	0	0.0%	3	10.3%	10	34.5%
1998	32	0	0.0%	1	3.1%	5	15.6%
1999	34	0	0.0%	1	2.9%	2	5.9%
2000	14	0	0.0%	0	0.0%	0	0.0%
2001	2	0	0.0%	0	0.0%	0	0.0%
2002	10	0	0.0%	1	10.0%	2	20.0%
2003	1	0	0.0%	0	0.0%	0	0.0%
Total	**565**	**18**	**3.2%**	**100**	**17.7%**	**190**	**33.6%**

Neil Bonnett started his career in 1974 when he drove in two races at Talladega. He soon began expanding his schedule and in 1977 drove in 23 races, winning two of them. His last win was this one at Rockingham in 1988.

Born in Bessemer, Alabama, on July 30, 1946, Neil Bonnett was the youngest member of the famed "Alabama Gang." He began racing in the cadet division at Montgomery, Alabama, in April 1969, and his first feature win came two months later at Birmingham International Raceway. Bonnett started racing on the short tracks near his hometown of Hueytown, Alabama, and he won everything in sight, including 80 percent of his starts in 1972. After cutting his teeth on short tracks and learning from Bobby Allison along the way, he moved to the Winston Cup circuit in 1974. He won his first Winston Cup pole at Nashville in 1976 and won his first race at Richmond in 1977.

During his career, he won several high-profile races, including the 1980 Talladega 500 and the Southern 500 in 1981, and captured victories at Charlotte and Daytona. During his career, he drove for legendary car owners such as the Wood Brothers, Junior Johnson, and Richard Childress. An accident at Darlington in 1990 interrupted Bonnett's racing career and forced him into a lengthy period of rehabilitation. During this time, he became one of the best color commentators in sports and hosted a weekly TV show, (*Winners on TNN*). While Bonnett was excellent in the broadcast booth, he still yearned to drive a race car. He received clearance from the doctors to begin testing race cars, and on July 25, 1993, Bonnett resumed his Winston Cup career at his "home" track, Talladega. Unfortunately, his comeback did not last long. On February 11, 1994, Bonnett was killed in a single-car crash during a practice session at Daytona International Speedway.

Throughout his career Neil was one of the most popular drivers on the circuit, partly because of his heavy right foot, but also because of his personality. He was always accessible and friendly, usually adding humor to a situation. Neil Bonnett excelled in everything he did. In addition to being a NASCAR Winston Cup star and an accomplished television broadcaster, he was a top-notch hunter and fisherman. Bonnett finished his Winston Cup career with 16 victories.

(right) In 1979, Neil began driving for the Wood Brothers. In a four-year partnership, they put together nine victories. He would rejoin the team in 1989 and would run another 31 races in the famed team's car.

(below) From 1984 through 1986, Neil piloted Junior Johnson's Chevrolet and captured three wins.

Year-by-year Performance

	Races	Wins		Top 5		Top 10	
1974	2	0	0.0%	0	0.0%	0	0.0%
1975	2	0	0.0%	0	0.0%	0	0.0%
1976	13	0	0.0%	1	7.7%	4	30.8%
1977	23	0	0.0%	5	21.7%	9	39.1%
1978	30	0	0.0%	7	23.3%	12	40.0%
1979	21	3	14.3%	4	19.0%	6	28.6%
1980	22	2	9.1%	10	45.5%	13	59.1%
1981	22	3	13.6%	7	31.8%	8	36.4%
1982	25	1	4.0%	7	28.0%	10	40.0%
1983	30	2	6.7%	10	33.3%	17	56.7%
1984	30	0	0.0%	7	23.3%	14	46.7%
1985	28	2	7.1%	11	39.3%	18	64.3%
1986	28	1	3.6%	6	21.4%	12	42.9%
1987	26	0	0.0%	5	19.2%	15	57.7%
1988	27	2	7.4%	3	11.1%	7	25.9%
1989	26	0	0.0%	0	0.0%	11	42.3%
1990	5	0	0.0%	0	0.0%	0	0.0%
1993	2	0	0.0%	0	0.0%	0	0.0%
Total	**322**	**16**	**5.0%**	**77**	**23.9%**	**143**	**44.4%**

Dale Earnhardt was one driver who truly captured the hearts of fans and the attention of his competitors. While he was a skilled and calculating driver, he carried himself like a modern-day gun-fighter with a Chevrolet in his holster.

Any discussion of the greatest all-time drivers cannot go far without mentioning Dale Earnhardt. His hard-charging driving style combined with a cocky attitude, which he backed up on the track, made him one of the most-loved drivers in the sport's history. He was born April 29, 1951, in Kannapolis, North Carolina. As the son of Ralph Earnhardt, Dale was born into a racing environment, but he had to earn his own way in the sport.

He drove the short tracks of North Carolina, working at odd jobs to keep his racing effort alive. In 1975 Dale started his first Winston Cup race, driving a Dodge for Ed Negre at Charlotte Motor Speedway. Dale finished the race in 22nd position (ironically the 23rd-place finisher was Richard Childress). Over the next few years, Dale ran a handful of Cup races for various owners before he got his first big break. It was Rod Osterland who was impressed with a young Dale Earnhardt and backed his first true Winston Cup effort. In 1979 Dale drove in 27 races for Osterland, and in the 16th race of the year won his first race, the famed Southern 500 at Darlington. His phenomenal rookie year ended in a 7th-place finish in the Winston Cup points and Rookie of the Year honors.

The next year Dale followed with an even more impressive effort, winning five races and running in the top 10 in 24 of the season's 31 races. It was good enough to win Earnhardt the first of his seven Winston Cup Championships. In doing so he became the first driver to win the Rookie of the Year and the Winston Cup Championship in consecutive years. Dale stayed with Osterland until 1981, also driving part-time for Jim Stacy and Richard Childress that year. In 1982 Dale began a two-year run with Bud Moore. He still ran well, but it was his next career move that was to provide him with a permanent home.

In 1984 he joined Richard Childress on a full-time basis, and the two never looked back. They won twice in their first year together, and with the exception of 1997, they won every year that they were together. In 1986 they won five races and their first championship (Dale's second). The next year they won 11 races and another championship. In 1990 and 1991, they won back-to-back championships, and in 1993 and 1994 they did the same. Dale finished in the top eight in the point standings in every year from 1979 to 2000, with the exception of 1982 and 1992, when he finished 12th.

Dale never peaked in the sport, because his whole career was a peak. Through a quarter-century of Winston Cup racing, he was always a threat to win races and championships. When his life ended on the high banks of Daytona in 2001, he had amassed 76 wins and had finished second 70 times. His total of seven championships is only matched by Richard Petty, and by no one in the Modern Era of NASCAR racing.

In 1984, Earnhardt joined Richard Childress Racing and would never leave. While driving for Richard Childress, he won 67 times and became the Winston Cup champion six times.

While he took a while to win at Daytona, Dale did not have a problem winning at other restrictor-plate tracks. He often dominated at Talladega, where he captured the checkered flag 10 times in 44 attempts.

Year-by-year Performance

	Races	Wins		Top 5		Top 10	
1975	1	0	0.0%	0	0.0%	0	0.0%
1976	2	0	0.0%	0	0.0%	0	0.0%
1977	1	0	0.0%	0	0.0%	0	0.0%
1978	5	0	0.0%	1	20.0%	2	40.0%
1979	27	1	3.7%	11	40.7%	17	63.0%
1980	31	5	16.1%	19	61.3%	24	77.4%
1981	31	0	0.0%	9	29.0%	17	54.8%
1982	30	1	3.3%	7	23.3%	12	40.0%
1983	30	2	6.7%	9	30.0%	14	46.7%
1984	30	2	6.7%	12	40.0%	22	73.3%
1985	28	4	14.3%	10	35.7%	16	57.1%
1986	29	5	17.2%	16	55.2%	23	79.3%
1987	29	11	37.9%	21	72.4%	24	82.8%
1988	29	3	10.3%	13	44.8%	19	65.5%
1989	29	5	17.2%	14	48.3%	19	65.5%
1990	29	9	31.0%	18	62.1%	23	79.3%
1991	29	4	13.8%	14	48.3%	21	72.4%
1992	29	1	3.4%	6	20.7%	15	51.7%
1993	30	6	20.0%	17	56.7%	21	70.0%
1994	31	4	12.9%	20	64.5%	25	80.6%
1995	31	5	16.1%	19	61.3%	23	74.2%
1996	31	2	6.5%	13	41.9%	17	54.8%
1997	32	0	0.0%	7	21.9%	16	50.0%
1998	33	1	3.0%	5	15.2%	13	39.4%
1999	34	3	8.8%	7	20.6%	21	61.8%
2000	34	2	5.9%	13	38.2%	24	70.6%
2001	1	0	0.0%	0	0.0%	0	0.0%
Total	**672**	**76**	**11.3%**	**281**	**41.8%**	**428**	**63.7%**

Few names in racing are as recognizable as that of A. J. Foyt. Whether he was in an Indy car, a road racing car, or a stock car, he was always a threat to win.

Anthony Joseph Foyt was born on January 16, 1935, in Houston, Texas. As the son of a race car driver, he was destined to race. Few drivers have had as impressive a career as A. J. Primarily known as an Indy car racer, A. J. drove just about anything, and he could win in just about anything, from USAC dirt to the Indianapolis 500. He could change race cars as easily as most of us can change shoes. During his "part-time" NASCAR career, A. J. won seven Winston Cup races, including the 1972 Daytona 500. While he will always be remembered first for his Indy car record, we can only wonder how great a stock car racer he could have been, had he driven NASCAR full-time.

Foyt decided at an early age that he wanted to drive a race car, and by the time he was 18, he was winning on Midwestern racing circuits. He went from there to sprint cars and then on to Indy cars, quickly becoming a winner. He won the Indy 500 for the first time in 1961, at the age of 26. He won again in 1964 and 1967, and became Indy's first four-time winner in 1977. For his career, Foyt won a record 67 Indy car races and captured seven Indy Car championships, also a record.

While he was dominating Indy car races, Foyt took time to compete successfully in other series, winning the Daytona 500, six other NASCAR races, and 41 USAC stock car events. He also won 50 USAC sprint, midget, and dirt track races. He is the only driver to ever win the Daytona 500, the Indianapolis 500, and the 24 Hours of Le Mans, considered by many to be the three greatest races in the world. Foyt retired after the 1993 Indianapolis 500, but came out of retirement the following year to race in the inaugural Brickyard 400.

He now owns two Indy Racing League (IRL) teams and began fielding a team in the NASCAR Winston Cup Series in 2000.

Toward the end of his NASCAR career, Foyt drove this Oldsmobile, which he owned. Although his last win came in 1972, A. J. was a competitor until he ran his last race— the inaugural Brickyard 400 at Indianapolis in 1994.

Foyt was in and out of NASCAR for 30 years, but he never ran more than seven races in a year and sometimes only competed in one a season. Regardless, he was able to win seven times in 128 starts. Here, he pilots the Wood Brothers Mercury to a third-place finish in the Daytona 500.

Year-by-year Performance

	Races	Wins		Top 5		Top 10	
1963	5	0	0.0%	2	40.0%	2	40.0%
1964	6	1	16.7%	2	33.3%	2	33.3%
1965	4	1	25.0%	1	25.0%	2	50.0%
1966	4	0	0.0%	0	0.0%	0	0.0%
1967	7	0	0.0%	2	28.6%	2	28.6%
1968	4	0	0.0%	0	0.0%	1	25.0%
1969	4	0	0.0%	3	75.0%	3	75.0%
1970	3	1	33.3%	1	33.3%	1	33.3%
1971	7	2	28.6%	4	57.1%	4	57.1%
1972	6	2	33.3%	5	83.3%	5	83.3%
1973	3	0	0.0%	1	33.3%	1	33.3%
1974	4	0	0.0%	2	50.0%	2	50.0%
1975	7	0	0.0%	1	14.3%	1	14.3%
1976	5	0	0.0%	1	20.0%	1	20.0%
1977	6	0	0.0%	1	16.7%	3	50.0%
1978	2	0	0.0%	1	50.0%	1	50.0%
1979	2	0	0.0%	1	50.0%	2	100.0%
1980	1	0	0.0%	0	0.0%	0	0.0%
1981	3	0	0.0%	0	0.0%	1	33.3%
1982	2	0	0.0%	0	0.0%	0	0.0%
1983	3	0	0.0%	0	0.0%	0	0.0%
1984	3	0	0.0%	0	0.0%	0	0.0%
1985	7	0	0.0%	1	14.3%	1	14.3%
1986	5	0	0.0%	0	0.0%	0	0.0%
1987	6	0	0.0%	0	0.0%	0	0.0%
1988	7	0	0.0%	0	0.0%	0	0.0%
1989	7	0	0.0%	0	0.0%	0	0.0%
1990	3	0	0.0%	0	0.0%	0	0.0%
1992	1	0	0.0%	0	0.0%	0	0.0%
Total	**127**	**7**	**5.5%**	**29**	**22.8%**	**35**	**27.6%**

Harry Gant racked up 18 wins in his 22-year NASCAR driving career and left the sport as one of its most-beloved drivers.

Harry Gant was born on January 10, 1949, in Taylorsville, North Carolina. He got a late start driving, by racing standards, entering the sport in 1964 at the age of 24. He was considered one of the best Sportsman drivers ever in the Southeast. Harry had been racing for almost a decade before he ran his first Winston Cup event. He ran one race in 1973, and for the next five years he could only manage to start 11 events.

In 1979, at the age of 39, Harry was finally able to run his rookie Winston Cup season. He drove a Race Hill Farm Chevrolet, and in 29 starts he carded five top-10 finishes and achieved his dream of being a full-time Winston Cup driver. As a result, Harry remains the cornerstone for all dreamers who, without his example, might believe themselves too old even to dream. Harry got his first win in 1982 at Martinsville, driving the Mach 1 Racing Buick, and he won again at Charlotte later in the year. In the mid-1980s Harry was always a threat, and when he did not win, he ran well. For instance, in 1984 he finished in the top 10 in almost 77 percent of the season's races.

His green-and-white Skoal Bandit car became one of the most recognizable race cars in the sport. In 1991 Harry won five races, including Darlington, Richmond, Dover, and Martinsville all in a row. This feat of four consecutive wins ties the Modern Era record, and, considering the level of competition in the sport, will not soon be broken.

Harry retired after the 1994 season with 474 starts, 123 top fives, and 18 wins. Few drivers have been loved and respected as much as Harry. With his unassuming manner and gentle smile, Harry was one of those drivers about whom you seldom heard a bad remark, as he was respected by fans and drivers alike.

Among Harry's many accomplishments was his feat of winning four races in a row in 1991, the year he piloted the Skoal Bandit Oldsmobile for Leo Jackson.

In 1993, Leo Jackson switched from Oldsmobile to Chevrolet. Harry drove the Lumina in 1993 and 1994, scoring 19 top-10 finishes, but no wins. He retired at the end of the 1994 season.

Year-by-year Performance

	Races	Wins		Top 5		Top 10	
1973	1	0	0.0%	0	0.0%	0	0.0%
1974	3	0	0.0%	0	0.0%	1	33.3%
1975	1	0	0.0%	0	0.0%	0	0.0%
1976	1	0	0.0%	0	0.0%	1	100.0%
1977	1	0	0.0%	0	0.0%	0	0.0%
1978	5	0	0.0%	0	0.0%	1	20.0%
1979	25	0	0.0%	0	0.0%	5	20.0%
1980	31	0	0.0%	9	29.0%	14	45.2%
1981	31	0	0.0%	13	41.9%	18	58.1%
1982	30	2	6.7%	9	30.0%	16	53.3%
1983	30	1	3.3%	10	33.3%	16	53.3%
1984	30	3	10.0%	15	50.0%	23	76.7%
1985	28	3	10.7%	14	50.0%	19	67.9%
1986	29	0	0.0%	9	31.0%	13	44.8%
1987	29	0	0.0%	0	0.0%	4	13.8%
1988	24	0	0.0%	0	0.0%	3	12.5%
1989	29	1	3.4%	9	31.0%	14	48.3%
1990	28	1	3.6%	6	21.4%	9	32.1%
1991	29	5	17.2%	15	51.7%	17	58.6%
1992	29	2	6.9%	10	34.5%	15	51.7%
1993	30	0	0.0%	4	13.3%	12	40.0%
1994	30	0	0.0%	0	0.0%	7	23.3%
Total	**474**	**18**	**3.8%**	**123**	**25.9%**	**208**	**43.9%**

ERNIE IRVAN

Ernie Irvan's career is defined by highs, lows, hard luck, and comebacks. He began on the Winston Cup circuit in 1987 at Richmond when he drove a Chevrolet owned by Mark Reno with support from Dale Earnhardt.

Ernie Irvan was born on January 13, 1959, in Salinas, California. He began racing karts at the age of nine, winning the California Championship at the age of 15. In 1974 he finished second in his class at the national kart championship races. At the age of 16, he graduated to stock car racing at the Stockton 99 Speedway, where he was victorious in his first race on asphalt.

In 1982 he loaded all he owned into a pickup and homemade trailer and, with $700 in his pocket, headed to the center of NASCAR—North Carolina. It wasn't long before he was in the Charlotte Motor Speedway, not as a racer, but as a welder installing new grandstands. While campaigning to get a Winston Cup ride, Ernie worked on race cars and ran late models at Concord Speedway. In 1987 Ernie made his Winston Cup start at Richmond Fairgrounds Raceway, driving a Monte Carlo sponsored by Dale Earnhardt Chevrolet. He raced later that year at Charlotte, finishing 8th. He finished the year with five starts, and he was on his way.

In 1988, driving for D. K. Ulrich, Ernie raced in 25 of the 29 Winston Cup events and lost the Rookie of the Year honors by three points. Ernie started all 29 races in 1989, his first full year in the Winston Cup Series, finishing with four top-10 finishes and 22nd in the final point standings. He then began the 1990 season driving for Junie Donlavey, but after three races moved to the Morgan-McClure team. His first win came in the Morgan-McClure car at the 1990 Busch 500 at Bristol Motor Speedway, in his 79th start. The team started the next year in style, winning the 1991 Daytona 500. At the end of the year Ernie had two wins, 11 top 5s and 19 top 10s, finishing fifth in points, a career best.

Ernie and Morgan-McClure were successful, but after the death of Davey Allison, Ernie took the job driving Robert Yates' No. 28 Ford, beginning in 1993. With Yates, Irvan became one of the sport's top drivers. They consistently ran well, and they won races. However, in a practice session at Michigan Ernie hit the turn 2 wall at over 170 miles per hour. He was severely injured and was given only a 10 percent chance of surviving the night. But he was much tougher than the doctors thought, and within weeks he was back in Charlotte, where he spoke to the fans before the fall race. Ernie worked hard on his recovery and was back driving in the 1995 season, and in 1996 he was back in victory lane. In 1997 he won at Michigan, where he had almost lost his life.

Irvan left Yates at the end of the season and joined MB2 Motorsports. In 1999 while practicing his Busch car, Ernie again crashed at Michigan and was once again airlifted to a hospital. This time Ernie put family before all else and announced his retirement. He ended his career with 15 victories, 22 poles, 68 top fives, 124 top tens, and the honor of being named one of NASCAR's 50 greatest drivers.

Ernie began driving for Robert Yates in 1993 after Davey Allison's death, and in the team's first 29 races, he won five times before being seriously injured at Michigan. After that, he would not race again for more than a year.

Irvan finished his career in the Nelson Bowers Pontiac. He was injured before the team could get a win, though, and was forced to retire from racing.

Year-by-year Performance

	Races	Wins		Top 5		Top 10	
1987	5	0	0.0%	0	0.0%	1	20.0%
1988	25	0	0.0%	0	0.0%	0	0.0%
1989	29	0	0.0%	0	0.0%	4	13.8%
1990	29	1	3.4%	6	20.7%	13	44.8%
1991	29	2	6.9%	11	37.9%	19	65.5%
1992	29	3	10.3%	9	31.0%	11	37.9%
1993	30	3	10.0%	12	40.0%	14	46.7%
1994	20	3	15.0%	13	65.0%	15	75.0%
1995	3	0	0.0%	0	0.0%	2	66.7%
1996	31	2	6.5%	12	38.7%	16	51.6%
1997	32	1	3.1%	5	15.6%	13	40.6%
1998	30	0	0.0%	0	0.0%	11	36.7%
1999	21	0	0.0%	0	0.0%	5	23.8%
Total	**313**	**15**	**4.8%**	**68**	**21.7%**	**124**	**39.6%**

Bobby Isaac raced off and on for 15 years. In six of those, he won 37 races.

Robert Vance Isaac was born to a large family on August 1, 1934. At the age of 12 he took his first job, in a sawmill, and as he worked, he saved his money for his first purchase, a pair of shoes. After working in the sawmill and watching local racers towing their cars to the track, Bobby decided he wanted to make a living racing. His first attempt at driving was cut short when the track promoter would not let him race because he was only 15. This didn't deter Bobby, and over the next few years he continued driving wherever he could.

While he also spent some time in Fords and Chevrolets, Bobby had most of his success in Dodge products.

Isaac was an intense competitor with a bad temper, and his early NASCAR years were filled with fights, suspensions, and reinstatements, but by 1962 Bobby was a North Carolina short track legend. He drove Smokey Yunick's Chevrolet in the 1963 National 400 at Charlotte, giving it a whale of a ride before a tire blew. Afterward, Yunick praised Isaac's driving skill. That endorsement impressed Ray Nichels, who put Isaac in his Dodge for the 1964 season, and the young driver was on his way to greatness. Isaac's name was associated with Dodges throughout his stellar career. He won three races in 1967, and in 1969 he appeared to be unbeatable, winning 17 times.

In 1970 consistency paid off, as Bobby drove the Nord Krauskopf's K&K Insurance Dodge to the Winston Cup Championship. He won 11 races, and his car accounted for nearly 54 percent of the total points that earned Dodge the manufacturer's championship, breaking a seven-year stranglehold by Ford. Isaac, Krauskopf, and legendary crew chief Harry Hyde decided to cap the season by going to Talladega Superspeedway, the world's fastest track, to try for a closed-course record. On a raw, blustery day (November 24, 1970), Isaac circled the track at 201.104 miles per hour to trump Buddy Baker's old record of 200.447 miles per hour.

Isaac felt that 1970 was the pinnacle of his career, although in September 1971 he went on to set 28 world-class records on the Bonneville Salt Flats in his Dodge. Many of his records still exist to this day. Isaac drove in selected races until he retired after the 1977 season.

During the 1969 and 1970 seasons, when he was in one of Nord Krauskoph's K&K Insurance Dodges, Isaac was a force to be reckoned with.

Year-by-year Performance

	Races	Wins		Top 5		Top 10	
1961	1	0	0.0%	0	0.0%	0	0.0%
1963	27	0	0.0%	3	11.1%	7	25.9%
1964	19	1	5.3%	5	26.3%	7	36.8%
1965	4	0	0.0%	1	25.0%	1	25.0%
1966	9	0	0.0%	2	22.2%	3	33.3%
1967	12	0	0.0%	3	25.0%	5	41.7%
1968	49	3	6.1%	27	55.1%	35	71.4%
1969	50	17	34.0%	29	58.0%	32	64.0%
1970	47	11	23.4%	32	68.1%	38	80.9%
1971	25	4	16.0%	16	64.0%	17	68.0%
1972	27	1	3.7%	10	37.0%	10	37.0%
1973	19	0	0.0%	5	26.3%	6	31.6%
1974	11	0	0.0%	1	9.1%	5	45.5%
1975	6	0	0.0%	0	0.0%	1	16.7%
1976	2	0	0.0%	0	0.0%	1	50.0%
1977	6	0	0.0%	0	0.0%	1	16.7%
Total	**314**	**37**	**11.8%**	**134**	**42.7%**	**169**	**53.8%**

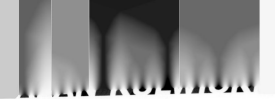

Alan Kulwicki drove five races for Bill Terry in 1985 to begin his Winston Cup career. In 1986, he started the year with Terry but later in the season became an owner-driver. He never drove another race in a car that he did not prepare himself.

Alan Kulwicki was born in Greenfield, Wisconsin, far from the heart of NASCAR racing, yet he managed to do great things in Winston Cup racing—and he did them his way. After earning an engineering degree from the University of Wisconsin, Alan decided to go racing. He ran on short tracks and was a successful competitor on the American Speed Association circuit. He sold all his ASA equipment (so he could not go back) in 1986 and joined the ranks of Winston Cup competitors.

Even though he lacked experience, Alan entered the sport as an owner-driver and was one of the first to bring a true technical engineering approach to the Winston Cup Series. In 1986 he won the Rookie of the Year title, running his team on a shoestring budget. He survived with the help of friends and volunteers, as he had only a two-man pit crew and throughout the 1986 season used only two race cars. After this great season, he obtained a bigger sponsor, Zerex Antifreeze/Coolant, which enabled him to become a real force in the sport.

Alan earned the reputation of a hardworking, no-nonsense competitor. His first win came in Phoenix in 1988, and it was there he made his first clockwise post-race lap, dubbed by the media the "Polish Victory Lap." He won again in both 1990 and 1991, but 1992 was the season that Alan's dream came true. Kulwicki's team had won races at Bristol and Pocono but was still 278 points behind, with just six races left in the season. In those six races, Alan had a pair of 2nds, a 4th, and a 5th—enough to take the title by 10 points over Bill Elliott. Competing with teams whose budgets dwarfed his, Kulwicki became the first owner-driver since Richard Petty in 1979 to win the Winston Cup. Tragically, Kulwicki, the reigning Winston Cup champion, died in a plane crash on his way to a race at Bristol in April 1993.

Alan was a young driver with great engineering talent, but many people thought he was not making a smart move when he started his own team so early in his career. He proved them wrong. His first win came in 1988 in a Ford sponsored by Zerex.

With Hooters as a sponsor, Kulwicki reached the pinnacle of the sport when he won the 1992 Winston Cup Championship.

Year-by-year Performance

	Races	Wins		Top 5		Top 10	
1985	5	0	0.0%	0	0.0%	0	0.0%
1986	23	0	0.0%	1	4.3%	4	17.4%
1987	29	0	0.0%	3	10.3%	9	31.0%
1988	29	1	3.4%	7	24.1%	9	31.0%
1989	29	0	0.0%	5	17.2%	9	31.0%
1990	29	1	3.4%	5	17.2%	13	44.8%
1991	29	1	3.4%	4	13.8%	11	37.9%
1992	29	2	6.9%	11	37.9%	17	58.6%
1993	5	0	0.0%	2	40.0%	3	60.0%
Total	**207**	**5**	**2.4%**	**38**	**18.4%**	**75**	**36.2%**

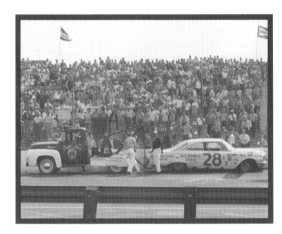

While most of Fred Lorenzen's career was in the Grand National days, he did compete in the Modern Era's first year and proved he was still competitive. He ended his career with 26 wins and finished in the top 10 in over half of the races he entered.

Fred Lorenzen was born in Elmhurst, Illinois, on December 30, 1934. He caught the car bug early. At age 13, he built his own small car, using junk parts and a washing machine motor. He could not keep it, however, as the police confiscated it because it was too fast. Later, while still in high school, he entered a demolition derby and won the event, and $100. He was doing what he had always wanted—making money driving.

Lorenzen began racing modifieds throughout the Midwest before moving to late models. In 1957 he drove in the USAC Series, racing a Chevrolet four times and finishing in the top 10 each time. The next year he switched to Fords and won five of seven events. Known as "Fearless Freddie," he moved to NASCAR in 1960 driving his own car. But as he could not beat the factory teams, he joined one, Holman-Moody. In 1961 he won three times, including his first visit to a superspeedway, at Darlington. From 1961 to 1966, Fred had multiple-win seasons. He was good everywhere, but especially on the longer and faster tracks like Atlanta and Darlington. However, he could still swap paint on the short tracks and had wins at Bristol, Martinsville, and North Wilkesboro.

His best year was in 1964. He entered only 16 races and won half of them. During the early- and mid-1960s, Fearless Freddie became a force to be reckoned with, winning 26 Grand National races. In 1967 Fred unexpectedly announced his retirement; however, he remained in retirement only three years, coming back to racing in 1970.

It was a good thing, as Fred was good for the sport. He was handsome, he was articulate, and he could certainly drive. Fred competed off and on until he retired again in 1972, ending his career with 26 wins and a career average of almost 50 percent of his starts resulting in top-five finishes.

(right) Much of Lorenzen's success came driving Fords for Holman-Moody in the mid-1960s.

(below) By 1970, Fred's career was slowing down, but he was still fast on the track. He won the pole at Atlanta in a Ray Fox Dodge.

Year-by-year Performance

	Races	Wins		Top 5		Top 10	
1956	7	0		0		0	
1960	10	0	0.0%	3	30.0%	5	50.0%
1961	15	3	20.0%	6	40.0%	6	40.0%
1962	19	2	10.5%	11	57.9%	12	63.2%
1963	29	6	20.7%	21	72.4%	23	79.3%
1964	16	8	50.0%	10	62.5%	10	62.5%
1965	17	4	23.5%	5	29.4%	6	35.3%
1966	11	2	18.2%	6	54.5%	6	54.5%
1967	5	1	20.0%	2	40.0%	2	40.0%
1970	7	0	0.0%	1	14.3%	1	14.3%
1971	15	0	0.0%	7	46.7%	9	60.0%
1972	8	0	0.0%	3	37.5%	4	50.0%
Total	**159**	**26**	**16.4%**	**75**	**47.2%**	**84**	**52.8%**

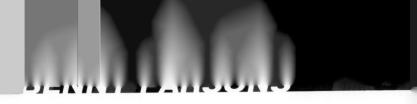

Benny Parsons won one race in the Grand National days and 20 in the Modern Era. His first win came at South Boston Speedway in 1971. He was driving a Ford. His last came in 1984 at Atlanta, when he was driving a Chevrolet.

Benny Parsons was born July 12, 1941. His path to the Winston Cup ranks was through the Automobile Racing Club of America (ARCA). Between 1965 and 1969, Benny won 16 ARCA races and won the ARCA Championship in 1968 and 1969.

He began his NASCAR career driving in one Grand National race in 1964 at Weaverville, qualifying 9th and finishing 21st. It wasn't until 1969 that Benny was back running with the top ranks of NASCAR. He drove four races in 1969, finishing with two top 5s, three top 10s, and one DNF. It was enough to put Benny on the top circuit full-time. His first full-time ride was with L. G. DeWitt. Benny drove in 45 races that year and finished in the top 10 in over half of them. He won his first race in 1971 at South Boston. Two years later, in 1973, Benny had one win, 15 top 5s, and 21 top 10s. The effort was enough to win Benny the championship in only his fourth full year on the circuit.

In 1975 Benny won the big one when he took the checkered flag in the Daytona 500. Benny won two or more races from 1976 to 1981. In 1982 he became the first driver to qualify at over 200 miles per hour when he ran 200.176 miles per hour to win the pole for the 1982 Winston 500 at Talladega Superspeedway. In 1988 Parsons retired, after 526 career NASCAR starts to become a full-time broadcaster and maintain his own automotive parts business. In his NASCAR career, Benny won 21 Winston Cup races, finished in the top 5 199 times, and in the top 10 283 times. His 21 wins rank him 24th on the all-time win list.

With Bud Moore as the owner and Melling Oil Pumps as a sponsor, Benny drove to three victories in the No. 15 Ford.

Year-by-year Performance

	Races	Wins		Top 5		Top 10	
1964	1	0	0.0%	0	0.0%	0	0.0%
1969	4	0	0.0%	2	50.0%	3	75.0%
1970	45	0	0.0%	12	26.7%	23	51.1%
1971	35	1	2.9%	13	37.1%	18	51.4%
1972	31	0	0.0%	10	32.3%	19	61.3%
1973	28	1	3.6%	15	53.6%	21	75.0%
1974	30	0	0.0%	11	36.7%	14	46.7%
1975	30	1	3.3%	11	36.7%	17	56.7%
1976	30	2	6.7%	18	60.0%	23	76.7%
1977	30	4	13.3%	20	66.7%	22	73.3%
1978	30	3	10.0%	15	50.0%	21	70.0%
1979	31	2	6.5%	16	51.6%	21	67.7%
1980	31	3	9.7%	16	51.6%	21	67.7%
1981	31	3	9.7%	10	32.3%	12	38.7%
1982	23	0	0.0%	10	43.5%	13	56.5%
1983	16	0	0.0%	4	25.0%	5	31.3%
1984	14	1	7.1%	7	50.0%	10	71.4%
1985	14	0	0.0%	1	7.1%	6	42.9%
1986	16	0	0.0%	2	12.5%	4	25.0%
1987	29	0	0.0%	6	20.7%	9	31.0%
1988	27	0	0.0%	0	0.0%	1	3.7%
Total	**526**	**21**	**4.0%**	**199**	**37.8%**	**283**	**53.8%**

For most of his career, David Pearson was a part-time driver, but when it was all over, he was a full-time legend. His 105 win total is surpassed only by Richard Petty, who started in more than twice as many races as Pearson did.

David Pearson was born on December 22, 1934, in Whitney, South Carolina, and though no one knew it at the time, one of the greatest racers ever had entered the world. David started racing in 1952, driving a 1940 Ford at a hobby race in Woodruff, South Carolina. Although he won only $13, he liked the experience so much that he knew racing was what he wanted to do for a living.

Early in his career, Pearson had maxed out in Limited Sportsman, but couldn't get a ride in NASCAR's Grand National circuit. He finally broke into the series in 1960, when he drove in 22 events in his own car and was able to finish seven times in the top 10. With that type of performance in a non-factory team, Pearson quickly turned some heads. The next year his career took off. He only drove 12 races in his own car and seven for Ray Fox Sr. In those seven he won three times, and all of them were big races. He took the checkered flag in the World 600, the Firecracker 250, and the Dixie 400. He also won the Rookie of the Year award.

Pearson went winless during the next two seasons, driving for different owners. In 1963, however, he began driving for Cotton Owens, and in 1964 he had a banner year. He won eight times and finished second eight times, finishing in the top 10 in almost 70 percent of the races. In a few short years, Pearson had become one of the sport's premier drivers. He won the NASCAR Championship in 1965, and after moving to Holman-Moody, he won two more in 1968 and 1969. In 1968 he won 16 times and finished second another 12 times. In 1969 he won 11 times and had another 18 2nd-place finishes. Throughout the 1970s, Pearson often competed on a limited schedule, driving for the Wood Brothers, whom he joined in 1972. He extended his winning streak from 1964 to 1980.

In 1973 in the new Winston Cup Series, he won an amazing 11 times in only 18 races. In 1976 he won 10 events in just 22 starts. His last win came in 1980, and for the next few years he cut back his already limited schedule, running his last race in 1986. He did so driving a car he owned, going out of the sport the way he came in. In any good argument on the sport's all-time best, Pearson should get serious consideration. He ended his career with 105 wins, ranking him second on the all-time win list. His career-winning percentage of 18.3 percent is the best of all major retired Modern Era drivers.

In the mid-1960s, Pearson drove Dodges for Cotton Owens. In four years, the team put together 27 wins.

After leaving Cotton Owens' team, David began driving Fords for Holman-Moody. From 1967 to 1971, the team would win 30 races, including this 1971 victory at Bristol. Note that at one point during the Bristol race, David's car was facing the wrong direction.

Year-by-year Performance

	Races	Wins		Top 5		Top 10	
1960	22	0	0.0%	3	13.6%	7	31.8%
1961	19	3	15.8%	7	36.8%	8	42.1%
1962	12	0	0.0%	1	8.3%	7	58.3%
1963	41	0	0.0%	13	31.7%	19	46.3%
1964	61	8	13.1%	29	47.5%	42	68.9%
1965	14	2	14.3%	8	57.1%	11	78.6%
1966	42	15	35.7%	26	61.9%	33	78.6%
1967	22	2	9.1%	11	50.0%	13	59.1%
1968	48	16	33.3%	36	75.0%	38	79.2%
1969	51	11	21.6%	42	82.4%	44	86.3%
1970	19	1	5.3%	9	47.4%	11	57.9%
1971	17	2	11.8%	8	47.1%	9	52.9%
1972	17	6	35.3%	12	70.6%	13	76.5%
1973	18	11	61.1%	14	77.8%	14	77.8%
1974	19	7	36.8%	15	78.9%	15	78.9%
1975	21	3	14.3%	13	61.9%	14	66.7%
1976	22	10	45.5%	16	72.7%	18	81.8%
1977	22	2	9.1%	16	72.7%	16	72.7%
1978	22	4	18.2%	11	50.0%	11	50.0%
1979	9	1	11.1%	4	44.4%	5	55.6%
1980	9	1	11.1%	4	44.4%	5	55.6%
1981	6	0	0.0%	0	0.0%	2	33.3%
1982	6	0	0.0%	2	33.3%	2	33.3%
1983	10	0	0.0%	1	10.0%	4	40.0%
1984	11	0	0.0%	0	0.0%	3	27.3%
1985	12	0	0.0%	0	0.0%	1	8.3%
1986	2	0	0.0%	0	0.0%	1	50.0%
Total	**574**	**105**	**18.3%**	**301**	**52.4%**	**366**	**63.8%**

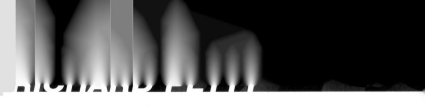

Richard Petty followed in his father's footsteps and became a race car driver. Few knew in 1958 when Richard ran his first Grand National race that over the next 35 years he would win 200 races and would be crowned "The King" of stock car racing. Richard Petty's start total is as impressive as his win total. While many drivers stayed home, he was always racing, giving fans at the smaller tracks an opportunity to see their driving hero.

Richard Petty was born on July 2, 1937, in Level Cross, North Carolina, and was destined to grow up in the racing world. His father, Lee Petty, was a three-time Grand National Champion. His brother, Maurice, choose a career as an engine builder, and his mother, Elizabeth, scored races for Lee. The Petty's more or less lived at the track.

In 1958 Richard ran nine Grand National races, finishing with one top-10 finish. In 1959 he expanded his schedule to 22 races, including a run in the first Daytona 500, and won the Rookie of the Year award. He ran an expanded schedule of 40 races in 1960, winning three times. He ran 30 times in the top 10, proving a consistency that continued through his career and led to seven championships. He had eight wins in 1962 and 14 in 1963. He won his first championship and nine more races in 1964. In 1965 Petty ran in only 14 races, winning four, but he came back to full speed in 1966 and won eight of the 39 races he started.

Petty won more races in 1967 than most drivers win in a lifetime. In 48 races that year, he won 27 and was runner-up in seven more. He finished in the top five in 79.2 percent of his races and won his second championship. For the next four years, Petty scored double-digit wins. He had 16 wins in 1968, 10 in 1969, and 18 in 1970. In 1971 he won 21 of his 46 races, along with his third championship. It was the last year of the long seasons.

In 1972 the Grand National Series became the Winston Cup Series, and the schedule was limited to about 30 races a year. It did not slow Petty down. He added championship trophies to his shelf in 1972, 1974, 1975, and 1979. In 1974 and 1975, he again scored double-digit wins, and he continued winning until 1984, when he won his 200th race, the 400-mile summer race at Daytona. Richard continued to race until he retired from driving in 1992.

Although he left the driver's seat, he is still a regular figure on the NASCAR circuit, as his team still competes. Throughout his career, Richard was called "The King," and it is certainly a title that he earned. His long list of accomplishments are impressive. He leads in all-time wins with 200, running a total of 1,185 races. He won seven Daytona 500s and 127 poles sixty-one of his wins were from the pole, he had the most consecutive wins (10) and the most wins in a season (27).

But Richard is The King both for his accomplishments and his manner— a gentleman from the tip of his boots to the top of his feathered hat. He always has had time for fans and media alike and has been a worthy ambassador for the sport. Richard Petty is in large measure responsible for its growth and success.

Petty's persistent work ethic and natural driving skill resulted in a total of seven Grand National and Winston Cup championships, and his contribution to NASCAR goes far beyond his performance on the track. His gentlemanly, unassuming manner and his tireless relationship with fans made him the sport's greatest ambassador.

After a brief, but successful, run in Fords in 1969, Petty was back in a Plymouth in 1970 and switched to Dodge in 1972. During this decade, he racked up 84 more Mopar wins. His last race in a Dodge came in this outing at Talladega.

Year-by-year Performance

	Races	Wins		Top 5		Top 10	
1958	9	0	0.0%	0	0.0%	1	11.1%
1959	22	0	0.0%	6	27.3%	9	40.9%
1960	40	3	7.5%	16	40.0%	30	75.0%
1961	42	2	4.8%	18	42.9%	23	54.8%
1962	52	8	15.4%	32	61.5%	39	75.0%
1963	54	14	25.9%	30	55.6%	39	72.2%
1964	61	9	14.8%	37	60.7%	43	70.5%
1965	14	4	28.6%	10	71.4%	10	71.4%
1966	39	8	20.5%	20	51.3%	22	56.4%
1967	48	27	56.3%	38	79.2%	40	83.3%
1968	49	16	32.7%	31	63.3%	35	71.4%
1969	50	10	20.0%	31	62.0%	38	76.0%
1970	40	18	45.0%	27	67.5%	31	77.5%
1971	46	21	45.7%	38	82.6%	41	89.1%
1972	31	8	25.8%	25	80.6%	28	90.3%
1973	28	6	21.4%	15	53.6%	17	60.7%
1974	30	10	33.3%	22	73.3%	23	76.7%
1975	30	13	43.3%	21	70.0%	24	80.0%
1976	30	3	10.0%	19	63.3%	22	73.3%
1977	30	5	16.7%	20	66.7%	23	76.7%
1978	30	0	0.0%	11	36.7%	17	56.7%
1979	31	5	16.1%	23	74.2%	27	87.1%
1980	31	2	6.5%	15	48.4%	19	61.3%
1981	31	3	9.7%	12	38.7%	16	51.6%
1982	30	0	0.0%	9	30.0%	16	53.3%
1983	30	3	10.0%	9	30.0%	21	70.0%
1984	30	2	6.7%	5	16.7%	13	43.3%
1985	28	0	0.0%	1	3.6%	13	46.4%
1986	29	0	0.0%	4	13.8%	11	37.9%
1987	29	0	0.0%	9	31.0%	14	48.3%
1988	29	0	0.0%	1	3.4%	5	17.2%
1989	25	0	0.0%	0	0.0%	0	0.0%
1990	29	0	0.0%	0	0.0%	1	3.4%
1991	29	0	0.0%	0	0.0%	1	3.4%
1992	29	0	0.0%	0	0.0%	0	0.0%
Total	1,185	200	16.9%	555	46.8%	712	60.1%

Racing observers will always ponder what could have been when they think about Tim Richmond. He drove in only 183 races in his short career and won 13 of them.

Tim Richmond was born in Ashland, Ohio, on June 7, 1955. He became known as one of the most spectacular drivers that the sport of stock car racing has ever seen. Early in his career, Tim raced in the USAC sprint cars and the Silver Crown Series and was the 1978 Sprint Car Rookie of the Year. This got him other rides, including a short career in Indy cars, where he competed in nine races and won the 1980 Indianapolis 500 Rookie of the Year award.

From 1983 to 1985, Tim drove Raymond Beadle's Old Milwaukee Pontiacs. He won two races with the team before moving into a Rick Hendrick Chevrolet after the 1985 season.

Tim then made the move from the lightweight open-wheel cars to the heavier Winston Cup race car, competing in five races for D.K. Ulrich in 1980. He went Winston Cup racing full-time in 1981 and garnered six top-10 finishes; won the Rookie of the Year award; and, more importantly, gained valuable experience piloting the heavier cars. He had it figured out in 1982 when, driving for J. D. Stacey, he won at Riverside twice. In 1983 Tim moved to Raymond Beadle's Blue Max Team and together they won a 500-mile event at Pocono. Tim's performance was improving, and his finishes showed it.

In half of Tim's 1983 starts, he finished in the top 10. From 1980 to 1985, Tim drove in 148 races, winning four times with 26 top-5 and 57 top-10 finishes. Tim switched teams in 1986, joining Hendrick Motorsports and crew chief Harry Hyde. Harry and Tim did not see eye to eye in the beginning, and for the first dozen races of the year they did little but argue. Eventually the two learned to appreciate each other and to work together, and when they made the turn they really made the turn. In the last 17 races of the year, they won seven and finished the year with 13 top-5 and 17 top-10 finishes.

It was Tim's best season, but unfortunately it was his last full one. Tim was soon out of the sport, suffering from AIDS at a time when you didn't talk about having AIDS and few treatment options were possible. Rumors swirled about his condition. While quite ill, Tim returned in 1987, claiming his sickness was pneumonia. He was able to run in eight races. In true Tim Richmond style, he won a quarter of them, taking the checkered flag at Pocono and Riverside. He finished four of his races in the top 10, driving his last event at Michigan on August 16, 1987.

Tim died on August 7, 1989, ending his short career just as it was taking off. In his brief time at the wheel, Tim won 13 races, leaving everyone to wonder what might have been.

In 1986, Tim Richmond was in Rick Hendrick's Folgers Chevrolet, and the results were impressive. The team put together seven wins. In 1987, Tim raced eight times in the car when he was very ill and still won twice.

Year-by-year Performance

	Races	Wins		Top 5		Top 10	
1980	5	0	0.0%	0	0.0%	0	0.0%
1981	29	0	0.0%	0	0.0%	6	20.7%
1982	26	2	7.7%	7	26.9%	12	46.2%
1983	30	1	3.3%	10	33.3%	15	50.0%
1984	30	1	3.3%	6	20.0%	11	36.7%
1985	28	0	0.0%	3	10.7%	13	46.4%
1986	29	7	24.1%	13	44.8%	17	58.6%
1987	8	2	25.0%	3	37.5%	4	50.0%
Total	**185**	**13**	**7.0%**	**42**	**22.7%**	**78**	**42.2%**

In the early years of Darrell Waltrip's career, he was heckled by fans and criticized by his fellow drivers. By the time he retired from driving, he was one of the sports most-loved personalities and a great ambassador of the sport.

Darrell Waltrip raced in NASCAR's Winston Cup Series for the first time in 1972—the first year of NASCAR's Modern Era. He ran five races in 1972, running a car he owned. He managed to finish the five races with a top 5 and three top 10s. He ran limited schedules in 1973 and 1974, again in his own car, and also ran five for Bud Moore. His finishes continued to improve.

He won his first race in 1975, in a car owned by his wife, finishing first at the Nashville Fairgrounds Speedway, two laps up over his closest competitor. He added another win later in the year in a car owned by Bill Gardner. Darrell had finished in the top 10 in well over 50 percent of his races over two years. He was good, and he knew it, but his brashly confident style had rubbed many the wrong way. Darrell had earned the nickname "Jaws" from veteran competitors. But while Darrell did some talking off the track, he backed it up when he was on the track. From 1975 to 1980, he stayed with Bill Gardner, and the combination was impressive. Darrell won six races in 1977, six more in 1978, seven in 1979, and five in 1980. In 1981 he began a six-year stay with Junior Johnson's team. If he was impressive before, after he hooked up with Junior, he was deadly. Darrell won 12 races in 1981 and 12 more in 1982. Over the next few years, if Darrell didn't win, he was threatening to win. In 1987 Darrell left a top team for another successful employment, this time with Rick Hendrick. His stay with Hendrick garnered more wins, including a six-win season in 1989. It was a sweet year for Darrell, as he finally added a Daytona 500 win to his long list of accomplishments. It was also a good time for Darrell off the track, as his reputation with fans and competitors had gone full circle, and he won back-to-back Most Popular Driver Awards in 1989 and 1990.

Darrell left Hendrick Motorsports to start his own team in 1991 and for a while was quite successful. He won twice in 1991 and three times in 1992, taking the checkered flag at Pocono, Bristol, and Darlington. The Darlington victory was Darrell's 84th and last win. During the later years of his career, Darrell ran worse and worse. He had pretty much been written off as a competitive driver until 1998, when he filled in for an injured Steve Park in a Dale Earnhardt Incorporated Chevrolet. All of a sudden, Darrell was running well again, and he had a top 5 and two top 10s in the 13 races he ran for DEI. It was plain to see that in a top-line car, Waltrip could still drive with the best of them.

After the 1999 season, Darrell was through driving Winston Cup cars and began his broadcasting career, although he still sneaks out and drives a race in the Craftsman Truck Series every now and then. Over his career, Darrell won over 10 percent of the races that he started and is one of only seven drivers to win at least three Winston Cup Series titles. He is the all-time Modern Era pole leader with 59 poles; his total of 84 wins ties him with Bobby Allison for third on the all-time win list; and, of course, he ranks first in Modern Era wins.

Behind the wheel of the DiGard Chevy, Darrell drove to 25 of his 84 victories.

From 1991 through part of the 1998 season, Darrell was an owner-driver. With Western Auto as a sponsor, he won five races.

Year-by-year Performance

	Races	Wins		Top 5		Top 10	
1972	5	0	0.0%	1	20.0%	3	60.0%
1973	19	0	0.0%	1	5.3%	5	26.3%
1974	16	0	0.0%	7	43.8%	11	68.8%
1975	28	2	7.1%	11	39.3%	14	50.0%
1976	30	1	3.3%	10	33.3%	12	40.0%
1977	30	6	20.0%	16	53.3%	24	80.0%
1978	30	6	20.0%	19	63.3%	20	66.7%
1979	31	7	22.6%	19	61.3%	22	71.0%
1980	31	5	16.1%	16	51.6%	17	54.8%
1981	31	12	38.7%	21	67.7%	25	80.6%
1982	30	12	40.0%	17	56.7%	20	66.7%
1983	30	6	20.0%	22	73.3%	25	83.3%
1984	30	7	23.3%	13	43.3%	20	66.7%
1985	28	3	10.7%	18	64.3%	21	75.0%
1986	29	3	10.3%	21	72.4%	22	75.9%
1987	29	1	3.4%	6	20.7%	16	55.2%
1988	29	2	6.9%	10	34.5%	14	48.3%
1989	29	6	20.7%	14	48.3%	18	62.1%
1990	23	0	0.0%	5	21.7%	12	52.2%
1991	29	2	6.9%	5	17.2%	17	58.6%
1992	29	3	10.3%	10	34.5%	13	44.8%
1993	30	0	0.0%	4	13.3%	10	33.3%
1994	31	0	0.0%	4	12.9%	13	41.9%
1995	31	0	0.0%	4	12.9%	8	25.8%
1996	31	0	0.0%	0	0.0%	2	6.5%
1997	31	0	0.0%	1	3.2%	4	12.9%
1998	33	0	0.0%	1	3.0%	2	6.1%
1999	27	0	0.0%	0	0.0%	0	0.0%
2000	29	0	0.0%	0	0.0%	0	0.0%
Total	**809**	**84**	**10.4%**	**276**	**34.1%**	**390**	**48.2%**

Cale Yarborough won 83 races in only 560 starts, but only drove full-time in the series from the mid-to late-1970s. His career spanned 31 years, though, and he won back-to-back Winston Cup championships in 1976, 1977, and 1978.

Cale Yarborough must be counted as one of the greatest drivers the sport has ever seen. He was born on March 27, 1940, in Timmonsville, North Carolina, and after unsuccessful careers in football and turkey farming, he decided to earn a living through racing.

He started his racing career in 1957, and over the next couple of years he drove primarily on short tracks in Sportsman events. While he occasionally ran a Grand National race in his own car, he usually did not finish if he started. In his first 12 races, Cale carded 10 DNFs. Things began to improve in 1965 when he got his first win while driving for Ken Myler. During the 1966 season, Cale changed drivers and joined the Wood Brothers—then his career really took off. While he still ran a limited schedule, Cale won multiple races every year from 1967 to 1970. In 1968 he ran only 21 races but won the Daytona 500, the Firecracker 400, the Atlanta 500, and the Southern 500. Cale left the Wood Brothers after the 1970 season. In 1971 and

1972 combined, Cale only drove in nine races, again in a car that he owned. His results were less than spectacular.

He jumped back into the sport full-time in 1973, this time driving for Junior Johnson. For the next eight years, Cale and Junior were a force to be reckoned with. They won four races their first year out and followed it in 1974 with a 10-win season. In 1976 the partnership hit its stride, and over the next three seasons, Cale won 28 races and became the only driver to win three championships in a row. After the 1980 season, Cale left Junior's team and again drove a limited schedule, this time for M. C. Anderson. He continued to win in the mid-1980s, driving for Harry Ranier.

Cale left Ranier after the 1986 season and for the next two years drove select races in his own race car. After a 10-race effort in 1988 that resulted in three top 10s, Cale retired from the sport. While spending much of his stock car racing career as a part-time stock car driver, he had amassed 83 wins, 50 of them on superspeedways.

In 1974, Cale ended the year with 10 victories. He started that season in the No. 11 Kar-Kare Chevrolet owned by Richard Howard and won six races. He switched mid-year to a Junior Johnson Chevrolet and won four more times.

In 1981, Yarborough began driving for
M. C. Anderson and continued his
winning ways. Here, they celebrate a
Firecracker 400 victory at Daytona.

Year-by-year Performance

	Races	Wins		Top 5		Top 10	
1957	1	0	0.0%	0	0.0%	0	0.0%
1959	1	0	0.0%	0	0.0%	0	0.0%
1960	1	0	0.0%	0	0.0%	0	0.0%
1961	1	0	0.0%	0	0.0%	0	0.0%
1962	8	0	0.0%	0	0.0%	1	12.5%
1963	18	0	0.0%	3	16.7%	7	38.9%
1964	24	0	0.0%	2	8.3%	9	37.5%
1965	46	1	2.2%	13	28.3%	21	45.7%
1966	14	0	0.0%	3	21.4%	7	50.0%
1967	16	2	12.5%	7	43.8%	8	50.0%
1968	21	6	28.6%	12	57.1%	12	57.1%
1969	19	2	10.5%	7	36.8%	8	42.1%
1970	19	3	15.8%	11	57.9%	13	68.4%
1971	4	0	0.0%	0	0.0%	1	25.0%
1972	5	0	0.0%	1	20.0%	4	80.0%
1973	28	4	14.3%	16	57.1%	19	67.9%
1974	30	10	33.3%	21	70.0%	22	73.3%
1975	27	3	11.1%	13	48.1%	13	48.1%
1976	30	9	30.0%	22	73.3%	23	76.7%
1977	30	9	30.0%	25	83.3%	27	90.0%
1978	30	10	33.3%	23	76.7%	24	80.0%
1979	31	4	12.9%	19	61.3%	22	71.0%
1980	31	6	19.4%	19	61.3%	22	71.0%
1981	18	2	11.1%	6	33.3%	10	55.6%
1982	16	3	18.8%	8	50.0%	8	50.0%
1983	16	4	25.0%	4	25.0%	8	50.0%
1984	16	3	18.8%	10	62.5%	10	62.5%
1985	16	2	12.5%	6	37.5%	7	43.8%
1986	16	0	0.0%	2	12.5%	5	31.3%
1987	16	0	0.0%	2	12.5%	4	25.0%
1988	10	0	0.0%	0	0.0%	3	30.0%
Total	**559**	**83**	**14.8%**	**255**	**45.6%**	**318**	**56.9%**

The
Grand

DAREL DIERINGER
RALPH EARNHARDT
FONTY FLOCK
TIM FLOCK
PAUL GOLDSMITH
DAN GURNEY
PETE HAMILTON
DICK HUTCHERSON
NED JARRETT
JUNIOR JOHNSON
PARNELLI JONES
TINY LUND

National Days

HERSHEL MCGRIFF
COTTON OWENS
MARVIN PANCH
JIM PASCHAL
LEE PETTY
FIREBALL ROBERTS
HERB THOMAS
CURTIS TURNER
JOE WEATHERLY
REX WHITE
GLEN WOOD
LEE ROY YARBROUGH

In 1964, Darel drove Mercurys for both Bill Stroppe and Junior Johnson. Here, his engine gets a tune-up during practice.

Darel Dieringer was born on June 1, 1926, in Indianapolis, Indiana. During much of his racing career, he was called the "King of the Used Cars." Darel was a basketball player in high school. He drove in his first race at age 19, in 1955. After a couple of years of driving, Darel worked at various other jobs, including spending time on the Firestone tire changing crew. In 1962 he returned to driving. A big, broad-shouldered man, Darel was a pioneer in the area of safety tires promoted by Goodyear. A resident of Charlotte, North Carolina, he also had successful businesses away from racing, a factor that prompted his retirement. In his career, Darel ran in 181 Grand National races, winning seven of them and finishing in the top 10 a total of 79 times. He also took nine pole positions. He ran in his first Grand National race in 1957 and his last in 1975.

During the 1967 season, Darel drove a Junior Johnson–prepared big-block Ford to six poles and one victory before switching to Cotton Owens–owned Dodges towards the end of the year.

Ralph Lee Earnhardt was born February 23, 1928, in Kannapolis, North Carolina. It was from there, in a garage behind his home, that he began his life's work—building race cars, both for himself and for others. He drove some of these cars to hundreds of wins and countless state and short track championships. He won the NASCAR Sportsman Championship in 1956, finished in the top 10 of the NASCAR National Sportsman point standings for six years, and finished 17th in the NASCAR Grand National (now Nextel Cup) point standings in 1961.

Generally he raced all during the week on short tracks close to his home and family instead of traveling to distant races. He did, however, drive over 50 races in the Grand National circuit for renowned car builders such as Cotton Owens and Lee Petty. Ralph was an innovator. He was one of the first to use tire stagger to improve the handling of his race cars and also pioneered the use of steel bars in the driver's door area for protection during side impacts.

According to Ned Jarrett, "Ralph Earnhardt was absolutely the toughest race driver I ever raced against. On the dirt and asphalt short tracks in Sportsman competition, when you went to the track you knew he was the man to beat." Ralph Earnhardt's career spanned 23 years of racing in NASCAR's Modified, Sportsman, and Grand National ranks. Through it all, he won more than 350 NASCAR races. He died from a heart attack on September 26, 1973, at the age of 45.

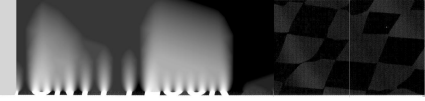

Fonty Flock raced in the Grand National Series from 1949 to 1957. While the sport was still in its early years, he brought both driving ability and style to the track.

Truman Fontell "Fonty" Flock was born in Fort Payne, Alabama, on March 21, 1921. Like many of the early stock car racers, his first experiences with performance driving came with a trunk of moonshine, and his competitors were the local sheriffs. He later admitted to deliberately seeking out the law for the fun of it, knowing his was the better car and he was the better driver. Flock's early hero was racer Ted Horn, who would come by his house for breakfast when he was in town.

Fonty probably won more races than anyone racing in the years before the sport was well organized. In 1957 after a bad wreck at Darlington, Fonty left the sport, only to return in 1964 to work on a fan club program for NASCAR, promoting the sport with wild tales of his racing career. On July 15, 1972, at age 51, Fonty died in Atlanta after a long illness. In his Grand National career, he drove in 153 races and started 33 of them from the pole position. He won 19 times, had 72 top-five finishes, and 83 top-10 finishes.

Fonty drove in an era where race cars were almost identical to stock cars. Drivers manhandled big cars with limited power and lots of body roll on dirt tracks. Nonetheless, he racked up 19 wins and 72 top-five finishes in his 153 official starts.

Tim Flock raced from 1949 to 1961 and won his first race at Charlotte in 1950 while driving for Harold Kite. Here, Tim pilots his Lincoln to a 9th-place finish at the second race in Charlotte in 1950.

Tim Flock was the younger brother of racers Bob and Fonty Flock. Tim was a superstitious racer. He never shaved on race day, wore green, or allowed peanuts anywhere near his car. Born on May 11, 1924, Tim saw his first race at age 13 and was hooked. At age 19, he began to get driving experience—behind the wheel of an Atlanta taxi. He worked as a firefighter and then a parking lot attendant until 1947, when he began driving a race car for his sister Ethel and her husband.

His best year of racing was probably 1952, when he won eight out of 34 races and the NASCAR Grand National Championship for the Hudson Motor Car Company. In 1955, another great year for Tim, he won 18 Grand National races (and 18 poles) during the season while driving a Chrysler 300 for Carl Kiekhaefer. The performance won Tim his second championship. Julius Timothy Flock was, in the fledgling years of NASCAR's Grand National circuit, more than a champion. He was a genuine character, joining the likes of Curtis Turner, Joe Weatherly, and his own brother Fonty as the rowdy daredevils who were the sport's pioneer drivers. Over his 13-year career, he won 40 races with 102 top 5s and 129 top 10s.

(above) In 1952, he won eight races in his Ted Chester-owned Hudson. Here, he passes Herb Thomas (also in a Hudson) on the low side.

When Tim began driving a Carl Kiekhaefer Chrysler, the results were disastrous—for the competition. For most of 1955 and part of 1956, he competed in a total of 46 races and won 21 of them.

Paul Goldsmith views the remains of his 1964 Ran Nichels–owned Plymouth after crashing only 55 laps into a race at Atlanta.

Paul Goldsmith was born October 2, 1927, in Parkersburg, West Virginia. At the age of 19, he began his racing career—on motorcycles. After spending some time in the merchant marine, Paul decided to leave the ships and try to make a living in racing. He was quite successful, as he won the American Motorcycle Association crown in 1952, 1953, and 1954. In 1953 he began racing cars. In 1956, with Smokey Yunick, Paul won one race and in the next year won four times.

He was quickly accepted in the NASCAR community because of his performance in his first race at the old Charlotte, North Carolina, Fairgrounds track. Paul proved his commitment to the sport when he flipped his car, landed on his wheels, and continued the race, finishing seconds behind the legendary Curtis Turner. Paul also won the final race on the old beach road course at Daytona. In his career, Paul raced motorcycles and stock cars and also spent some time running both Indy and SCCA events. In his 11-year Grand National career, he won nine races in 127 starts, with eight poles and 59 top 10s.

At Daytona in 1964, Goldsmith set a qualifying record of 174.919 miles per hour. A few days later, he finished third in the Daytona 500.

Many racers get into the sport because their fathers are racers. Not Dan Gurney. He was born April 13, 1931, at Port Jefferson, New York, the son of an opera singer. Since Dan could not sing, the only logical career choice was racing. He was one of the most methodical and intense competitors the sport has ever seen.

Learning to drive on dirt roads around Riverside, California, Dan became a master of road racing. He also had success in drag racing, Indy cars, and record speed runs on the Bonneville Salt Flats. He was always pulled back to road racing. From Corvettes to Ferraris, Dan drove them all. He dusted the NASCAR regulars in 1963 at Riverside to win the 500-mile event. He did the same for the next three years, until his streak at Riverside was broken in 1967. He came back to win the event in 1968, making it five wins in six starts. In all Dan ran in only 16 NASCAR races but walked away with five wins and 10 top 10s.

Dan Gurney was a Grand National racer for 10 years and drove a total of 16 races, capturing all of his five victories at Riverside. He also drove in events at Daytona and Atlanta. Here, his Wood Brothers Ford is a car length away from being involved in an early race accident.

Pete Hamilton was the son of a Harvard Ph.D., spoke impeccable English, and was possibly the neatest man in automobile racing. (He even kept his fingernails clean when he was working on cars.) He was born July 20, 1942, and grew to be a man of stature, weighing 175 pounds and standing 6 feet, 2 inches, tall. In 1967 he got the attention of NASCAR owners when he won the National Late Model Sportsman Crown.

In 1968, running a limited schedule of 16 races, Pete had six top-10 finishes and won the Rookie of the Year award. Richard Petty picked him as number two driver for Petty Enterprises in 1970, because he was willing to work on the automobiles and learn how to drive in the "Petty manner." It paid off, as Pete won the 1970 Daytona 500. Pete's NASCAR career was relatively short, lasting from 1968 to 1973. He ran 64 races, winning four of them and finishing over half in the top 10.

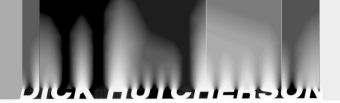

DICK HUTCHERSON

Dick Hutcherson made a rare decision for a driver. He climbed from behind the wheel, left the job of driving to others, and became a crew chief and mechanic for David Pearson's Holman-Moody Ford. While racing, Dick was a cautious driver who took care of his car and his results proved how good he was.

Dick was born November 30, 1931, and learned to drive starting in 1956 on the dirt track in his hometown of Keokuk, Iowa. In the early 1960s he began traveling south to run the higher-paying NASCAR events. His NASCAR career started in 1964 when he ran in four races, winning two poles and having two top-five finishes. He made the move to the Grand National circuit full-time in 1965 and battled Ned Jarrett for the Grand National Championship. In 1965 he ran in 52 races, driving to nine poles, winning nine races, and amassing 32 top fives and a 2nd-place finish for the Grand National Championship.

Dick won three times in 1966 and 1967. After winning the Dixie 500 at Atlanta, Dick was picked by the top dogs at Ford to be a factory driver. However, his driving career was coming to an end. In 1967 Dick became operations manager for Holman-Moody, and he was an integral factor in that team's 1968 and 1969 Grand National Championships.

Over a short four-year career, Dick Hutcherson won 14 races in only 103 starts. He won races driving No. 29 Fords owned by either Holman-Moody or Bondy Long.

Ned Miller Jarrett was born near Newton, North Carolina, on Columbus Day in 1932. His love of cars began early, and by the age of nine, he was allowed to drive the family car to church on Sundays. When Ned was 17, he quit school to join the family lumber business. He ran his first official race in 1952 at Hickory, North Carolina, and, although he was inexperienced, he still managed to finish in 10th place.

Ned's parents did not like him driving the car and wanted him to limit his racing role to being a mechanic. This arrangement lasted until one night when the car's driver was sick. Ned drove in his place, using the sick driver's name, and finished in 2nd place. He continued driving, and after a few wins, Ned's father found out and changed his mind about Ned's driving. After success in Sportsman racing, Ned decided to go Grand National racing and bought a used Ford from Junior Johnson. Ned wrote Junior a $2,000 check on Friday (which his account could not cover). He won enough money racing the car over the weekend to cover the check on Monday. He was on his way to becoming a racing legend.

(opposite) From 1959 to 1965, Ned Jarrett was one of the most dominant drivers in Grand National racing. He won 50 races over those seven years, including triumphing 15 times in 1964.

(below) In 1964, Ned took the checkered flag at Atlanta in his Bondy Long Ford.

When his career was over, he had won 50 races and two championships. Only two of Ned's 50 wins were on superspeedways, but when it came to the tough short tracks, he was one of the best ever. In 1960 Ned won five races, but in 1961 he won only at Birmingham, Alabama. However, he was among the top five in 22 races, enough to win the Grand National Championship. In 1965 Jarrett won 13 races and another Grand National Championship (he was in the top five 42 times in 54 races). A year later, Jarrett was again in the championship hunt, but Ford withdrew from NASCAR. Jarrett retired at a young age, still at the top of the sport. Over his career, Jarrett finished in the top five an astonishing 54.1 percent of the time and the top 10 69.9 percent of the time. These stats are the highest of all retired Modern Era drivers.

Here, Ned Jarrett narrowly escapes trouble in his No. 11 Ford, but this wreck ended the day for Parnelli Jones, Jimmy Pardue, and Dan Gurney.

If only one driver could be picked to represent the early years of NASCAR, it would be Junior Johnson. The part-time moonshiner, part-time race driver racked up 50 wins in 14 years of racing.

One of the all-time great racing legends, Junior Johnson, came from Ronda, North Carolina, and was born on June 28, 1931. He was one of the drivers who bridged the gap as NASCAR changed from the chaos of early dirt track racing to the more regulated sport running on paved tracks. Junior was a cagey, shrewd racer, saving the car when he had to and charging when necessary. He learned to drive on the back roads of North Carolina, running moonshine in his youth. Junior did not always get away, and he served time for moonshining before becoming a racer.

His professional driving career was often part-time and spanned 14 years. In that time he ran in 313 races. When he left the sport he had 50 wins, 121 top 5s, 148 top 10s, and 46 poles. He retired from driving after the 1966 season, still at the top of the sport. While he was not driving, Junior was still active in the sport, becoming one of the greatest car owners in stock car racing history. As an owner, he won 139 races, ranking him second on the all-time owner win list. Away from racing, Junior has been very successful in the construction rental business and as a chicken farmer.

Some of Junior's best runs came in Chevrolet car owned by Ray Fox and sponsored by Holly Farms Poultry.

When he was not driving for another owner, Junior drove a car he owned. His legend as a car owner continued long after his driving days were over.

Rufus Parnelli Jones was born on August 12, 1933, in Texarkana, Arkansas, and moved at a young age to Torrance, California. When he was a kid he went by Rufus, a name that ensured combat with other youngsters from the beginning. An aunt helped Jones, nicknaming him Parnellie; he liked that name better, and later dropped the "e." He learned to drive in the fields around his home, sometimes intentionally "rolling" cars like a stunt driver.

He was racing hot rods by the age of 17 and then began racing in sprint cars, winning his first title in 1960. Whether it was sprint cars, Indy cars, NASCAR, or the Pike's Peak climb, Parnelli could win. In his 12-year part-time Grand National career, he started 34 races and won four of them. After retiring from driving, Parnelli was successful as a car owner and in business interests away from the track.

From 1956 to 1970, Parnelli Jones drove in only 34 races, but he managed to win four of them. He primarily raced on road courses and short tracks on the West Coast but did occasionally venture into the Southeast. He won in this No. 115 Ford at Riverside in 1967.

Tiny Lund was a fixture on the circuit from 1955 until his death in 1975. He won five times in 303 starts.

At 6 feet, 5 inches tall, and 270 pounds, Tiny Lund was anything but tiny. He was born on March 3, 1936, in Harlan, Iowa. He played both football and basketball in his youth, but later fell in love with racing. At the age of 15 he began racing motorcycles, and then moved to sprint cars and midgets. His size, however, made racing these cars difficult, so he moved to modifieds. Before he became a NASCAR star, he spent four years as a flight engineer in the U.S. Air Force, specializing in jets.

After he was out of the Air Force, he returned to racing and in 1963 went to Daytona without a car, just hoping to work on someone's pit crew. What happened was like a story from a movie. Marvin Panch was driving a Maserati experimental car in practice when the car became airborne, slid on its top, and burst into flames. Tiny was the first man to reach the car, and he pulled Marvin from the fire. Because of his burns, Panch could not drive in the 500, and he persuaded the Wood Brothers to let Tiny drive their Ford in the Daytona 500. They agreed, and much to everyone's surprise, Tiny won the race. He was later awarded the Carnegie Medal for Heroism for his actions at the track that day.

His heroic act set in motion a career that ultimately ended with Tiny being the all-time winner in Grand American racing, with 41 victories. During Tiny's career, he won over 500 features and 49 major races. He was a four-time champion in the Grand American division, winning titles in 1965, 1970, 1971, and 1974. In his 20-year Grand National career, he ran in 303 events, winning five times and finishing in the top 10 a total of 119 times. His career was cut short when he was killed in a racing accident in 1975.

By 1965, Tiny was driving this Ford Galaxie owned by Lyle Stelter. He won one race that year at the Colombia Speedway.

*In the late 1960s, Lund was running a
very limited schedule. Here his Dodge
gets ready to head out onto the track.*

Hershel McGriff was born December 14, 1927, in Portland, Oregon. His racing history actually consists of two different careers. Early on he raced in series other than stock cars, including a win in the 1950 Mexican Road Race, which covered 2,135 miles over six days of racing. He then began to race stock cars in NASCAR's early years. McGriff left his home in the northwest in 1953 to go south and race with the country's best stock car racers. His battles with Lee Petty were among some of the most classic the sport had ever seen. Hershel ran in NASCAR's premier series part-time for over four decades. His first race was in 1950, and his last was in 1993. When it was over, he had started in 85 events, winning four times and capturing five poles, with 31 top-10 finishes.

Hershel McGriff ran 24 races in 1954 and won four of them. For the rest of his career (which spanned from 1950 to 1993), he pretty much only competed when the circuit visited the tracks where drivers turn right.

Cotton raced throughout the 1950s and well into the 1960s before leaving the sport. He won nine races in a career that consisted of only 160 starts.

Born May 21, 1924, Cotton Owens received his nickname because of his head of white hair. He was a quiet, soft-spoken man and regularly gave 10 percent of his income to his church. When he was a boy, he would climb trees so that he could see over the fence and watch the races at the local track. His father owned a garage, so Cotton grew up around cars and formed the base of his automotive knowledge. After he was out of school, he spent time in the U.S. Navy. When he was released, he got his first chance to drive in a race in 1947. In an ill-handling race car, he finished second in the race, and his career had begun. He then drove in the modified division and during the 1950 and 1951 seasons, he won 54 main events, and in one stretch he won 24 in a row. His success carried over to his time on the Grand National circuit. He drove on the Grand National circuit from 1950 to 1964, starting 160 races, winning nine of them and finishing in the top 10 a total of 84 times.

In 1956, Cotton drove this Jim Stephens Pontiac to a third-place starting position for the race on the Daytona Beach Course, but he finished in a disappointing 61st position.

Marvin Panch raced from 1951 to 1966, racking up 17 wins. Six of them came in 1957.

Marvin Panch was born May 28, 1926, in Menomine, Wisconsin. He became a race car driver and was good at it, but he became one only after trying a number of other sports. After high school football and baseball, and an unsuccessful boxing career, Marvin decided to be a race car driver. While helping to support his widowed mother in Oakland, he worked in a garage where he was exposed to the racing scene. He began entering a car in local races as a car owner and first drove when his driver failed to show up at the track. He won the race and, figuring he no longer needed to pay a driver, took over the duty himself. In 1949 Marvin ran his first NASCAR late-model race at Bay Meadows, finishing third. After a brief stay in the U.S. Army, he returned to racing in 1957. Marvin continued to race up through the 1960s mainly in NASCAR's premier Grand National Series and retired from the sport with 17 Grand National victories after running in 216 races. He also won 21 poles and finished in the top 10 in well over half of the races that he entered over his entire career.

James Roy (Jim) Paschal was born on December 5, 1926, near High Point, North Carolina. All he ever wanted was a farm with chickens and cattle and enough land to grow some crops—and a victory at the Southern 500. He began racing in 1947, running modifieds at the old Daytona Beach course. In 1953 he joined the circuit full-time, finishing seventh overall in points. Throughout the 1950s and 1960s, Jim ran a limited schedule, choosing his races and only racing when he wanted to. Over his 23-year Grand National career, he raced in 421 races and walked away from the sport with 25 wins and 230 top-10 finishes. He won his last race, the World 600, in 1967. After that Jim raced very little, choosing instead to spend time with his chickens, cattle, and crops on the farm that he always wanted.

Jim Paschal's career spanned the entire existence of the Grand National Series as well as one race in the Winston Cup Series. He won 25 times in his 421 starts.

In 1955, Paschal visited victory lane three times in an Ernest Woods-owned Oldsmobile, winning races at Hillsboro, Colombia, and Charlotte. In 1955, he visited victory lane three times in an Ernest Woods-owned Oldsmobile, winning races at Hillsboro, Colombia, and Charlotte.

LEE PETTY

When Lee Petty began racing on the NASCAR circuit in 1949, he began a legacy that continues to this day. His son Richard retired as the sports all-time win leader, his grandson Kyle continues to race, and his great-grandson Adam competed in a Winston Cup race before his death.

Lee Petty started his racing career as hobby. Born March 14, 1914, he was 25 years old when he drove the family's Buick in a race at Charlotte Fairgrounds—and rolled the car four times. The experience did not deter him, and from then on he began to be serious about racing. He owned and maintained the cars he drove, and soon involved sons Richard and Maurice in the business.

During 12 of his 16 years of racing in the Grand National ranks, Lee never placed lower than sixth in the championship. He won three championships: in 1954, 1958, and 1959 (the same year his son Richard won the Rookie of the Year award). The 1959 season was his best, with Lee finishing 41 of 49 races and winning 11 times. The year included a win at the new Daytona International Speedway in the inaugural Daytona 500, a race that ended in a photo finish between Petty and Johnny Beauchamp. The problem was it took NASCAR awhile to find someone with a photo of the finish, and it was three days before Petty was declared the winner.

A crash at Daytona in 1961 was the end of Lee's full-time racing career, but until his retirement in the early 1970s, Lee remained involved in the family business of racing. In his career, he won 54 races in 433 starts, finishing in the top five a phenomenal 231 times.

During his 16-year career, Lee Petty proved himself to be one of the sport's greatest drivers. His 54 wins rank him high on the all-time winner list.

Petty was always a threat in the No. 42 car. While most drivers hired out to different owners, Lee ran only one race behind the wheel of a car that he did not own. If he drove, he drove for the same Petty Enterprises that is still fielding cars on the Nextel Cup Circuit.

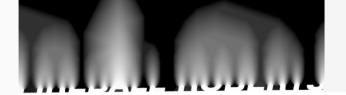

When he began his career, Fireball Roberts only needed three tries before he won his first Grand National race. During his fifteen-year career, he added 32 more victories while driving for legendary owners such as Smokey Yunick, Banjo Mathews, and Holman-Moody.

Born Edward Glen Roberts Jr. on January 20, 1931, in the Daytona Beach area, he was dubbed "Fireball" in his youth due to the speed of his fastball. Fireball's first race was on February 15, 1948, at the Daytona Beach course. A year later, Fireball started on the NASCAR circuit full-time. Fireball was always fast. During his racing career, he set over 400 different records at various tracks. On the new superspeedways that were being built in the late 1950s and early 1960s, Fireball was always a threat. He won the Firecracker 250 at Daytona International Speedway in 1959. In 1962 he won the Daytona 500 and the Firecracker, becoming the first driver to win both of the track's two premier events in a single season.

In 1960 he won the Dixie 500 at the new Atlanta International Raceway, but Darlington was his favorite superspeedway. When he was driving at Darlington, Roberts was one of NASCAR's best. He won the Rebel 300 in 1957 and 1959 and the Southern 500 in 1958 and 1963. In 1964 Fireball was involved in a crash with Ned Jarrett and Junior Johnson at Charlotte. He was severely burned and died of pneumonia 37 days later. In his Grand National career Fireball Roberts ran in 204 races and won 33 of them.

Fireball seldom drove in more than 20 races a year and often less than 10. For instance, he drove in only 10 races in 1958, but he finished his short season with six wins.

In 1963, Roberts moved from a Pontiac to a Holman-Moody Ford and won four races out of 15 attempts in the car. In 1964, he had won one of nine races in the car before he suffered fatal injuries in a crash at Charlotte.

HERB THOMAS

Born on April 6, 1923, in Barbecue Township, North Carolina, Herb Thomas worked in his father's sawmilling business, supplying wood for the military during World War II. After watching his first race, he was convinced he could drive as well as anyone he saw on the track. He scraped together enough money and parts to run his own car and began running in local races. When NASCAR was formed in the late 1940s, Herb joined up. He won his first Grand National race in 1950, driving a Plymouth at Martinsville, Virginia, and won the Grand National Championship in 1951, driving a Hudson Hornet. He won a second championship in 1953.

When he wasn't winning the championship, he was close, finishing second in 1952, 1954, and 1956. During the early part of his career, Herb had maintained his first job, continuing to run the family's sawmill. Herb however eventually sold the sawmill so that he could devote more time to racing. During the mid-1950s he teamed up with Smokey Yunick to build one of the most dominant teams the sport has ever seen. In 1956 Herb was seriously injured in an accident that ended his career. When it ended, he had 48 wins to his credit, placing him 12th on the all-time win list.

When Herb Thomas was in his prime during the mid-1950s, he was as good as anyone in the sport. Time after time he won in his self-owned car.

Herb's weapon of choice, the Hudson Hornet, was the hottest car in the sport in the early 1950s. After he began driving the car late in the 1951 season, Thomas won five out of 13 races. In the next four years, he added 33 more Hudson-powered wins to his record.

Curtis Turner raced on the Grand National circuit from 1949 to 1968. He competed in 17 seasons, running a total of 183 races. Of those, he captured 17 victories. The car owners he competed with were the who's who of racing. He drove for the Wood Brothers, Holman-Moody, Smokey Yunick, and Junior Johnson. Many of his early wins came driving an Oldsmobile for John Eanes.

Curtis Turner was born on April 2, 1924, in Floyd, Virginia. A large man—6 feet, 2 inches tall and weighing 220 pounds—Curtis had supreme confidence in himself on and off the track. While drivers today have to remain wholesome and proper to please their sponsors, Curtis was not restricted in such a way. It probably would not have made a difference—Curtis was a hard charger on the track and the party scene. More than once he came straight from a party to the race, but nevertheless, he could handle a stock car like few others.

Supposedly Curtis (like other stock car pioneers) learned to drive the old-fashioned way—hauling moonshine. He began racing in 1946 at a small track in Mount Airy, North Carolina, ending the race with a last-place finish. The confident Turner won the second race he entered, and by the end of his career he was considered by many to be the best dirt track driver that ever lived. His first nickname was the "Blond Blizzard from Virginia," but he was later renamed "Pops" because he routinely "popped" competitors off the track. Curtis won 22 races in NASCAR's old convertible division and 17 races in the Grand National division.

His involvement with racing went beyond driving. One of his gifts to the sport is the Charlotte International Speedway, which he built but later lost. Turner tried to organize the drivers in a union and was promptly banned from NASCAR for life. He was allowed back five years later, mainly because the sport needed the name of Curtis Turner. He was killed in a plane crash in 1970.

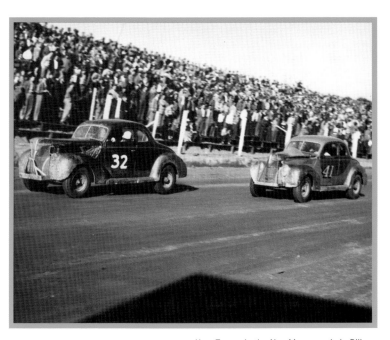

Here Turner, in the No. 41 car, reels in Bill Haddock in the No. 32 car during an early dirt track race.

Joseph Herbert Weatherly was born in Oak Grove, Virginia, on May 29, 1922. Joe's father was killed in a car accident when he was nine years old, and times were tough. Joe had to go to work delivering papers to help his mother make ends meet. He fought in World War II and lost two teeth when a sniper shot them out. When Joe came back from the war, he began his racing career on motorcycles—and he was good at it.

He won three American Motorcycle Association (AMA) Championships, but in 1950 he began to also drive stock cars. (The word was that he was tired of the impact suffered in motorcycle accidents.) In 1952 he won 49 of the 83 races that he started in the lower ranks of stock car racing. The following year, he won NASCAR's Modified crown, this time winning 52 races. He drove his first Grand National race in 1952 and got his first win in 1958. Over the next few years, he drove for both the Ford and Mercury factory teams. By the early 1960s he was one of the hottest drivers on the circuit. He accumulated 25 wins and won the 1962 and 1963 Grand National Championships. In 1964 Joe was killed in a crash at the Riverside International Raceway, cutting short a great career that was on the rise.

Joe Weatherly's first wins came in a Holman-Moody–prepared Ford. He later moved to a Bud Moore Pontiac and continued to be successful on the track. In 1964, he was killed in a crash.

Rex spent most of his career in a Chevrolet before switching to Mercury. From 1958 to 1962, he won 28 times, with most of his wins coming in a self-owned car.

It was said that Rex White developed his smooth driving style while gathering eggs from farmers around Taylorsville, North Carolina, and getting them to market over rough dirt roads without breaking them. From the top of his crew cut, Rex stood 5 feet, 4 inches tall and often had trouble just reaching the pedals. But in racing big things sometimes come in small packages, and few have had the spirit and talent of Rex White.

He came to Silver Spring, Maryland, to work as a short order cook, and it was there that his racing career began. Rex won with consistency, taking care of the car, just like the eggs, throughout the race. His first Grand National race was in 1956, and by 1960 he won the Grand National Championship. He narrowly missed winning championships in both 1959 and 1961. Rex was injured after the 1964 Pan American road race, which kept him out of racing until 1965. After that, Rex only competed in some Sportsman racing events. He ended his career with 25 Grand National victories, ranking him in a tie for 20th in all-time wins.

Here, Rex moves to the inside of another Chevy.

Glen Wood drove on the Grand National circuit for 11 years and ran partial schedules. Although he ran in only 62 events, he won four times. He usually drove in a car prepared by him and his brother. After Glen retired, he and his brother formed the Wood Brothers racing team, which became one of the greatest racing organizations that the sport had ever seen.

During the Modern Era of NASCAR, Glen Wood has been known for being half of the famous owners of the Wood Brothers Racing team. But before he was a successful car owner, he was a driver. He formed the team in 1950 to run modifieds on dirt. Glen was the driver and what started as a part-time hobby ultimately became a business for the next generation of his family. Glen's driving ensured that the team was soon successful. In 1954 he won the North Carolina Sportsman Championship, and three years later he finished third in the NASCAR Convertible Division Championship.

In the Grand National ranks, Glen usually only drove a couple of races a year, although he won four races in his 62-race career and in 1959 was named NASCAR's Most Popular Driver. In 1960 he won three races, twice at Winston-Salem and once at Martinsville. After Glen drove his last Grand National race, in 1964, he became the car owner for a list of drivers that reads like a Who's Who of NASCAR. Drivers Cale Yarborough, David Pearson, A. J. Foyt, Fireball Roberts, Curtis Turner, Joe Weatherly, Marvin Panch, Tiny Lund, and Ricky Rudd all spent time behind the wheel of Glen's race cars. Although his driving career was not of great length, Glen Wood is still one of NASCAR's 50 Greatest Drivers, and few have equaled his overall contribution to the sport.

LEE ROY YARBROUGH

Lee Roy Yarbrough was born September 17, 1938, in Jacksonville, Florida. He decided early in his life to be a racer, and his journey in the sport of auto racing is legendary. When he was 14 years old, he quit school and lied about his age to get his driver's license. He started racing and out-classed the other competitors at the local dirt tracks. At least one promoter reportedly paid a bonus to anyone who could beat him. He drove in both the Sportsman and the modified classes in his early career and moved up to Grand National in 1960, at the young age of 22.

That year he won a single race, and it was the start of Yarbrough becoming a household name. He drove selected races every year until 1972, running as many as 30 races some years and as few as six in others. His best year was in 1962, when he won seven of the 30 races he entered. Even with his limited schedule, he was a top driver, especially on the longer tracks. He was a rare combination of a hard charger who could take care of his car mechanically and still stay out of trouble. When he left the Grand National ranks, he had 14 wins in only 198 starts, and he finished in the top 10 in almost half of the races that he entered. Not bad for a part-time stock car racer.

While all of Lee Roy's 14 Grand National wins came in cars owned by other people, he was still an accomplished mechanic and car tuner. He left Grand National racing after the 1972 season.

Index

318